ENVIRONMENTAL
POLICY
IN CHINA

ENVIRONMENTAL POLICY IN CHINA

LESTER ROSS

INDIANA UNIVERSITY PRESS
Bloomington and Indianapolis

Manufactured in the United States of America

Library of Congress Cataloging-in-Publication Data

Ross, Lester.
Environmental policy in China.

Bibliography: p.
Includes index.
1. Environmental policy—China.   I. Title.
HC430.E5R67   1988   363.7'056'0951   87-45587
ISBN   0-253-31837-8

1 2 3 4 5 92 91 90 89 88

CONTENTS

TABLES

FIGURES

To Ai'de and Luo Lingling, xiao pengyou *ambassadors of goodwill, and the apples of their father's eye.*

ACKNOWLEDGMENTS

For their support during the writing of this book, I wish to express my gratitude to the Andrew W. Mellon Foundation for a fellowship awarded through the American Council of Learned Societies, and to the Committee on Scholarly Communication with the Peoples Republic of China of the National Academy of Sciences, which funded a year's research leave in China. During my year in China, I was hosted by the Institute of Environmental Management Science of the Chinese Research Academy of Environmental Sciences, under the able leadership of Li Kang and his deputy, Cheng Weixue. Among those who read and commented on the manuscript at different times, I wish to particularly thank Michel Oksenberg for his guidance and encouragement throughout, Cathy Enderton, Fritz Gaenslen, Tom Hammond, Mike Lampton, Jim Nickum, Mitch Silk, and Pete Suttmeier. I thank the Department of Political Science at Purdue University, particularly Jill Brady, Deanna Johns, and Jennifer Redden, for processing this manuscript from handwritten illegibility into a professional-looking document. An earlier version of chapter 5 was published in *Comparative Political Studies*, July 1986. Last but never least, I thank my wife, Claudia, for being everything that she is, and for tolerating everything that I am.

ABBREVIATIONS

APSR	*American Political Science Review*
AS	*Asian Survey*
BR	*Beijing Review*
CBR	*China Business Review*
CD	*China Daily*
CQ	*China Quarterly*
CUFM	Joint Economic Committee (1982). *China under the Four Modernizations*. Washington: U.S. Government Printing Office.
DZ	*Dili Zhishi* (Geographical Knowledge)
FAO	Food and Agriculture Organization of the United Nations
FBIS	Foreign Broadcast Information Service, *Daily Report: People's Republic of China*
GR	*Guangming Ribao* (Brilliant Daily)
H	*Huanjing* (Environment)
HB	*Huanjing Baohu* (Environmental Protection)
HK	*Huanjing Kexue* (Environmental Science)
HQ	*Hong Qi* (Red Flag)
JAS	*Journal of Asian Studies*
JG	*Jingji Guanli* (Environmental Management)
JPRS	Joint Publications Research Service, following series:
CAG	*China Report: Agriculture*
CEA	*China Report: Economic Affairs*
CRF	*China Report: Red Flag*
CPS	*China Report: Politics and Sociology*
CST	*China Report: Science and Technology*
PSM	*China Report: Political, Sociological, and Military Affairs*
WWEQ	*World-Wide Report: Environmental Quality*
JR	*Jingji Ribao* (Economics Daily)
JY	*Jingji Yanjiu* (Economic Research)
LJ	*Linye Jingji* (Forestry Economics)
LJW	Agricultural Economics Research Institute, Chinese Academy of Social Sciences (1982). *Linye Jingji Wenti* (Problems of Forestry Economics). Beijing: Zhongguo Shehui Kexue Chubanshe.
LK	*Linye Kexue* (*Scientiae Silvae*)
NJJ	*Nongye Jingji Jishu* (Agricultural Economics and Technology)
NJW	*Nongye Jingji Wenti* (Problems of Agricultural Economics)
NYT	*New York Times*
PR	*Peking Review* (predecessor of BR)

RR	*Renmin Ribao* (People's Daily)
ZBN	*Zhongguo Baike Nianjian* (Chinese Encyclopedia Yearbook)
ZHK	*Zhongguo Huanjing Kexue* (Chinese Environmental Science)
ZL	*Zhongguo Linye* (Chinese Forestry)
ZNB	*Zhongguo Nongmin Bao* (Chinese Peasant News)
ZNN	*Zhongguo Nongye Nianjian* (Chinese Agricultural Yearbook)
ZRGGYG	*Zhonghua Renmin Gongheguo Guowu Yuan Gongbao* (PRC State Council Gazette)
ZS	*Zhongguo Shuili* (Chinese Water Conservancy)
ZTN	*Zhongguo Tongji Nianjian* (Chinese Statistical Yearbook)
ZZ	*Ziran Ziyuan* (Natural Resources)

ENVIRONMENTAL
POLICY
IN CHINA

I.

STRATEGIES FOR IMPLEMENTATION

Work on Chinese politics has consisted largely of chronologically based narratives intended exclusively for an audience of area specialists, with only incidental attention to broader theoretical issues. Although this work is rich in descriptive content, its value is diminished by the absence of a theoretical perspective or comparative research design. This volume is different. It is an interpretative case survey, employing policy implementation and public goods theory to explain the empirical reality of China. In this way, it expands the social science data base and at the same time places China in the broader theoretical context so necessary for comparative research (Lijphart 1971).

This book analyzes Chinese environmental policy and assesses the efficacy of alternative modes of policy implementation: plan and regulation, moral suasion, and the market. Through an examination of several related policy sectors (afforestation and forest management, water resources use and development, natural hazards management, and pollution control), this study concludes that bureaucratic planning and moral suasion have largely failed to solve environmental problems despite major investments in political and other resources. Conversely, it demonstrates that markets have a considerable potential to enhance the environment that has only recently been recognized by China's leaders.

An explanation for the differential performance of these policy modes demands investigation because both China and environmental policy are polar cases. Few other countries have ever assembled so broad an array of the political controls needed to pursue a strategy of moral exhortation. Environmental degradation for its part is usually regarded as a signal case of market failure crying out for governmental regulation. If this study can demonstrate that market instruments outperform the alternatives even in so inhospitable a context, then the theoretical justification for their application to a broad spectrum of policies and political systems is strengthened.

In addition to its theoretical significance, this book presents a detailed study of the evolution of environmental policy in China, something that has received little attention to date. The particular focus is the critical period since the landmark Third Plenum in 1978, but extensive background on earlier periods is also provided. Moreover, this book highlights the technical side of policy decisions without neglecting the political considerations involved. In particular, it analyzes the bureaucratic and academic debates over critical decisions affecting environmental policy, thereby illuminating the policy process in China.

Introduction

Environmental management is one of the great challenges of modern times. As with superpower diplomacy, the urgency of management has increased as a result of man's ingenuity in devising ever more sophisticated and powerful technologies. But the risks arising from pollution, the unintended by-product of economic activity, are far more subtle and pervasive than nuclear war in terms of poisoned air, contaminated water, and a toxified food chain. Once confined to the industrialized world, industrial pollution has spread to developing countries, where a lack of regulation frequently makes it more severe. Nevertheless, most of the Third World is endangered more by traditional forms of environmental overload, such as unhealthful water, deforestation, and soil erosion, than by modern industrial pollution. Regardless of which is the more serious threat, environmental policy is an important determinant of each country's potential for economic development and improving the quality of life of its citizens.

How then is the environment to be managed? Environmental problems can be tackled in strikingly different ways. To some critics, environmental quality is a product of the distribution of power and the nature of a society's ethical beliefs. Pollution is considered part of the seamy underside of capitalism in which avaricious businessmen pursue profit at the expense of human health. Through advertising and marketing, business entices consumers to buy nonbiodegradable containers and gas-guzzling cars instead of natural or more humane alternatives. These analysts charge that business deliberately shuns such environmentally benign technologies as solar power in order to sell more profitable products like electricity generated from fossil fuels or nuclear power. These critics of business generally argue that people must make an ethical commitment in their private lives to refrain from environmentally damaging behavior before a turn for the better can be expected (Cahn 1978, Ophuls 1977).

William Ophuls is one of the most articulate exponents of this perspective. In his prize-winning book *Ecology and the Politics of Scarcity* (1977), he wrote:

> (I)t is clear that we have been living in an age of rampant individualism that arose historically from circumstances of abnormal abundance. It seems predictable, therefore, that on our way toward the steady state we shall move from individualism toward communalism. . . . As the community and its

rights are given increasing social priority we shall necessarily move from liberty toward authority. . . . Because the free play of market forces and individual initiative produces the tragedy of the commons, the market orientation typical of most modern societies will have to be abandoned. . . . The character of economic life will change totally. Ecology will engulf economics: we shall move away from the values of growth, profligacy, and exploitation typical of "economic man" toward sufficiency, frugality, and stewardship. . . . Finally the steady-state society will undoubtedly be characterized by genuine morality, as opposed to a purely instrumental set of ethics. It seems extremely unlikely, for example, that a real commitment to stewardship could arise out of enlightened self-interest; it will require a change of heart. (226–31)

Although moralists like Ophuls believe that strong governmental action is an essential ingredient in the building of an ecological utopia, others are more suspicious of the strong hand of government. They regard governmental controls as a threat to the personal freedom and individual responsibility that are essential in an organic society. Some even recognize that bureaucracy can pose as big a problem for the environment as private business. They believe in the power of morally charged theocracies like the Buddhist state of Schumacher (1973) or decentralized communities of committed individuals capable of governing society in an ecologically sound fashion.

A second perspective places less faith in the potential for value change, predicting instead that polluters will continue to selfishly pursue their own interests at the expense of the public good. Because individuals acting alone cannot resist powerful economic interests, adherents of this perspective favor an expanded role for government as owner of resources and planner and regulator of economic activity in order to protect the environment.

Such a change in the posture of government under capitalism can only be obtained through electoral politics and strong and continuous interest group activity of the kind carried out by Ralph Nader's family of public watchdog organizations. The Nader groups played a critical part in encouraging a wider governmental role through a series of widely publicized investigative studies in the late 1960s and early 1970s on water and air quality, among other subjects. Other groups, such as the Sierra Club, the National Wildlife Federation, and the Natural Resources Defense Council, have been more influential on a continuing basis. Such interest group activity is most likely to occur in an open political system that provides extensive opportunities for freedom of assembly and citizen access. The result has been a great expansion in the government's responsibilities for the environment in the United States despite a strongly individualistic political culture that has inhibited development of a welfare state.

The path is much easier in communist countries, where the state automatically assumes the dominant position with regard to economic activity. All that is required there is for the state to plan and regulate environmental quality in the same fashion that it manages the economy as a whole. Some observers (Parsons 1977, Kapp 1974) have naively assumed that that gives communist countries an inherent advantage with regard to environmental quality, somehow ignoring their checkered record with regard to economic performance.

By contrast, a third perspective accepts the need for public action to correct the problems of market failure but declines to endorse either bureaucratic controls or the abolition of avarice as the solution. Instead, advocates of the market approach reaffirm the basic superiority of a system under which self-interested individuals strive for a maximum return. What is needed is not the elimination of markets but rather their reform so that environmental goods get their due just like any other resource. Prices then serve the same communication function for the environment as they do for raw materials, energy, or labor. Rising prices would indicate an excess of demand leading to added production and the introduction of substitute commodities, while falling prices would lead to a reduction in output until the excess of supply had disappeared. In this fashion, resources would be directed to their most efficient use.

Proponents concede that market imperfections result in environmental problems but argue that modifications in incentives and property rights can make markets more suitable instruments of public policy. From this point of view, environmental problems have two basic causes. On one hand, common property resources such as water or air typically lie outside the realm of private ownership and instead are regarded as community property. Although community ownership sometimes builds a sense of reverence that leads to conservation, all too often it results in a free-for-all scramble. Because such common property resources are free for the taking, there is an incentive to overconsume them. In an agrarian economy, that may lead to overgrazing of the community pasture if population density increases, as in Garrett Hardin's classic parable, "The Tragedy of the Commons" (1968). As society industrializes, manufacturers will discharge their wastes untreated into rivers and the atmosphere because neither individuals nor government agencies have strong incentives to protect the resource (Kneese and Schultze 1975). Just as there is a tendency to overconsume a resource's assimilative capacity, there also is little incentive to increase the supply of renewable common property resources such as grasslands because the community cannot restrict entry and thus prevent degradation by overgrazing or other activities.

The more general explanation for environmental problems involves externality or spillover effects. Externalities are side effects that are borne by those not party to a transaction. For example, hillside farming may increase the danger of downstream flooding, while careless dumping of toxic wastes may contaminate an entire community's water supply. Flood victims and drinkers of contaminated water have no recourse to express their demand for a safer environment because they do not participate in the real estate, farming, or waste-disposal markets. In this respect, problems related to common property resources may be regarded as a subset of externalities.

Some externalities—a beautiful vista or wetlands preservation, for example—may of course be beneficial. The literature distinguishes between "pecuniary" and "real" externalities. The former refer to such indirect transactions as a new technology displacing an old one. Existing jobs may be lost, but the economy as a whole may benefit. "Real" externalities involve direct transactions such as pollution (Russell 1982). But even some "real" externalities are positive. Silt derived from upstream erosion may enrich the soil of downstream farms. But just as increased pollution arises from the inability of consumers to express their preferences for pollution control in the market, such positive externalities as natural habitats tend to be underproduced because remote beneficiaries do not contribute to increased acquisition.

In rare instances, environmental improvement can be obtained through purely private action. Wilderness advocates can buy fragile sites and insulate the property from unwanted intrusions, particularly if the property is an island or entry can otherwise be restricted. The Nature Conservancy operates in precisely this manner; so did the estates maintained as hunting preserves by wealthy and powerful families in earlier days. Similarly, victims of pollution may bargain with polluters for relief or file suit in court.

In most cases, however, environmental improvement cannot be obtained through purely private action. For example, the conservation of whales, grizzlies, and other migratory or fugitive species is exceedingly difficult to privatize because of their vast spatial requirements. Moreover, environments often are so complex, with so many parties involved, that pollutants cannot easily be traced back to their sources. Group action generally is necessary whenever people lack the money to buy rights to development or to induce polluters to take greater care in waste handling, but it is often hard to form groups and enforce group decisions.

Because the transaction costs as well as the financial costs are severe, citizens turn to government for environmental relief. Democracies provide ample opportunities for citizens to organize and seek governmental action through lobbying and the ultimate threat of electoral defeat. The impact is uneven, however, because most groups of like-minded individuals remain in a "latent" state. As Olson (1965 and 1971) demonstrated, individuals have an incentive to take a free ride or to disguise their true preferences except when the marginal additional benefits to them personally exceed their costs of participation. The only groups that will succeed are the "privileged" ones—in the sense that enough individuals have a positive net calculus of participation to keep the groups in existence despite the existence of free riders—or those that are able to provide "selective incentives" or side payments to individuals to overcome the tendency to free ride.

The consequence often is that too little environmental protection is provided, while at other times too much is supplied. Until environmentalists organized, wilderness and other values tended to be slighted in the United States (Nash 1982). Once such groups became established, however, the contrary danger of too much protection at the expense of unorganized groups developed. For example, Tucker (1977) showed how an essentially innocuous pumped storage facility along the Hudson River in New York was delayed and eventually killed for vague and contradictory reasons despite its promise of providing a reliable nonpolluting energy source.

Although environmental improvement thus presupposes government intervention in the economy, proponents of the market approach prefer a limited role for government in contrast to the traditional response to market failure, namely, planning and regulation under which the government prescribes social behavior. By contrast, they argue that the most efficient solutions depend on improving the functioning of markets so that the behavior of self-interested individuals becomes more compatible with community concerns without the need for inculcating "good motives" (Amacher et al. 1976: 25–26).

With regard to externalities, this market approach involves the clarification and legal enforcement of property rights so that individuals who suffer from pollution enjoy the right to compensation, either through mutual transactions or ultimately by judicial action. For example, shared ownership of a groundwater aquifer tends to result in "mining," in which case withdrawals exceed replenishment because each owner has an incentive to take as much as he can as quickly as he can, lest others act first and pump him high and dry. The solution may involve instituting a system of correlative rights in which each individual's consumption is constrained by the obligation to preserve the other parties' consumption unimpaired in terms of quantity and quality. Once each individual rightholder is assured a fixed portion of the resource in perpetuity, he will have an incentive to use it efficiently rather than wastefully, since his allotment can be neither increased nor decreased. To ensure an optimal social outcome, however, rights can be made transferable so that the most productive user can buy out his less productive neighbors (Anderson 1983). In the United States, several states in recent years have begun to move in this direction with regard to both surface and groundwater rights.

In other instances, common property resources normally held by government might be transferred to private producers through either leasing or permanent arrangements. That is because government agencies thrive on the basis of their success in winning budgetary appropriations rather than by maximizing profits. If, for example, some national forestland were transferred to the private domain, the most productive lands probably would be managed more efficiently, resulting in an increase in timber production. Although these lands would henceforth be managed as plantations rather than as natural woodlands, the increased productivity per acre probably would ease pressures to open more marginal lands for production. The end result could be more production at lower cost plus increased reservation of marginal lands for wilderness and other less intensive uses (Hyde 1981).

In many instances, of course, private operation would not be sufficient by itself to assure the provision of such social values as recreation and conservation. Rather than rely upon moral exhortation to do the right thing, market proponents recommend the purchase of public easements to restrict the private operator's options only with regard to the designated purpose. For example, improvements in soil science and hydrology now enable policymakers to identify lands that are the biggest contributors to soil erosion. The market approach recommends the purchase of easements or the negotiation of performance contracts to restrict cultivation or other adverse practices on fragile sites. That eases the direct burden of conservation on individuals who farm such lands while at the same time enabling government to focus scarce funds on the most erosion-prone areas. The Soil Conservation Service has been moving in this direction in recent years, in contrast to its historical emphasis on equal attention to all farm operators without regard to performance (Brubaker and Castle 1982), and such a provision was incorporated in the Food Security Act of 1985.

In cases like air quality, where it is impossible to physically divide the resource into individual parcels, market advocates favor reliance on economic incentives by government. That might involve the setting of charges based on the volume and composition of pollutants released into the atmosphere or the creation of markets for pollution rights. In the latter instance, government would have to determine thresholds of acceptability for environmental quality. Rights to pollute below administratively determined ceilings would be auctioned or otherwise allocated among firms that then could spend, save, or sell their pollution rights. Alternatively, emissions charges would be assessed against polluters in accordance with their discharges into common property resources, especially air and water. The less one pollutes, the lower one's charges would be (Anderson et al. 1977).

Market advocates concede that such mechanisms sometimes are inappropriate, as when pollutants are so highly toxic that no level of ambient concentration can be considered acceptable. In such instances, direct regulation ranging up to outright prohibition may be preferable (Baumol and Oates 1979, Bower et al. 1977). Economists argue, however, that clarifying property rights and establishing incentive structures raises efficiency. Of course, there can be technical problems associated with quasi-market mechanisms for environmental management. For example, monopolistic behavior may result from high barriers to market entry. Problems of access to remote regions may result in few bidders for the right to manage public lands, or charges for pollution may be set so high that new firms cannot afford to enter production. When few transactions take place, the markets become thin, making prices highly susceptible to wide fluctuations (Noll 1982). It is also argued that the requirements for metering emissions or withdrawals are too demanding for the government or any private association to undertake, with the result that artificial markets will dissolve in epidemics of cheating. But metering in general is not appreciably more difficult in a market than under bureaucratic regulation. With the passage of time many problems have been worked out and economic mechanisms have been introduced more widely in industrialized capitalist countries, although often in conjunction with direct regulation rather than on an exclusively market-oriented basis (Schelling 1983, Tietenberg 1984, Reese 1983, Downing and Hanf 1983, Anderson, 1983).

Thus, the fundamental difference between the three approaches to environmental policy is less a matter of feasibility than of ideology or politics. Advocates of the market approach regard environmental management not as a moral crusade but as a set of circumstances demanding limited government intervention. The morals of polluters are largely incidental to the policy process, in part because some degree of pollution is actually considered preferable whenever the costs of control exceed the costs of pollution. The crucial consideration is to ensure the widest possible scope for a decentralized choice structure in comparison with its less efficient alternatives.

By contrast, environmentalists place more stress on moral or spiritual values. They correctly perceive that markets convert environmental amenities into fungible assets, a practice they reject as an infringement on the organic balance of nature. Some may concede that if the ecological values of fragile wetlands could be fully priced, some wetlands assuredly would be preserved because their prices would rise in response to scarcity. Nonetheless, environmentalists are skeptical that nature can ever be incorporated into the price structure because of the environment's transcendental value, as argued by John Muir or as pictured by Ansel Adams (Nash 1982: 167–70; cf. McCloskey 1983). Even if environmental values could be fully priced, sites precious to someone or to the sentient earth itself would inevitably be developed. In more practical terms, environmentalists distrust markets because they refuse to concede the moral irrelevance of limited pollution or the death of even one whale, lest individuals become further accustomed to subordinating their social obligations to selfish interests.

The Chinese Political Economy

The debate over environmental policy originated in free-market economies. Were pollution exclusively a by-product of capitalism, this book's message would be rather simple: wherever possible, free-market economies should imitate their communist counterparts. That would involve increased emphasis on central planning and moral exhortation. Indeed, to the extent that classical Marxist thinkers, including Engels (1940), gave thought to environmental issues, they assigned the blame to shortsighted profit seeking by capitalists. Moreover, some social scientists in recent years have identified specific features of Soviet-style systems that allegedly enhance environmental management. In particular, central planning has been held to enhance the flow of information on environmental problems and facilitate the making of decisions with regard to the interests of the whole, as opposed to special interests. Since environmental integrity is a public good, the result is a higher level of environmental quality than in decentralized, profit-driven systems (McIntyre and Thornton 1978a and 1978b, Kapp 1974).

Most analysts of the Soviet Union who have looked at this issue disagree with this analysis. They begin by explaining pollution in terms of economic development, population pressure, and other universal phenomena that are substantially independent of the nature of the political economy. They then go on to observe that pollution and loss of natural habitat are actually more severe in the Soviet Union despite lower levels of economic output. That is attributed to the political economy, which concentrates power in a political elite dominated by producer interests with little opportunity for contrary interests to be expressed, takes little account of environmental values in the planning process, and features enormous amounts of built-in slothfulness and waste (Goldman 1972, Gustafson 1981, Taga 1976, Ziegler 1980 and 1982).

With the exception of the Soviet Union, there has been remarkably little attention paid to environmental policy in communist countries. This circumstance limits the generalizability of conclusions because findings from one country may not necessarily be applicable even to similar countries. It is particularly serious with regard to China because of its huge size and long-standing geopolitical rivalry with Moscow.

From a theoretical perspective, the Chinese case also is important because of the wide range of variation that it presents in terms of policy instruments. China has had more extensive social controls and more conscious manipulation of moral values than most other countries in the world. Yet China also has witnessed a remarkable series of fluctuations in terms of policy instruments. While the system generally resembles a Soviet-style economy, at particular junctures, such as the Great Leap Forward and the Cultural Revolution, the political and planning apparatus has been subordinated to the frenzy of a moral crusade. Of greater long-term consequence is the shift toward economic reform since 1978 that has assumed unprecedented proportions in terms of foreign trade and investment, enterprise autonomy, price reform, and market transactions.

These changes have affected environmental management as well as other sectors of society. In contrast to the early 1970s when official spokesmen trumpeted China's inherent superiority, the tone nowadays is one of serious concern over the state of the environment, coupled with a search for effective policy. It now is conceded that no system is immune to such problems as "resource exhaustion," "environmental pollution," and "ecological imbalance," and, more importantly, that they may be more severe in China than elsewhere (FBIS, Dec. 2, 1983: K12–17).

The apparent paradox is that this more sober approach to environmental problems is the result of a reform trend predicated upon the fostering of self-interested behavior. Many analysts would argue that self-interest is fundamentally incompatible with protecting a public good like environmental quality. The major purpose of this book is to resolve this apparent paradox. The key step is to analyze the historical record, which reveals substantial variation in choice of policy instruments. These instruments then can be compared in terms of their performance in order to determine their relative effectiveness.

In particular, three distinct types of implementation strategy or ways of carrying out policy can be identified. They are the bureaucratic-authoritative approach, the campaign-exhortation approach, and the market-exchange approach. These types vary along several critical dimensions: comprehensiveness, centralization of authority, role of the Communist party, role of administrative departments or governmental bureaucracy, incentives for compliance, and distribution of property rights. Some of these dimensions, such as the role of the party and incentives for compliance, are familiar to China specialists. Others, especially property rights, are not.

Property rights refer to sets of rules defining the ownership and use of goods. Although the initial distribution of property rights may or may not satisfy any particular set of moral criteria, a well-defined system of rights is efficient in the sense that it forces each individual to assume the full cost of his actions rather than foisting the burden off on his neighbors or the public at large. Property ownership is structured in terms of bundles or packages of rights rather than as an indivisible entity, so ownership and use can be held by separate parties and each right can be governed by various conditions, e.g., limitations on the right to alienate or transfer property. Moreover, the concept of property is not restricted to real goods but rather has expanded over time to include various forms of intellectual property, recently including copyrights for computer software in the United States and patents for inventions in China.

The form in which property rights are held, especially communal vs. private, represents a major dividing line between political economies, with liberalism predicated upon private property rights. Moreover, efficiency, including the resolution of externality problems, is facilitated when property rights are distinctly defined and made enforceable (Alchian and Demsetz 1973). An investigation of China in terms of property rights is particularly important because new systems of rights are emerging rapidly. Such an investigation not only permits comparative analysis but also offers an intriguing opportunity to study how rights are determined, instead of relying on the Hobbesian and Lockeian fiction that the existing distribution of rights is derived from nature.

I will begin by discussing each policy implementation type. Then I will spend the next three chapters examining several policy sectors involving different aspects of environmental policy. The focus on several policy sectors broadens the scope of this book. Confidence in its conclusions will be enhanced to the extent that the findings for each case are similar. Then I will discuss how changes in the policy process take place in terms of agenda setting before I summarize and elaborate upon the analysis in the concluding chapter.

Bureaucratic-Authoritative Implementation

Bureaucratic-authoritative implementation involves the setting of political priorities by the Communist party and the leading echelons of government, especially the State Council and the State Planning Commission.* These priorities are compiled in sets of imperative plans or commands that are then communicated downward through the bureaucracies for implementation. Ideally, lower echelons comply fully with the orders of their superiors, and that results in a highly uniform process of implementation in which decisions are made in accordance with the interests of the whole as defined by the central elite.

This form of implementation has been the norm in China, in part because of its resonance with traditional governmental institutions but primarily because of borrowing from the Soviet Union. It is distinguished not so much by the existence of hierarchy per se, but rather by its ranking on several other dimensions, including comprehensiveness, centralization, compliance, the role of the party, and property rights.

Comprehensiveness. The planning process in China is directed toward setting priorities for all major values. This process primarily refers to the economy, not so much in terms of interest rates, foreign exchange values, and other macroeconomic levers that play only a minor role, but primarily with regard to capital investment, the production and distribution of commodities, and even production processes. Planning involves the setting of Soviet-style material balances in which requests for supplies are reconciled with production capabilities. Although in principle the planning process ought to govern all commodities, in practice no more than several hundred

---

*Bureaucratic-authoritative implementation should not be confused with the concept of a bureaucratic-authoritarian political system formulated by Guillermo O'Donnell (Collier 1979). Bureaucratic-authoritarianism refers to a technocratically and militarily dominated regime that arises under special conditions of international economic dependence following the failure of a development strategy based on import substitution. In de Janvry's words (1981: 191), "the military and the bureaucracy dominate the state, which is managed according to technocratic principles without concern for popular mobilization and with widespread use of repression to create social stability and a favorable investment climate for disarticulated accumulation. The military and technocratic fractions of the bourgeoisie become the guardians of the interests of the disarticulated alliance." Bureaucratic-authoritative implementation in China by contrast is imposed by the civil authority, in this case the party, rather than the technocracy or military, and arose in conditions of minimal dependence on the capitalist world.

major agricultural and industrial commodities have ever been subject to full controls.* Other commodities, especially finished goods, items of lower strategic importance, or goods in relative abundance, have been subject to lesser degrees of control (Cheng 1982). However, the regime generally has been able to strongly influence production of all goods through tight control of principal intermediate goods and production functions, e.g., grain procurement quotas that limit the opportunity for agricultural production units to plant other crops.

Although comprehensiveness is most apparent with regard to economic policy, the bureaucratic approach is also applicable to society as a whole in the sense that the private realm, which involves "negative freedom" as described by Sir Isaiah Berlin (1958), is greatly restricted. The regime in this respect defines the milieu in which writers and artists may operate, as well as the content of school curricula, in order to produce socialist cultural works and to prevent the spread of unorthodox thoughts.

In reality, the planning process has always been incomplete and hampered by a lack of administrative capacity. Poorly educated and undertrained officials, faced with administering the most populous country in the world despite primitive communications and analytical systems, deserve a measure of sympathy. In this respect, China has been governed more by imperfect or inconsistent planning than by strong planning. Nevertheless, the approach is marked by its determination to maximize control over society.

Centralization. The bureaucratic approach typically involves a high degree of centralization in order to set priorities for society as a whole. It is constitutionally acceptable in China thanks to the existence of a unitary state led by a mass party governed by the principles of democratic centralism. In practice, centralization has been most pronounced with regard to the instruments of coercion, namely the armed forces and the public security organs, in order to ensure that force is employed only as intended.

With regard to the economy, centralization has at times been reduced through administrative decentralization, as in the 1957–58 period. The purpose in part was to restore some flexibility to the system. However, it primarily involved conflict between Mao Zedong and his supporters in the party who favored more rapid development than orthodox planners considered acceptable. The resulting administrative decentralization involved a transfer of authority from Beijing to the provinces where Mao's support was greater (Chang 1978: 47–64, Schurmann 1968: 195–210). After Mao's

---

*Agricultural commodities ordinarily are classified in three categories. First-category goods are produced by the state on a planned basis, and include grains, edible oils, and other items of great importance. Second-category goods are subject to purchase by the state, but above-norm production may be sold at a premium by the producer to the state or on the free market. Third-category goods can be sold somewhat freely. For more on this point, see Cheng (1982: 201–4). This system was greatly altered in the 1980s through the introduction of market reforms.

policies proved unsuccessful during the Great Leap Forward, however, Chen Yun led the planners in a move to recentralize authority in the name of "treating the entire country as a chessboard." This development indicates that the natural tendency under planning is for centralization to increase, although some degree of decentralization for operational decisions is of course inevitable.

Compliance. The bureaucratic approach is predicated upon the concept of obedience to authoritative commands. Recruits assume careers in an organization where they agree to accept the orders of their superiors in exchange for security of tenure, fixed compensation, and other considerations. In a public bureaucracy, the acceptance of authority is bound up with the legal basis for the superior's commands in the Weberian sense of rational-legal authority, although the relationship can be defined more generally in terms of a contract. In Coase's terms (1960), an employee voluntarily surrenders his freedom on the job in return for financial and other rewards that reflect his qualifications and employment conditions. China's principal departures from the Weberian ideal lie in the absence of free labor markets and the emphasis on political or ideological conformity, as opposed to task performance, as a major criterion for employment and advancement.

In practice, as Barnard (1938, 1964) noted many years ago, the acceptance of authority by subordinates is conditional upon the behavior of their superiors. Good leaders inspire their subordinates to do more than is expected of them, while poor or mediocre leadership brings on evasion and a slipshod effort by subordinates. Organizational leaders in China generally have had few resources under their control to elicit superior performance because of the regime's ideological abhorrence of unemployment. Job tenure tended to be inviolate as symbolized by the term *iron rice bowl.* Major exceptions involving transfers to lower echelons *(xia fang)* or administrative rectifications took place in response to central party directives of broad scope, so organizational officials have had limited influence over the number of employees to be seconded downward. Those unfortunate enough to be selected interpreted their treatment as the product of political persecution or bad luck, which in neither case could be countered by superior performance. Such positive incentives as promotions and pay raises are also of limited scope because of budget restrictions and a tendency to treat all personnel alike regardless of their performance ("sharing rice out of the big pot").

Conflict occurs at all levels within the system, of course, although its existence is often denied. It occurs among the senior leaders and also at the nexus between the top party leadership and agency heads who may constitute a threat to the former's freedom of action. As Harding (1981) showed, Mao's fundamental distrust of bureaucracy led him to experiment with drastic reform strategies involving normative incentives that nullified many of the rationalizing features of the system. By contrast, Liu Shaoqi,

Chen Yun, and other leaders were more satisfied with bureaucracy and tried instead to perfect the system in terms of command and compliance.

The role of the party. The power of the Communist party is supreme in the sense that the party leadership selects the implementation instrument. But the party's role as an organization varies depending on which approach is chosen. Under the bureaucratic model, as discussed by Suttmeier (1974) in his analysis of scientific policy, the party shares authority with professionally trained administrators on the premise that the party's overall political power goes unchallenged. In other words, the party itself becomes structurally differentiated in a pattern paralleling the institutional divisions within the government itself. As a consequence, the party tends to lose some of the unity and flexibility that it enjoyed when its responsibilities for governance were less onerous. Moreover, the party becomes more responsive to the separate claims of bureaucratic interests and less responsive to its own higher leadership when the two are in conflict, which in turn induces the leadership to consider nonbureaucratic approaches.

It also should be understood that the party's sharing of authority with professional officials frequently hampers policy performance by injecting political biases and an emphasis on conformity into essentially routine matters. More generally, survival and expansion of the organization tend to be stressed even at the expense of performance. In the scientific realm, for example, research support typically is allocated to each institute on the basis of historical funding patterns without attention to productivity. Within each institute, senior researchers are favored. Junior researchers and everyone outside of the academy system enjoy less opportunity for funding because the system only incidentally rewards merit (BR, Jan. 21, 1985: 6–7).

Property rights. Formally speaking, the ultimate goal of socialism is the transfer of all ownership as well as other property rights to the state as agent for the whole people. That has been the pattern for natural resources since the founding of the People's Republic; it became the dominant system in industry after the socialization drives of the 1950s. The principal exception is agriculture, where, in contrast to the Soviet Union, almost all land is held in common by collectives that are considered part of the people but not agents of the whole people.

Regardless of whether property is state-held or collectively held, the practical consequence is the assignment of property rights to particular organizations or bureaucracies entrusted with their operation, e.g., the Ministry of Textile Industry for textile plants or the Ministry of Chemical Industry for petrochemicals. The structure extends down within vertical systems *(xitong)* all the way to individual units, each of which is highly impermeable to external influence. Although the central authorities retain overall power with regard to interagency transactions and can reorganize their individual functions, each agency retains enormous power over its own property. Housing and other emoluments typically are available only through membership in a unit *(danwei)* that allocates scarce goods largely according to internal criteria. Once an agency acquires property, even quasi illegally, it can be very difficult for the former owner to dislodge it, as was true in the case of many university campuses and public parks that were occupied by the army during the Cultural Revolution. Even the higher leadership's ultimate authority is constrained by the tight control each organization exercises over internal information through both formal and informal channels. The consequence is continuous rivalry between the central planning authorities and individual bureaucracies over the control of funding, real estate, and other property even when central policies encounter no overt opposition.

Campaign-Exhortation Implementation

Campaigns are short-term or intermittent organizations with flat hierarchies and a simple division of labor, involving mobilization of some or all of the populace by a governmental or private entity. Campaigns can exist anywhere, with prominent examples in the United States being political campaigns and health-related campaigns such as immunization drives. They are attractive whenever broad participation is required for brief intervals, since they can bring together large numbers of people without incurring the fixed costs of a bureaucratic organization. Campaigns are more common, however, in a mobilizational regime such as the People's Republic of China, where the governing authorities have much greater ambitions regarding the transformation of popular values through political participation, and where the traditional political culture emphasizes the emulation of morally virtuous elites rather than the rule of law (Chu 1979). Moreover, as we shall see, campaigns can provide the higher leadership with an implementation approach other than the bureaucratic norm to be used against political opponents or a sluggish bureaucracy.

Following Yu (1967) and Cell (1977), campaigns can be grouped into several types according to their primary goals: economic, ideological, and struggle. Economic campaigns such as the Great Leap Forward or annual afforestation exercises are intended to increase economic performance through changes in social institutions, the popularization of new technologies, or increased labor inputs, all of which are dependent on mass mobilization. Ideological campaigns are designed to transform social values in the direction favored by the regime; examples include "Learn from the PLA (People's Liberation Army)" and "Build a Socialist Spiritual Civilization." Struggle campaigns such as the antirightist campaigns and the Cultural Revolution are designed to stigmatize segments of the populace designated as enemies of the people in order to advance ideological goals. All three types depend on mass mobilization and share similar characteristics. Because this book's primary focus is on economic campaigns, it will not be possible to analyze the other types of campaigns directly. Our findings nonetheless have broader significance in light of Cell's finding that economic campaigns are the most successful. In other words, should the most successful campaigns prove less capable than previously thought, the case for campaigns in general is weakened.

Comprehensiveness. Campaigns sometimes are linked together in waves of mobilization. During political high tides such as the Great Leap Forward, one campaign followed another in wavelike sequence with the political ripples extending across the policy map. The antirightist political campaign of 1957, for example, was orchestrated to squelch domestic opposition. In turn it emboldened the believers in the power of mobilization as an organizational tool, while weakening potential opponents. A greatly enlarged winter waterworks construction campaign led in turn to further mobilization in the countryside with the encouragement of Mao Zedong and other party leaders. The Great Leap, of course, ultimately extended to urban areas and industry as well as agriculture.

The Great Leap exemplifies the broad and far-reaching scope of campaigns. Nevertheless, campaigns in general do not strive for balance or evenhandedness. Rather, they proceed in uncoordinated spurts in the belief that a breakthrough on one front can lead to decisive results on other fronts. Thus, the Great Leap was predicated on the notion that massive labor reserves had only to be awakened for agriculture to accomplish decades of work in a few years. Similarly, campaigns may be initiated to highlight an issue and force action by an otherwise unresponsive bureaucracy.

Although Mao personally relished the juggling of imbalances as part of his leadership repertoire, many of his colleagues came to regard the Great Leap and similar forays as blind adventures into the unknown. Therefore, they resolved after his death and especially after the Third Plenum in 1978 to narrow the scope of campaigns. Rather than involve all policy sectors simultaneously, campaigns were restricted to particular sectors where they might be most appropriately employed. Their intensity also was diminished lest they spin out of control, creating unforeseen problems and destroying the stability on which any long-term development strategy rests. Future campaigns, therefore, are likely to be relegated to secondary status with regard to implementation.

Centralization. Campaigns typically are highly centralized in the sense that the decision to proceed is usually issued from Beijing. Guidelines on the conduct of the campaign are communicated downward through the mass media and the organizations responsible for conducting the campaign. For the most part, however, the administrative structure is thin and the content of instructions sketchy. That in part results from bypassing the regular bureaucracies. Priority is placed on local initiative in the spirit of grassroots mobilization, but the frequent result is disorganization as localities interpret the campaign to suit their own circumstances. Thus, what begins as a highly centralized initiative sometimes culminates in chaos.

Compliance. Instead of promises of material gain or career advancement, campaigns characteristically rely on a mixture of normative incentives and coercion to secure compliance. Hortatory appeals are made in behalf of the campaign's formal goals in order to stimulate participation. Campaign organizers cultivate "backbone elements" among the politically reliable to serve as the nucleus, then agitate their constituency as a whole through mobilization meetings, the popularization of model heroes, and other devices. Although the ideal campaign might obtain participation solely on the basis of enhanced identification with the regime's values, in practice any campaign also embodies a mixture of artificially stimulated social pressure and threats of coercion. Indeed, some campaigns of the ideological type rely heavily on violence directed against designated enemies of the regime. Personalization of the target through scapegoating graphically instructs everyone else on the dangers of being labeled an enemy of the people, thus increasing the incentives for participation. Reliance on the inculcation of fear suggests, however, that campaigns may be more effective at deterring unorthodox behavior than at eliciting change in positive values (Goldman 1979).

Nonetheless, the capacity of campaigns to elicit participation has fallen markedly since the Cultural Revolution. The decline in responsiveness has been felt throughout the populace but most of all among younger generations forced to adjust to sudden policy reversals and newly aware that China lags far behind Taiwan and nearby countries. Youths who participated in the Cultural Revolution felt betrayed when Mao abruptly withdrew his support in 1968 and ordered them to the countryside. Their sense of disillusionment grew with the realization that their lack of sound education and skills meant that their years of activism had been wasted in terms of future career prospects. Meanwhile, the post-Cultural Revolution generation became skeptical about socialism and inclined to pursue personal interests over politics. The party and its auxiliaries, especially the Communist Youth League, faced internal crises as they were forced to adjust to reduced roles for themselves and increasingly cynical and individualistic constituencies (Rosen 1985, Hooper 1985).

The decline in the normative mobilization power of campaigns represents a sharp reversal from the situation in the mid-1970s. Then, the radical left was still vying for power, and some Western analysts were led to identify continued reliance on the mass mobilization campaign as "the hallmark of Chinese communism" (Cell 1977: 6). Unless popular support for campaigns somehow expands once again, it seems unlikely that campaigns can ever regain as prominent a role as they enjoyed in the past. The likelihood instead is that future campaigns—even economic ones—either will be less intensive or will have to rely more extensively on coercion.

The role of the party. Campaigns are a quintessentially party product. Although extensive reliance on campaigns in the economy arose in the guerrilla war out of hardship, campaigns also represent the practical application of ideology to day-to-day tasks. Ideology serves not only to motivate participants but also to define problems and solutions in political terms. In terms of the initiation and leadership of campaigns, power is not distributed equally among the elite but instead is concentrated at the peak of the system and among those involved in party affairs and ideology or propaganda rather than economic management or technology. A typical campaign is decided upon by the higher leadership, often at the urging of party propagandists, and then disseminated downward for implementation, either through specially created work teams or through the regular administrative bureaucracies, but under the direct guidance of their party branches rather than line bureaus.

Thus, the initiation of campaigns is an intensely political choice that tends to align ideologues against their counterparts in the party who are more interested in modernization than in revolution. The post-Mao era saw a dramatic transformation in this regard when the purge of the Gang of Four, followed by the eclipse of the Whatever faction, which was still faithful to Mao's precepts, greatly reduced the power of the ideologues. In their place rose Deng Xiaoping and the pragmatists, who no longer held much faith in the power of shopworn ideology to modernize the country. Indeed, General Secretary Hu Yaobang among others argued that the party should henceforth concentrate on educating and persuading the people, beginning with its own cadres, rather than engaging in day-to-day involvement in administrative affairs often through coercive means (Hu Yaobang 1983: 7). In other words, managers and experts should be allowed much wider scope to run the country without interference by the party.

Naturally, Hu's prescription for a scaled-back party focusing on "human relations" in terms of organization theory ran into opposition. Within a year, China embarked on a Combat Spiritual Pollution campaign on the apparent initiative of the party's Propaganda Department with Deng Xiaoping's backing. When the campaign appeared on the verge of getting out of hand and upsetting intellectuals, foreign investors, and others whose contributions were needed for modernization, Deng withdrew his support and the campaign fizzled.

By the winter of 1986–87, the conservatives had regained the initiative and were able to deal a damaging blow to the pragmatists, with Deng Xiaoping himself forced to depose his erstwhile successor, Hu Yaobang. That signaled a slowdown to the reforms that had begun after Mao's death. Even on this occasion, however, the leadership took pains to announce limits: purges, reeducation, and other characteristic elements of campaigns would be allowed to continue (NYT, January 30, 1987). That meant that campaigns were unlikely to regain their past prominence without an even more drastic change in the political balance.

Moreover, because campaigns lack a permanent identity and autonomous expertise, they would still face the danger of routinization and capture by permanent organizations even if more political support were forthcoming.

For example, the annual winter season farmland capital construction campaigns never regained the transcendental promise of building a new social system that was theirs during the Great Leap Forward. Instead, they became a regular feature of the agricultural collectives and then declined when the power of the collectives was curtailed after the Third Plenum in 1978, especially in southern China.

Property rights. Campaigns are predicated upon eliciting self-abnegating behavior from the populace indicating that the ideal is for property rights to be held in common. A latter-day example of this phenomenon was the campaign to Build a Socialist Spiritual Civilization that took shape in 1981 in an effort to restrain the entrepeneurial and get-rich-quick impulses unleashed by the Four Modernizations. The campaign included a variety of civic programs in which individuals were expected to take part without compensation, not only to build up the public sector but also to reemphasize socialist values (Ross 1987). Most often, however, campaigns operate within the prevailing regime of nominally common property rights.

The challenge facing campaigns in this regard is their ability to overcome the tragedy of the commons, which involves the abuse of property that is either publicly owned or lacks clear title and assignment of usage rights. In China, such property ranges from stairwells in apartment buildings and the area between a unit's outer walls and the street to larger areas such as grasslands, forests, and waterways. Cell (1977) and Bennett (1976) argued that campaigns were highly successful precisely because they mobilized people in large numbers to do what individuals or small groups in ordinary circumstances could not accomplish. In other words, campaigns overcome the customary impediments to collective action and thereby can best resolve problems affecting the management of common property resources.

In actuality, the record of campaigns appears to be at best mixed and frequently negative. Because campaigns produce a rise in activity, they may appear to exert a positive impact that is loudly trumpeted in the press, but the accomplishments are often evanescent and fade quickly when attention turns elsewhere. For example, it is widely known that many natural predators were decimated during the Combat Pests campaigns of the 1950s before it was realized that they actually helped agriculture by devouring insects and other pests. It is less commonly known that periodic antipest campaigns relying on massive applications of toxic pesticides have continued, decimating predator populations through the accumulation of toxins in the fatty tissues of higher animals, thus worsening the problem of rat infestation while deflecting attention from other solutions (CD, Dec. 14, 1985).

Very often, in fact, campaign accomplishments are exaggerated by junior officials without fear of follow-up inspections or sanctions. Even in the 1950s when popular response to the normative appeals of a newly victorious revolutionary regime was higher, the results often were flawed. That problems have grown worse in more recent times suggests that campaigns in the long run are of limited effectiveness as society modernizes and becomes more structurally differentiated.

Market-Exchange Implementation

Markets are abstract yet highly flexible institutions that operate on the basis of mutually advantageous transactions between buyers and sellers. Markets can organize trade in specific, highly tangible commodities such as coal or clothing, in aggregations of commodities such as the market for consumer goods, or in such intangibles as services. The key element is the exchange of benefits between self-interested parties, none of whom participate unless they stand to gain from the transaction. Prices summarize information on aggregate supply-and-demand relationships, signaling producers and consumers when and how to participate. To the extent that prices accurately reflect scarcity, the market will be cleared, resulting in an equilibrium. Markets thus enable participants to interact with minimal direct contact or formal supervision in a manner that quickly responds to changes in supply or demand.

Markets for private goods under perfect competition and well-defined property rights function efficiently. Where competition is absent or flawed, the goods in question are collective or public (i.e., noncontributors or free riders cannot be excluded), or there are extensive externalities (i.e., effects on parties not involved in the transaction), then markets cannot spontaneously produce efficient outcomes. That does not always mean, however, that markets ought to be rejected in favor of planning or campaigns in such cases. Governments can design artificial markets, or the private goods components of public goods may be segregated to enable markets to operate in the private goods sector.

Markets, of course, were of only marginal importance in the Chinese political economy before the Third Plenum. Since then, their scope has greatly expanded through the relaxation and sometimes the elimination of state controls over many commodities and the privatization of property rights. In general, markets operate under the broad rubric of indirect or guidance plans, floating prices, and other controls, so they are not truly free markets. Nevertheless, they play an increasingly prominent role. Because of their rising importance, they warrant full consideration.

Comprehensiveness. Markets can be extended to most sectors of the political economy. The principal exceptions involve the kinship, family, or fraternal economy in which items of value are exchanged on the basis of love or as gifts rather than for direct personal advantage, although Becker (1981) has shown that even marriage and similar relationships can be creatively analyzed in terms of economic exchanges. In other cases, a lack of infrastructure or of buyers and sellers may inhibit the formation of markets, especially in a subsistence economy. Of more importance in the modern world are public goods such as those for national defense where noncontributors or nonpurchasers cannot feasibly be excluded from enjoyment, although even in such cases markets may be employed on the production side.

Centralization. Although there are some limitations on market scope, the more important feature is the general absence of explicit coordinating mechanisms. Markets consist of a highly decentralized process in which price and self-interest coordinate the activities of large numbers of actors despite geographical separation and the complexity of their transactions. Because they are decentralized, markets are likely to be opposed by most Marxists as well as anyone else who believes that conscious or "scientific" planning can outperform self-interested individuals. More specifically, the central planners are likely to condemn even limited markets out of fear that individuals or localities will acquire power sufficient to evade the planners' commands. Such appears to have been the case at the Central Work Conference of 1980 where Chen Yun and his allies forced a temporary halt to the process of economic reform that involved administrative decentralization as well as market measures per se (Solinger 1982). Chen was particularly exercised by the prospects of a decline in grain production, which he feared would lead to "social disorder" (CD, Sept. 24, 1985).

Compliance. Markets are distinguished by their singular reliance on material incentives and appeals to self-interest. Other factors may affect the process, but they are distinctly subordinate. This pattern inevitably causes conflicts because of the ideological tendency to condemn self-interest as a manifestation of exploiter-class mentality. That was most pronounced during the Cultural Revolution and the later power struggle over Mao's succession. Zhang Chunqiao (1975) and Yao Wenyuan (1975), two members of the Gang of Four, cited Marx's century-old injunctions against the "bourgeois right" to reject any effort to resume paying people according to their effort and skills rather then equally or on the basis of political virtue.

By contrast, Deng Xiaoping, Hu Yaobang, and Zhao Ziyang became convinced that material benefits and greater allowance for self-interest were essential ingredients in their modernization policy. That led to many policy adjustments involving not only wages and fringe benefits, but also credit, taxation, pricing, and property rights. Although it was recognized that some social stratification would inevitably result, such stratification was considered temporary and regarded as a necessary spur to laggards.

Role of the party. The party's organizational role in a market system is extremely limited because participants make decisions in accordance with their own self-interest rather than with an externally defined political interest. Opposition to the expansion of market methods therefore is likely to emanate from two sources. Ideologues and propagandists, whose power rests on their authority to articulate a governing political philosophy, can be expected to resist any innovation that threatens to relegate them to political impotence, especially one that denies the need for guidance in political and economic ethics. Proponents of planning also may object to a decline in party influence for this reason.

Nonetheless, it is the party itself that decides whether markets are to be expanded and thus whether its operating role in implementation should decline. This decision-making process requires strong, unified leadership to prevail against inertial forces as well as political opposition. For example, proponents recognized that the decisions taken in October 1984 to accelerate economic reforms in the urban areas and subsequently to proceed with price reform required some centralization of overall decision-making power (Tian Jiyun 1984: 19). However, illegal and quasi-legal behavior often is unleashed during the transitional phase of the reforms when markets are still highly imperfect, perversely jeopardizing the future of the reforms.

Property rights. The market approach features the disaggregation of property rights to individuals or corporate enterprises. While this approach achieves its purest form in a strictly private economy, there is nothing to prevent its application in a more limited group or collectively oriented property rights regime. So long as the transactions between entities are decided on the basis of mutual self-advantage, it matters little how large the entities are, or whether internal transactions are themselves market oriented or characterized by some form of solidary relations. As Williamson (1975) argued, the formal hierarchy characteristic of large corporations often has advantages over small companies even in a market economy because many individual transactions can be subsumed under broad employment contracts, thereby reducing transaction costs. In other words, the market itself helps to define the optimal scale of its own organization.

Similarly, although "local organizations" or voluntary cooperatives in many respects represent alternatives to the market as well as to bureaucracies, it is also apparent that their success in a market economy depends on their economic performance and internal cost accounting, as even sympathetic studies indicate (Esman and Uphoff 1984: 24 and 221). It is unclear whether local organizations represent a pure alternative to households, corporations, and bureaucracies, but the lack of associational freedom led to their virtual absence in China until the post-Mao era. Moreover, it is still not clear to what extent the rise of new "cooperative" *(hezuo)* forms of social organization since the Third Plenum in place of "collectives" *(jiti)* is due to the preferences of small cultivators and urban residents or to the regime's continuing need to maintain some form of control and ideological conformity over market participants.

Regardless of whether rights holders are private or corporate, the government's role becomes one of clarifying and enforcing property rights to be exercised by citizens, while retaining for direct administration only those property rights that cannot feasibly be transferred to private or corporate jurisdiction. The redefinition of government's role and the shrinkage of the commons are in dramatic contrast with the two approaches previously considered. Because the policies to be addressed in this book are among those considered least amenable to a market approach, they provide strong test cases for evaluating the limits to its effectiveness.

Of course, it is no easy task to create a property rights regime of this sort out of a highly controlled political economy of the central planning type. Not only is firm political leadership needed to prevail against domestic opposition, but a myriad of equity and technical problems also arise concerning the distribution as well as the definition of rights, the setting of prices, and the like. Since it is clear that efficient markets cannot be created in all cases, the task China faces is in part one of avoiding the temptation to extend the markets too quickly and to apply them in inappropriate situations.

Conclusions

The three implementation strategies identified in this chapter exhibit sharply divergent features. The bureaucratic-authoritative approach is a comprehensive, centrally directed system relying on commands. It concentrates information and authority in a small body of officials responsible for the overall governance of society. The paradox is that it depends on large bureaucracies that accumulate power unto themselves and tend to operate in accordance with internal needs even when these needs do not coincide with planners' preferences or the external environment. Bureaucracies can overwhelm the planning process by manipulating the flow of information upward as well as by modifying the execution of commands while engaging in mutual rivalries among themselves. The chief danger is that bureaucracies will usurp power from the higher leadership while exploiting the populace at large.

The exhortational-campaign strategy by contrast relies on inculcating a unity of values among the central authorities and the populace at large to carry out policies. The chief problem is that the values of parties in such widely disparate circumstances do not coincide, and, morality aside, the regime cannot always employ coercion to generate positive compliance by an otherwise reluctant populace. Without stronger linkages between center and periphery, power tends to accrue to grass-roots units that operate without any clear sense of direction, creating the danger of a collapse of political authority—as almost happened during the Cultural Revolution.

The market-exchange approach is predicated upon the pursuit of self-interest by individuals whose activities are coordinated impersonally without benefit of advance design. It ultimately represents a radical departure from the other two approaches because intervention from above and moral injunctions are relegated to secondary status. From the perspective of defenders of the status quo, the risk is a transfer of power from the party and government to corporate entities and individuals. From another perspective, the danger is the inability of autonomous participants to cooperate in behalf of shared purposes, resulting in what might be called "the tragedy of the private" because of market imperfections. The rise in crime during the early post-Mao era is a particularly salient example, and it may jeopardize the entire approach.

The major concern of this book is the relative effectiveness of each approach with regard to the implementation of public policy. As such, the book seeks to determine whether the approaches exhibit consistent influence on policy outputs. Nonetheless, no study of the policy process, particularly in a country as highly politicized as China, can escape the politics of policy implementation. Therefore, I will pay considerable attention to how and why policy choices are made, beginning with forestry and then proceeding to water resources and pollution control. In this manner I will be able to both map the policy process and analyze policy outcomes.

II.

FORESTRY POLICY

This analysis of environmental policy begins with forestry, a renewable biological resource. With sound management, the supply of forest products and forestry's ecological functions, like those of any other biological resource, can be sustained indefinitely. If policy is misguided, however, the resource stock will be degraded, to the misfortune of both producers and society at large. In this chapter, I will show that forestry growth during the Maoist era was slowed by deficiencies in central planning and by policy instability, despite substantial rhetorical support by the higher leadership. The problems included inadequate producer prices and a lack of coordination between growers and loggers. I will argue that the market approach presents substantial potential for improving resource management in the post-Mao era but that it remains subject to serious technical as well as political impediments.

Forestry has long been a matter of social and political concern in modern China. China ranks low among the countries of the world with regard to forest area and timber reserves, and her standing is even lower on a per capita basis because of her great population. Some summary numbers convey the severity of the problem. China has 115 million hectares (ha) of forest, with forest cover amounting to 12 percent of surface area. That compares poorly to a world average of 22 percent. Moreover, one-third of China's forests are considered poorly stocked (Luo Hanxian 1983, Forestry Development Section 1983). On a per capita basis, China has less than 0.12 ha per person, far below the world average of 1.1 ha. In both respects, China ranks about 120th among the countries of the world (Chi Weiyun 1982).

Timber reserves are also sparse, totaling just over 10 billion m^3, or about 10 m^3 per capita, of which about one-third is accessible. By contrast, the United States, with less than one-quarter of China's population, has 1.41 ha forest and 97.6 m^3 timber reserves per capita. Stocking is poor in China. Reserves average 70–75 m^3/ha but this figure is skewed by the remaining virgin forests in remote areas of the country such as Tibet. Stocking elsewhere averages only about 30 m^3/ha, far below the standards of advanced countries, and post-1949 plantations average only about 10 m^3/ha (Wu Jinghe 1983, Ministry of Forestry Technical 1983: 26–27).

The shortage of forest resources has severe consequences for industrial production and living standards. Timber distributed through state channels totals just over 50 million m³ per year, or 0.05 m³ per capita. That is far below average world consumption of 0.65 m³ per capita and less than one-thirtieth the level of the United States, even though China has fewer substitutes to choose from. Even after allowance is made for timber that is consumed on site or distributed outside state channels and for noncommercial wood products such as firewood, per capita consumption is still only about 0.2 m³ per capita (Yong Wentao 1982, *Linye Gongzuo* 7: 39).

The shortage of wood fiber affects the entire economy. Timber, like other building materials and energy, is officially classified as a scarce commodity and has been subjected to strict pricing and distribution controls (State Commodities General Administration 1981). Even so, not enough wood is available to meet the needs of the construction, mining, railway, paper, and other industries. Planned allocations are insufficient to begin with, yet enterprises often consider themselves lucky to receive what they have been promised. For example, in 1980 the construction industry received only about two-thirds of planned deliveries, and the deficiency contributed to chronic delays in project completion (Lin Senmu and Zhou Shulian 1981). Competition for timber became so severe in the early 1980s that prices rose sharply and the central government's priority projects languished for lack of supplies. To assure progress on key projects without causing inflation, the regime imposed strict controls on lower-priority construction projects and insisted on absolute compliance with fixed prices for scarce commodities (Chang 1984; BR, Aug. 15 1983: 7).

Timber scarcity acquires a more human complexion when the necessities of life are considered. The rural sector is home to 85 percent of China's population, most of whom rely on vegetative matter or biomass for part or all of their fuel needs (table 1). Biomass provides about 80 percent of

Table 1

Energy Sources for Daily Life in Rural China, 1979

Source	Volume (thousand tons)	Heat Value (calories/ kilo)	Standard Coal Equivalent (thousand tons)	Standard Coal Equivalent (% of total)
Untreated coal	39,300	5,000	28,070	10.3
Fuelwood	181,600	4,000	103,770	38.1
Plant stalks	231,800	3,400	112,590	41.3
Animal dung	9,400	3,000	4,030	1.5
Methane gas	703,760	5,000	500	0.2
Other	48,000	3,400	23,310	8.6
Total	1,213,860	--	272,270	100.0

SOURCE: Chen Tuyan (1983).

the rural fuel budget—which is typical of less developed countries. Wood accounts for about 38 percent of the total biomass used for energy, with stalks and other plant matter supplying the remainder (Sun Jingbo 1983). Yet into the late 1970s 42 percent of rural households were still short of fuel for heating and cooking for three months or longer each year and another 22 percent suffered from fuel shortages for briefer periods (FAO 1982: 242–43, Wu Wen and Chen Enjian 1982, Forestry Development Section 1983, *Linye Gongzuo* 8: 106). In desperation, people uprooted or chopped down vegetation, depriving the soil of organic nutrients and tilth, and plundered historical landmarks and other structures for wood (Chen Tuyan 1983; NYT, May 20, 1983; RR, March 27, 1985). For a long time furniture was also in short supply, which is hardly surprising since the allocation of timber for the furniture industry in 1979 was only half that for 1957, even though the population had grown by 300 million in the interim (Bernstein 1982: 145).

Although people and industry may cope with shortages of wood fiber by making do with less or relying more on concrete, bagasse, and other substitutes (Veilleux 1978: 102–3, Peterson 1982: 141), the long-term environmental consequences are severe. Deforestation increases water runoff and aggravates erosion. Soil loss can affect farming in the source areas, but far worse is the heightened danger of flooding in lowland areas because heavy sediment loads aggrade streambeds and clog natural drainage channels. The Yellow River is notorious for being the muddiest river in the world, carrying an average sediment load of 37.6 kg/m^3 and aggrading its bed by up to 10 cm a year. Its average annual erosion rate has been calculated at 1.5 cm over the entire basin, about ten times higher than the much smaller Eel River basin in northern California, which is the most heavily silted stream in the United States (Shen 1979: 546). What is worse, the sediment load is said to have increased by over 20 percent since the Communists gained power (Zhong Xingfan 1982). Meanwhile, many foresters and ecologists apocalyptically warn that China's greatest river, the Yangtze, is in danger of becoming a second Yellow River due to deforestation in the southwestern highlands (Ross 1983b, He Naihui 1982, Wang Mingzhong 1983).

Thus, China is a forest deficit nation in ecological, economic, and social terms. An enlarged forest resource base is in consonance with the ancient mandate for Chinese governments to harmonize relations between heaven and earth and between man and nature, a mandate that was manifested in repeated afforestation programs during periods of dynastic vigor (Chen Rong 1934). Afforestation also has been championed in the Soviet Union, particularly with regard to windbreaks or shelter belts in farming areas. In sum, forestry merited a big effort from the People's Republic of China both on practical grounds and in terms of tradition and ideology. The question is how successfully it has met this challenge. My task is to first trace the course of policy and then proceed to evaluate its effectiveness.

Historical Review

The Chinese Communist party (CCP) expressed an interest in promoting forestry soon after its locus of operations shifted to the countryside. Even before coming to power in 1949, the CCP had initiated afforestation programs in areas under its control, including the Jiangxi Republic (1931–34) and the Shaan-Gan-Ning Border Region (beginning in 1937). These programs were very modest in scale. They paled in comparison with the inevitable damage to forests that had been caused by agricultural reclamation and logging for economic and military reasons in these poor, hard-pressed areas (Ross 1980a: 41–54, Yu Guangyuan 1980: 18–19; cf. Schran 1976: 119–21). Far more important was the social aspect. The party's land reform policy, particularly in Jiangxi, threatened confiscation of private landholdings, thus encouraging liquidation both by the original landholders and by the new owners (Polachek 1983: 824, Ross 1980a: 41–54).

Our main interest, however, is the CCP's policy since 1949. Afforestation began on a small scale but soon grew to become an enormous program averaging four to five million hectares a year, not to mention many millions of trees planted in scattered lots and along roadways. It is the largest sustained tree-planting program in human history, involving great waves of human energy to transform the face of China from a treeless and often erosion-prone landscape into a sylvan vista bringing pleasure and prosperity to the people. The party's sentiments are aptly expressed in such phrases as "greenification of the motherland" (lühua zuguo) and "the great gardenification" (da yuanlinhua).

The CCP's forestry policy cannot be discussed without reference to land ownership, management, marketing, and organization. The party's fundamental goal was to assert public ownership of most forests as well as other natural resources and, ultimately, the economy as a whole. From the outset, in the Agrarian Reform Law of 1950 (article 18) and all future state constitutions, the state claimed ownership of all major natural forests as well as forests of special strategic or economic significance and forests whose ownership could not otherwise be determined. In this fashion, the state soon laid claim to ownership of 73 percent of the country's forests by area, although there were great regional variations. The state's control was greatest in such sparsely settled frontier regions as the rim of Manchuria, a remote vastness whose rich forest lands had only recently been opened up by the Japanese. By contrast, the remaining forests in long-settled regions, especially the South, were largely under private ownership (Ross 1980a: 67).

Private ownership flourished briefly in the early 1950s, when land reform actually increased the number of private woodlot owners by redistributing larger holdings confiscated from clans, temples, landlords, and so-called rich peasants. For a time, private forestry was the mainstay of afforestation while the government was preoccupied with reconstruction (Government Administration Council 1951). Even then, rural cadres showed hostility toward private owners, who were regarded at best as latent enemies of the revolution. Nevertheless, the party continued to follow a moderate line in the countryside. As late as the summer of 1953, the government issued a major directive that reminded officials of the important role that private forestry would yet play in the South. Households were promised respect for privately held plantations under the formulation *shei zhong shei you* (ownership to the planter). Cadres were warned that continued interference with harvest and marketing decisions and threats to seize woodlots would further dampen private interest in forestry and exacerbate deforestation (ibid. 1953).

Nevertheless, the demise of private forestry was in sight. Cooperative afforestation had been eagerly promoted from the outset as the key to developing forestry as well as to furthering social change (Ministry of Forestry 1952; Zhongguo Linye Editorial Committee 1953: 21). Although the pace of collectivization was originally intended to be fairly gradual, taking fifteen years or longer to complete, it soon sped up precipitously. Party chairman Mao Zedong feared that land reform would entrench a new class of wealthy peasants in power unless collectivization was accelerated. Mao furthermore believed that collectivization would unleash the productive power of the masses, resulting in a great increase in agricultural output through organizational change and ideological inspiration. He circumvented the opposition of his more cautious colleagues in Beijing, including Liu Shaoqi and Deng Zihui, by taking his case to the provinces and packing key decision-making bodies, especially the party Central Committee's Sixth Plenum in October 1955, with his supporters. Thus, collectivization essentially was completed by the beginning of 1956, over a decade earlier than originally planned (Chang 1978: 9–17, MacFarquhar 1974: 15–32). Moreover, the first stage of collectivization, which involved thirty to forty households per unit as well as continued private ownership of the means of production, was soon superseded by advanced collectives that were about ten times larger and in which the collective owned the major factors of production.

It is important to note that collectivization in forestry actually preceded the process for agriculture as a whole. By 1954, 70–80 percent of all afforestation was already being conducted by cooperatives, a remarkable increase in the span of only one year (ZL 1954 9: 1–4, Ross 1980a: 82). This increase was justified by the greater capital needs and economies of scale characteristic of forestry. The Ministry of Forestry seems to have accepted collectivization for these reasons, although foresters qualified their position by insisting that success depended on voluntary participation by the peasants. Foresters from the minister on down recognized that forced collectivization would only arouse resentment and sabotage (Liang Xi 1955, Compendia of Forestry Laws and Regulations 5: 422).

Social and organizational reasons were also behind the rapid pace of collectivization in forestry. As Shue (1980) argued, collectivization's relatively smooth welcome among the populace was heightened by the promise of improved access to credit, tools, seeds, and other inputs that the government used as a positive inducement. Private farmers by contrast faced increasing difficulty securing inputs and marketing their produce as the state tightened control over supply and marketing.

Nevertheless, with the exception of access to better land and tools owned by wealthier households, the principal attraction of collectivization to farmers was the promise of future prosperity. That made forests vulnerable to the ax because they represented standing capital that could be used to start off collectives in the black. Rural cadres in many instances encouraged unsustainably high levels of logging to provide their newly organized collectives with windfall profits. Very little of the value of the timber was paid to the original owners despite their nominal rights to continued ownership of the means of production because trees were considered a gift of nature rather than a product of labor and thus could not be assigned a value from a Marxist economic standpoint. That helps to explain why collectivization advanced faster in forestry than in agriculture as a whole (Ross 1980a: 91–95, ZL 1956 5: 17–19).

The collectivization of the rural sector not only proceeded faster than originally intended; it also went further. Collectivization was at first expected to result in small organizations averaging thirty households, corresponding in size to natural villages, with participants retaining title to the capital they had contributed in exchange for dividends or rent payments. By late 1956, however, almost all of these Agricultural Producers' Cooperatives had been transformed into much larger (100–300 households) Advanced Agricultural Producers' Cooperatives that took ownership of land without compensation, in effect becoming true collectives. The Great Leap Forward in 1958 saw a further dramatic expansion in which the collectives were combined into communes as large as 20,000 households each, although the norm was closer to 5,000. Indeed, for a time virtually the entire farm population of China was grouped into barely 25,000 communes. These communes were not merely agricultural organizations; they also incorporated industrial functions and especially the powers of government previously exercised by the township (*xiang*) (Walker 1965, Crook 1975, Chinn 1978, Compendia of Forestry Laws and Regulations 8: 90–97).

The Great Leap Forward was an economic disaster, largely because it was organized in haste, conducted without regard for reality, and based on impossibly large organizational units (MacFarquhar 1983). The consequences for forestry were especially severe. The backyard steel furnaces campaign, communal cooking, and a big upsurge in timber production aggravated the breakdown of existing ownership and management systems.

Entire regions of the countryside, especially in the South and Southwest, were laid waste.

Although the Great Leap marked the apparent end of the private sector and small-scale agriculture and forestry, the ensuing economic depression eventually forced a policy retrenchment in the early 1960s (Compendia of Forestry Laws and Regulations 9: 1–7 and 19–33). Substantial economic authority was decentralized down to the production brigades and teams, smaller constituent units within the communes roughly corresponding in size to the old higher and primary level collectives respectively. Although decentralization helped to restore production, it proved highly controversial and was subject to recurring efforts to recentralize power, although it was never actually reversed. Most noteworthy was the Learn from Dazhai campaign. Dazhai was a model agricultural brigade that Mao plucked from obscurity to become a symbol of asceticism, discipline, and the subordination of economic activities to political goals. Its fame rested upon its elimination of production teams while treating the brigade as the basic accounting unit, thereby reducing inequality and enlarging the scale of production. Although Dazhai was eventually denounced as a fraudulent product of phony statistics, unpublicized state aid, and political repression (RR, Feb. 12, 1981; Zhou Jinhua 1981), it dominated the rural policy scene for over a decade. As late as 1976, national conferences on learning from Dazhai in agriculture were convened while the brigade's former leader, Chen Yonggui, enjoyed the prestige of Politburo membership.

It was not until 1978, two years after the death of Mao, that reform of the economy, including the collective system, became the watchword for the countryside at the Third Plenum of the Eleventh Central Committee. The Rules and Regulations concerning Work in the Rural People's Communes from the early 1960s, widely known as the Sixty Articles, were updated and supplemented by a new statement of twenty-five articles. The new document confirmed the status of the smallish production team as the unit of account, reducing the power of the commune and brigade and beating back the challenge presented by the image of Dazhai. More importantly, the production responsibility system was legitimized, and that encouraged small work groups to contract with their production teams for the performance of various tasks (BR 23: 12, Mar. 24, 1980: 14–20). That in turn paved the way for the extension of similar grants of autonomy over the next several years to households and individuals who were encouraged to get rich on their own, without waiting for their neighbors to keep pace.

In this fashion, the production responsibility system reproduced several features of a household-based farm economy reminiscent of tenant farming. The principal qualification was the party's ban on the private ownership of land, with Hu Yaobang, then party general secretary, and Premier Zhao Ziyang maintaining that public ownership of land is one of the two fundamental criteria of a socialist society (the other being the distribution of income according to labor). Under the production responsibility system, the collective retained ownership of land, apportioning plots and tasks to individuals or small groups for management. The latter pledged that they would complete their contractual responsibilities in exchange for a share of the output plus eligibility for performance incentives. Over time, producer autonomy with regard to farming has been further eased, to the point that "specialized households" are often no longer part of the grain-dominated economy at all, while others engage in diversified agriculture.

In addition, a portion of the collective landholdings are divided among households on an equal per capita basis as private plots. These plots, tiny as they are, supply much of China's eggs, vegetables, pork, and similar commodities. In all, it is estimated that private plots and sideline occupations outside the collective structure contributed almost 40 percent of household income on average in the early 1980s. Although private plots remain under public ownership, they can be inherited and thus share many features of genuinely private property (Lin Wenshan 1983, Keidel 1983).

The collectives continue to perform some roles throughout the countryside, although their power is much reduced thanks to the separation of political and economic functions. They also continue to serve as intermediaries between the state and the households and may exercise a dominant role with regard to the management of many common property resources such as irrigation systems. As power within the "collectives" devolves down to the villages (the old production brigades) and as household autonomy rises, the collectives have been encouraged to evolve in the direction of "cooperatives," offering a varying mix of services based on voluntary rather than compulsory membership instead of trying to manage the entire economy.

It must be stressed, however, that the state plan remains a critical decision-making element in the rural sector as it does in the economy as a whole (Lardy 1983). The state sets aggregate production targets for priority (first-category) commodities such as grain and cotton that are then divided among the collectives. Under current arrangements, the collectives in turn contract with households or small groups for production (Du Runsheng 1984b: 19–20). Producers can determine how to work their land but do not have complete freedom to decide what to produce or how to market their produce and negotiate prices. There has, however, been a considerable expansion of autonomy with regard to the marketing of above-norm production even for tightly regulated commodities (FBIS, Dec. 5, 1983: P3–4; Zhao Ziyang 1985). If the role of compulsory delivery quotas in the agricultural economy continues to decline, producer autonomy and the role of markets will further increase.

The state's continuing power to shape the rural economy is clearest with regard to grain production. During the 1960s and early 1970s grain had highest priority under the slogans "take grain as the key link" and "dig deep and store grain everywhere." This command-based system resulted in sluggish production increases for grain and actual decreases in cotton, oils, and other less favored commodities still subject to compulsory deliveries (Lardy 1983). The economic reforms that began in the late 1970s spurred production of grain and other commodities, but also aroused a backlash among defenders of the plan who feared that grain would be neglected. They argued that planning is as essential a feature of socialism as public ownership and distribution of income according to labor and therefore should not be sacrificed for merely transitory gains, especially since they believed in socialism's ultimate superiority over capitalism. They were particularly worried by the decline in acreage devoted to grain caused by increased planting of more lucrative crops and the rural housing boom that resulted from the peasants' newfound prosperity. Ironically, adherents to planning do not seem to have attributed to planning deficiencies the loss of twenty million hectares of farmland (resulting in a net loss of seven million hectares) over the previous quarter century due to irrigation, urbanization, and other construction projects (BR 23: 12, Mar. 24, 1980: 14). In any event, the decline in grain production in 1985 led to a modest effort to restore grain production without fundamentally compromising the reforms (RR, Feb. 23, 1986).

This brief review reveals the three basic modes of forestry ownership and management in China: state, collective, and private. These three correspond quite closely to the implementation categories identified in the first chapter: bureaucratic-authoritative, campaign-exhortation, and market-exchange. The state system is essentially bureaucratic and relies largely on hierarchic commands to secure compliance; the collective sector features campaigns alongside plans; and the private sector relies largely on material incentives organized through market-type mechanisms. The prominence of each at any given time is largely a reflection of broader political dynamics, although the peculiarities of forestry also are involved. Inevitably there is some degree of overlap between the three sectors. Some market mechanisms now operate within the collective and state sectors. Nevertheless, the distinction between the three sectors is large enough to warrant treating them separately. To facilitate the narrative, most of this chapter will be organized under the state, collective, and private headings. Before proceeding, however, some additional background information on performance and problems is needed.

Policy Performance

Although statistics for China became much more comprehensive and widely available after Mao's death in 1976, it can still be very difficult to evaluate policy performance because of gaps and inconsistencies in the data. That is particularly true for forestry, where the infrequency and lack of uniform standards in resource inventories makes it hard to determine how large the resource base is at any given time, how fast it is growing, what the quality of the stock is like, and whether any changes in the numbers are due to increases or decreases in forest area and timber growth or to changes in inventory procedures (Zhou Xu and Chen Qizhong 1984). The ability to accurately measure China's resource base affects the regime's capacity to make sound policy decisions, and that in turn affects the future of timber production and ecological functions such as soil conservation.

For example, the Chinese tend to describe all land not being used in Chinese-style agriculture as "wasteland" (Enderton 1984: 23), yet there is no absolute criterion to decide when a site is in need of reforestation or whether a site that is scientifically suited to forestry is needed for agriculture, industry, or other uses. Although skilled foresters can agree on what constitutes full closure of the forest canopy or what the quality of a plantation is like, the lack of an immediate end product makes it easy for politically minded officials to misrepresent reality in order to exaggerate their accomplishments. The result is that forestry statistics are highly prone to vagueness and distortion, even in a political economy where the manipulation of numbers is a basic skill in the hands of politicians up and down the policy ladder.

It is claimed that forest cover in 1949 amounted to 8.6 percent of surface area, or about 82.8 million hectares, although one occasionally still encounters much lower claims of about 5 percent of surface area or 50 million hectares. The smaller figure is based on actual but incomplete survey data, while the larger number is more of an extrapolation (*Contemporary* 1985: 27). Following a decline during the early 1950s, Chinese sources report that forest cover expanded in an irregular fashion to 12.7 percent of surface area, or 122 million hectares, by the mid-1970s. By 1981, however, forest cover had retreated to 12 percent of surface area, or 115 million hectares (table 2). This decrease was a result of policy changes to be discussed later. Thus, there was a net rate of increase of about a million hectares a year during the PRC's first three decades, according to official sources. These same sources report that timber reserves also increased during the period, from about 5,800 million m^3 in 1949 to 9,500 million m^3 in the mid-1970s, before increasing to 10,260 million m^3 in 1980. That represents a net rate of increase of about 140 million m^3 a year, or a compound growth rate of 1.8 percent (LJ 1985, 6:40).

Unfortunately, these figures seem to exaggerate the gains that have been made. The starting point of 8.6 percent forest cover is almost certainly too low, which is not surprising given the absence of genuine inventories and the desire of forestry personnel to gild their accomplishments and to emphasize the need for additional investments in forestry (*Linye Gongzuo* 8: 141, Ross 1980b, Sheng Chijing 1950). This point is easily shown by subtracting newly afforested area from later, more reliable statistics. From 1949 to 1981, over 112 million hectares were afforested but only 28 million hectares, or about 25 percent, were successful (Chi Weiyun 1982, LJ 1985

Table 2

China's Forests

Classification	Area (10³ ha)	% of Forests	% of Surface Area
Fully Stocked (1981) (0.4+ closure)			
Timber	83,836	74.0	
Economic	11,280	10.0	
Shelter	10,002	8.8	
Fuelwood	3,693	3.3	
Special use	1,299	1.1	
Bamboo	3,200	2.8	
Total	113,308	100.0	
Taiwan	1,970		
Total	115,277		12.0
Lightly stocked (1976) (0.1-0.3 closure)	15,630	1.6	
Shrubs (1976)	29,570	3.1	
Newly planted (1976) (-0.1 closure)	4,310	0.4	
Nurseries (1976)	400	0.1	
Total forestland	165,187	17.2	
Afforestable wasteland	83,500	8.7	
Total	248,687	26.2	

SOURCES: Data for 1976 from Ministry of Forestry Technical Economics Research Section (1983), 19–20. Data for 1981 from LJ (1985) 6: 40; and Contemporary 1985, 608 and 614–615. All totals rounded to the nearest thousand.

6: 40). Since the mid-1970s inventory reported 122 million hectares of forest, it seems that forest cover cannot have been less than 94 million hectares, or 9.8 percent of surface area, in 1949 (table 3).

The net increase shrinks further when losses are factored in. Forest fires damage an average of 660,000 hectares a year. The rate fell in the early 1980s from an average of 870,000 hectares in 1966–78 and an extraordinary 1.5 million hectares in 1979, when political conditions were unsettled and before the post-Mao reforms had been implemented; it rose again in 1985–86 to alarming levels (CD, Aug. 13, 1985, and Feb. 28, 1986; *Linye Gongzuo* 5: 156–62, 6: 158–66, and 8: 270–74). Pests and disease, problems that receive little attention because of their lack of drama and visibility, infest almost 7 million hectares a year on average, including over 8 million hectares in 1981 (*Linye Gongzuo* 8: 163–64; RR, Mar. 14, 1986). Defores-

Table 3

Afforestation in China, 1950-1984

Year	Timber 10^3 ha	%	Economic 10^3 ha	%	Shelter 10^3 ha	%	Other 10^3 ha	%	Total 10^3 ha	%
1950	14	11			87	53			127	100
1951	77	17			255	56			451	100
1952	500	46			548	50			1,085	100
1953	447	40	13	1	417	37	236	21	1,113	100
1954	636	55	34	3	339	29	157	13	1,166	100
1955	947	55	288	17	393	23	83	5	1,711	100
1956	2,454	43	1,428	25	1,352	24	489	9	5,723	100
1957	1,735	40	1,350	31	994	23	276	6	4,355	100
1958	2,513	41	2,297	38	849	14	440	7	6,099	100
1959	2,246	41	2,033	37	742	14	429	8	5,450	100
1960	1,959	47	1,314	32	511	12	360	9	4,144	100
1961	717	50	377	26	185	13	162	11	1,441	100
1962	606	51	340	28	126	11	127	11	1,199	100
1963	689	45	470	31	175	11	196	13	1,530	100
1964	1,392	48	825	28	436	15	258	9	2,911	100
1965	1,727	50	932	27	447	13	320	9	3,426	100
1966	2,389	53	1,058	23	624	14	462	10	4,533	100
1967	2,232	57	848	22	538	14	286	7	3,904	100
1968	1,988	58	668	20	452	13	305	9	3,413	100
1969	2,097	60	741	21	335	10	306	9	3,479	100
1970	2,461	63	656	17	381	10	386	10	3,884	100
1971	3,123	69	641	14	328	7	433	10	4,525	100
1972	3,437	74	525	11	286	6	388	8	4,636	100
1973	3,697	74	461	9	354	7	471	9	4,983	100
1974	3,779	76	502	10	385	8	336	7	5,002	100
1975	3,651	73	533	11	428	9	362	7	4,974	100
1976	3,545	72	663	13	429	9	289	6	4,926	100
1977	3,309	69	702	15	476	10	306	6	4,793	100
1978	3,130	70	881	20	420	9	65	1	4,496	100
1979	2,931	65	935	21	546	12	77	2	4,489	100
1980	2,927	64	823	18	513	11	289	6	4,552	100
1981	2,531	62	630	15	631	15	312	8	4,110	100
1982	2,631	59	653	15	861	19	351	8	4,496	100
1983	3,805	60	820	13	1,098	10	601	10	6,324	100
1984									6,930	100

SOURCES: State Statistical Bureau (1985b), 80; 1984 from BR
17, 52 (Dec. 27, 1984): 10.
NOTE: Economic forests include oil, nut, rubber, and similar
trees grown for their seeds, oil, or bark, rather than for
their timber. Fruit orchards are separately classified as
an agricultural endeavor. "Other" includes fuelwood,
national defense, and amenity forests.

tation in the name of agricultural and grasslands reclamation is also severe, far exceeding newly afforested land in some parts of the country, especially Xinjiang, Qinghai, and elsewhere in the Northwest, as well as Hainan, Yunnan, and other frontier areas in the South (*Linye Gongzuo* 8: 162–63). Lags in the regeneration of harvested land are said to total 920,000 hectares, but that may be an underestimate since Heilongjiang alone had a backlog of 870,000 hectares in the early 1980s. Moreover, more than 70 percent of regeneration has occurred through natural means, which tend to be slower and less reliable than human intervention (*Contemporary* 1985, app. 15; RR, Nov. 6, 1978; ZNN 1982: 335; Liaoning Forestry Society et al. 1982: 448). Finally, there have been continuing and widespread incidents of deforestation (*luan kan lan fa*) by the rural populace.

To be sure, with the exception of the conversion of forest land to agricultural or other purposes, most burnt, diseased, or harvested land remains available for forestry use and some of the timber can be salvaged. Nevertheless, consideration of forestry losses as well as gains substantially qualifies China's record of accomplishments. The *net* increase in forested area is probably less than half the one million hectares a year reported to have been successfully afforested. This figure corresponds to Vaclav Smil's estimate (1984: 12 and 22–23) that 20 million hectares were deforested through the 1970s and that only 43 million hectares, or less than one-third of forestland, are actually productive.

Although this does not negate China's impressive achievements in ubiquitous village and roadside plantings, which are not always included in afforestation statistics,* it shows that the long-standing shortage of forest resources cannot be alleviated without major reforms. Reports of massive afforestation are misleading because they are frequently inflated and do not allow for high rates of failure. The exaggeration arises during afforestation campaigns when cadres are under pressure to overfulfill their targets. In the absence of a reliable inspection procedure, cadres have little reason to fear that their falsification will be exposed. As the first minister of forestry explained:

> As everyone knows, our afforestation statistics are not really based on actual measurements, but are fixed on the basis of mere eyeballing or guesswork. Consequently, there are mistakes, overestimates, and even totally unfounded reports. (Liang Xi 1956)

Although the post-Mao regime insists on statistical accuracy, the problem persists. Hubei in 1984 submitted acreage claims that were two-thirds larger

---

*Some areas do incorporate individual tree plantings in afforestation statistics at a rate of 5,000 trees per hectare (*Contemporary* 1985: 29, Yang Furong et al. 1982). The failure to do so reflects a professional bias among foresters against small-scale operations and further obscures the true state of the resource base.

than the real figures, and Ningxia, Guizhou, and other provinces also conceded exaggeration problems (RR, Jan. 5 and 31, 1985; JPRS CST–84–
029, Sept. 27, 1984: 235–38). These problems were so serious that national
afforestation area statistics were omitted from the official statistical com-
muniques and yearbooks for 1985–86.

The leaders must continue to impress upon lower-level officials the need
for factual reporting. However, the tendency of the latter to exaggerate is
reinforced by the ambiguity of performance measures. The dominant considerations have historically been the number of trees or the size of the
area planted, and secondarily, the number that survive *chenghuo*, which can
be interpreted to mean survival on the day a sapling is planted regardless
of its future prospects. This practice encourages officials to focus on mobilizing a big effort to plant trees without sufficient heed for subsequent
cultivation and management. In recent years, there has been a decided shift
toward *baocun*, which also means survival but implies closure or good prospects for future growth. This change is partly responsible for the solid
improvements in quality that have been observed in many parts of China
(FAO 1982).

Nevertheless, confusion persists in the minds of many officials, and top
leaders like Vice-Premier Wan Li have to remind people every year to adopt
the *baocun* standard and to stop filing misleading reports on the number
of trees planted and *chenghuo* rates (RR, Mar. 1, 1986). This tendency is
hard to reverse because campaigns draw political sustenance from rising
claims of success submitted during the planting season rather than three
or five years down the road (Liu Yun 1984). Moreover, the criteria for
success are remarkably casual; they include *chenghuo* rates of as low as 40
percent and stocking densities of as low as 0.4 (Chinese Forestry Society
1985: 86–91). Under such circumstances, it is not surprising that *baocun*
rates average only about 30 percent, one-third of which consists of "dwarf
stands" just over 1.5 meters in height (ZNN 1982: 106, Wang Dianwen
1985).

New regulations promulgated in 1986 partially address this problem by
setting a minimum canopy closure requirement of 0.3 for qualification as
forest cover, requiring the inclusion of the Four Arounds roadside and
village plantings in forest cover statistics, and setting an 85 percent minimum survival rate standard for new plantations. Amazingly, the new regulations persist in use of the term *chenghuo* rather than *baocun*, which will
only perpetuate the confusion and impair quality (ZRGGYG, May 30, 1986:
456, articles 14 and 15).

The incompatibility between inventories conducted at different times is
further revealed by an examination of table 4. A comparison of the 1955
and 1976 inventories indicates that forest land increased in all areas of the
country, with the largest rate of increase occurring in thinly forested North
China and the smallest in the Southwest. These figures obscure the fact
that declines were actually reported for a number of provinces in terms of

Table 4

Regional Distribution of China's Forest Resources

Region	Forest Cover (% of surface area)		Per Capita Forested Land (hectares)	Per Capita Timber Reserves (m^3)
	1955-56	1973-76		
Southwest	9	11.0	0.17	24.4
Northwest	1	2.6	0.13	10.3
Central South	9	25.3	0.10	2.4
East	13	24.6	0.07	2.0
North	2	9.2	0.04	0.9
Northeast	23	34.2	0.24	27.7
Total	100	100.0	0.13	9.5

SOURCES: <u>Senlin</u> <u>Gongye</u> <u>Tongxun</u> (April 1957): 43; Li Keliang (1982): Ministry of Forestry Technical Economics Research Section (1983); <u>Zhongguo</u> <u>Linye</u> <u>Gaikuang</u> (Chinese Forestry Conditions); Beijing; ZL Chubanshe, 24-25.

forest cover, particularly in the Southwest, where forest cover in Sichuan fell from 19 percent to 13.3 percent, and in Yunnan, from 35 percent to 24.9 percent (Ross 1983b: 214). That once again indicates that inconsistency in inventory procedures complicates the task of analyzing changes over time. But the fact that data from the 1981 inventory have been more fully reported is encouraging (table 5).

This problem unfortunately persists, albeit to a lesser degree, as indicated by the mid-1970s and 1981 inventories. The largest proportional change took place in Gansu, an arid, poverty-stricken province which became the focus of an intensive tree-planting campaign launched by Party General Secretary Hu Yaobang himself, as well as an important link in the "Great Green Wall" shelterbelt system being built across northern China. However, shelterbelt construction did not actively get under way until 1978, and the Gansu campaign only began in the fall of 1979. No matter how many trees were later planted, they could not account for so large an increase unless the *baocun* reporting procedures were ignored. This is particularly likely given serious problems with planting stock (RR September 19, 1985; Ross 1986; *Linye Gongzuo*, 5:162–68 and 6:81–130). Moreover, the absence of any change whatsoever in major provinces like Yunnan and Tibet indicates that the later inventory was never completed in these remote areas. On the other hand, the large decline in Fujian may have been as much an artifact of changes in inventory procedures as of increased logging.

Forest industry and timber production statistics are free of the problems associated with counting trees and estimating timber growth but are subject to their own complications. China has officially reported a rise in timber production over the years to just over 60 million m^3, which represents a

Table 5

Provincial Forestry in China

	Forested Land (10^3 ha)			Forest Cover (%)		
	1973-76	1981	Change	1973-76	1981	Change
Beijing	200	140	− 60	11.2	8.1	− 3.1
Tianjin	30	30		2.4	2.6	+ 0.2
Hebei	2,010	1,670	− 340	10.8	9.0	− 1.8
Shansi	1,090	810	− 280	7.0	5.2	− 1.8
Inner Mongolia	10,700	13,840	+3,140	9.2	11.9	+ 2.7
Liaoning	3,420	3,650	+ 230	23.5	25.1	+ 1.6
Jilin	6,510	6,080	− 430	34.5	32.2	− 2.3
Heilongjiang	16,660	14,930	−2,730	37.5	33.6	− 3.9
Shanghai	10	10		1.3	1.3	
Jiangsu	340	330	− 10	3.3	3.2	− 0.1
Zhejiang	3,960	3,430	− 530	88.9	33.7	− 5.2
Anhui	1,750	1,790	+ 40	12.7	13.0	+ 0.3
Fujian	5,900	4,500	−1.400	48.5	37.0	−11.5
Jiangxi	6,110	5,460	− 650	36.7	32.8	− 3.9
Shandong	1,320	900	− 420	8.7	5.9	− 2.8
Henan	1,790	1,400	− 390	10.9	8.5	− 2.4
Hubei	4,360	3,800	− 560	23.5	20.5	− 3.0
Hunan	6,580	6,880	+ 300	31.1	32.5	+ 1.4
Guangdong	7,480	6,020	−1,460	33.9	27.3	− 6.6
Guangxi	5,510	5,200	− 310	23.3	22.0	− 1.3
Sichuan	7,460	6,730	− .730	13.3	12.0	− 1.3
Guizhou	2,560	2,310	− 250	14.5	13.1	− 1.4
Yunnan	9,550	9,550		24.9	24.9	
Tibet	6,320	6,320		5.1	5.1	
Shaanxi	4,580	4,330	− 250	22.3	21.1	− 1.2
Gansu	1,870	2,627	+ 757	4.2	5.9	+ 1.7
Qinghai	190	190		0.3	0.3	
Ningxia	60	70	+ 10	0.9	1.0	+ 0.1
Xinjiang	1,440	1,120	− 320	0.9	0.7	− 0.2
Total	121,860	115,250	−6,610	12.7	12.0	− 0.7

substantial increase since the 1950s (table 6). Most commercial timber, however, is harvested and distributed outside the planning process and is therefore not included in the official statistical series. That is true especially of timber that is locally produced and consumed but also applies to large volumes of timber that are legally or quasi-legally transported across provincial boundaries. The total may amount to as much as 70 million m^3 a year. In Hunan, for example, locally consumed timber in the period 1979–82 was three times greater than planned production (ZL, April 1983: 38). Adjustments in statistical coverage made in 1984 as part of the "single-ledger" production permit system filled only a small portion of the gap.

In addition, fuelwood production totals as much as 180 million m^3 annually. Fuelwood consists largely of branches and other noncommercial wood fiber but includes over 70 million m^3 of roundwood despite official

Table 5

Provincial Forestry in China
(Part 2)

	Timber Reserves 1973-76 (10^3 m^3)	Gross Value Forestry Output 1984 (10^6 yuan)	Timber Production 1984 (10^3 m^3)	Gross Value Forest Industry Output 1984 (10^6 yuan)
Beijing	4,390	50	57	663
Tianjin	1,990	20	0	214
Hebei	73,230	467	122	237
Shansi	56,550	654	128	99
Inner Mongolia	818,510	460	4,785	645
Liaoning	87,130	373	689	430
Jilin	683,570	364	6,384	1,034
Heilongjiang	1,577,110	718	16,683	2,618
Shanghai	290	8	0	619
Jiangsu	12,590	278	3	407
Zhejiang	82,410	489	2,037	391
Anhui	46,950	392	464	239
Fujian	243,300	699	7,280	724
Jiangxi	262,530	587	3,744	598
Shandong	22,900	566	106	390
Henan	78,660	468	99	179
Hubei	96,300	633	731	349
Hunan	189,370	702	3,760	378
Guangdong	176,790	1,591	4,516	705
Guangxi	192,610	491	2,940	343
Sichuan	1,346,920	1,567	4,570	754
Guizhou	158,810	423	826	93
Yunnan	988,600	720	3,066	319
Tibet	1,436,170	12	219	18
Shanxi	238,930	451	458	171
Gansu	194,790	278	548	124
Qinghai	30,600	36	63	24
Ningxia	2,500	91	43	11
Xinjiang	236,810	145	477	105
Total	9,350,000	13,733	63,848	12,681

efforts to enjoin state forest farms from burning roundwood for their own energy needs (GR, Dec. 9, 1982; Wang Qingyi and Gu Jian 1983). In sum, total production is close to 300 million m^3 annually and is thus about four to five times greater than official statistics indicate (Wang Zhangfu and Wang Enling 1983: 7). More importantly, it exceeds the annual growth increment by perhaps 100 million m^3 a year (Yang Zhong 1983a; NJW, January 1984: 63; Chen Dongsheng 1980; Forestry Development Section 1983). The imbalance between growth and timber removals looms even larger when one factors in timber left to rot by loggers as slash and stumps that never gets to the grading station—amounting to 35 percent of timber

Table 5

Provincial Forestry in China
(Part 3)

SOURCES: 1973-76 inventory data from Ministry of Forestry
Technical Economic Research Section (1983), 19-27. Data on
1981 inventory from JR (Jan. 28, 1986). Data on 1984 output
and production from Chinese Statistical Yearbook 1985, 242,
325, and 355.
NOTES: Gross Value Forestry Output (GVFO) includes value of
tree cultivation (with the exception of tea and mulberry
groves and fruit orchards, which are classified under
agriculture); gathering of seeds, nuts, and oils; and value
of timber production at or below village level, i.e., from
production of GVFO, forest products for 23 percent, and
small-scale logging for 20 percent. Timber growth has been
rising in value more rapidly than other components in recent
years. State Statistical Bureau (1985b). Gross Value
Forest Industry Output includes heavy industry component
(7,422 million yuan in 1984, of which logging and
transportation above village level accounted for 4,305
million yuan, with the remainder accounted for by
processing), and light industry component (mainly items for
household or daily use), which totaled 5,259 million yuan in
1984. Chinese Statistical Yearbook 1985, 317-318 and 622.
Gross value data listed in 1980 prices.

by volume in the Northeast, which is China's leading timber-producing
region (Liaoning Forestry Society et al. 1982: 449).

Implementation Strategies

Although China, like other countries, will become proportionally less
dependent on forest products and other primary products over time in the
course of economic development—the ratio of the gross value of industrial
and agricultural output to timber production having almost tripled, from
6,569 yuan in 1952 to 18,616 yuan in 1984—consumption will continue to
rise in real numbers despite major efforts by the government to develop
timber substitutes and alternative energy sources and to otherwise
encourage conservation (Han Yongwen 1985). Although better policies
present great potential for eventually increasing timber production,
in the interim production will be constrained by the exhaustion of older
production centers, by growing recognition of the need to limit logging in
erosion-prone areas for ecological reasons, and even by rising demand for
recreation and habitat preservation, which is rapidly rising as shown by the
expansion in nature preserves—from little more than a handful several
years ago, to 274 in 1985 covering 16 million hectares, to a projected 429
by 1990 (CD, Feb. 7, 1985). Rising demand has already forced China to
greatly increase its imports of timber and other forest products to about 9
million m^3 a year by the mid-1980s. It also threatens further resource
degradation unless productivity increases. Since the average growth incre-

Table 6

Timber Deliveries in China, 1949-1986

Year	Domestic Production (10^3 m^3)	Imports (10^3 m^3)	Year	Domestic Production (10^3 m^3)	Imports (10^3 m^3)
1949	5,670				
1950	6,640	10	1970	37,820	81
1951	7,640	9	1971	40,670	72
1952	12,330	12	1972	42,530	225
1953	17,540	22	1973	44,670	653
1954	22,210	18	1974	46,070	934
1955	20,930	27	1975	47,030	281
1956	20,840	27	1976	45,730	738
1957	27,870	28	1977	49,670	539
1958	35,790	54	1978	51,620	534
1959	45,180	118	1979	54,390	579
1960	41,290	112	1980	53,590	1,812
1961	21,940	203	1981	49,420	1,553
1962	23,750	296	1982	50,410	4,827
1963	32,500	544	1983	52,320	6,498
1964	38,000	560	1984	63,850	7,910
1965	39,780	1,568		(58,000)	
1966	41,020	1,540	1985	63,230	9,710
1967	32,500	120	1986	65,020	7,152
1968	27,910	111			
1969	32,830	85			

SOURCES: Domestic production taken from State Statistical Bureau (1985a), 32; Chinese Statistical Yearbook 1985, 338; and RR, Mar. 1, 1986. Data on imports from Chinese Statistical Yearbook 1983, 438, and 1985, 518.
NOTE: 1984-86 figures reflect changes in reporting procedures to incorporate timber harvested from collectively owned forests used in rural construction by either collectives or individuals in accordance with "single-ledger" system. Unadjusted figure in parentheses.

ment is between 1.8 and 2.4 m^3 per year—about 60 to 80 percent of the world average and far below the standard attained in many developed countries (*Contemporary* 1985: 33, Zhang Jianguo 1982, Wu Jinghe 1983, Li Zhankui et al. 1982)—there is substantial biological potential for growth. The question is to what extent public policy can facilitate forestry development for both ecological and economic reasons, or whether there will be a return to policies that hamper growth. For answers, I will examine the properties of each implementation strategy beginning with the state sector.

The State Sector

The state sector comprises approximately 62 million hectares of forested land, or about 52 percent of the total, representing a gradual but accelerating decline from the state's 73 percent share in the early 1950s (*Contem-*

porary 1985: 373). State forests also account for 628 million m³ of timber reserves, or 61 per cent of the total, and 27 million m³, or about half, of planned logging (RR, Aug. 17, 1985; Liu Zhuangfei 1982). The state's share has fallen because it conducts less than 15 percent of afforestation while the collectives and private sector account for the remainder (State Statistical Bureau 1985b: 80). The small state role in afforestation is a result of the Chinese ideological preference for the collective in the rural economy; it is also attributable to collective labor costs that are off-budget and much lower than in the state sector. Most state forests are administered within the Ministry of Forestry system; the principal exceptions are modest holdings within the Ministries of State Farms and Land Reclamation (2.08 million hectares) and Water Conservancy and Electric Power, and plantations established by some industrial ministries such as Railways, Coal Industry, and Light Industry (paper manufacturing) for their own use (JPRS 83905 CAG 265, July 18, 1983: 6).

Most state forests are still unmanaged, so their growth and composition are governed by natural forces without benefit of scientifically guided human intervention. Where management exists, it is the responsibility of the 4,000-odd state forest farms (*guoying lin chang*). In major forest areas, these farms are in turn grouped into a smaller number of forestry administrations or bureaus (*linye ju*), which on average are in charge of 200,000 to 300,000 hectares and 30,000 to 40,000 people (Yang Furong 1985). The farms cover only 33 million hectares, of which only 22 million hectares are treed, and not all of the latter are actively managed (*Contemporary* 1985: 373). Virtually all farms are under the direct leadership of provinces (10 percent), prefectures (12 percent), and counties (78 percent) rather than the national government as a result of administrative decentralization, which often dates back to the 1950s. Nevertheless, they continue to be supervised by the Ministry of Forestry under China's system of dual (horizontal and vertical) authority. The central goverment's authority generally is highest in major logging areas such as Heilongjiang and lowest on scattered sites (ibid.: 381).

Management policy is clear in its intent. The regime's goal is to expand the resource base to 20 percent of surface area by the end of the century, with an ultimate goal of 30 percent. In addition to afforestation, this policy involves the formal requirement that timber production in any year should not exceed the volume of new growth to ensure that there is no decline in the volume of timber on the stump. Timber production targets are set in the expectation that regeneration will follow the harvest (Yang Furong et al. 1982, Forestry Law in Ross and Silk 1987).

That amounts to a policy of nondeclining even-flow sustained yield, which has a very conservative import. If carried out successfully, the policy assures that production in the future will never be less than in the present. But it ignores the fact that old-growth timber grows very slowly and has a higher mortality rate. This silvicultural system thus disregards the potential for speeding the introduction of more vigorous new trees by accelerating the

harvest of old-growth timber. It similarly ignores the costs arising from a
failure to replace living capital that is vulnerable to disease and the elements
while on the stump.

Nondeclining even-flow sustained yield cannot be justified on either economic or biological grounds, especially in the case of uneven aged natural
forests like those in much of China. Nevertheless, this silvicultural system,
which originated in Germany, has been written into the statute books not
only in China but alsc in the United States and other countries (Dana and
Fairfax 1980: 331–34, Parry et al. 1983) out of fear that timber harvests
would otherwise soon deplete the resource base. Foresters often believe
that they must impose an easily comprehensible limitation on logging to
enhance forestry conservation regardless of its suitability.

The record indicates, however, not only that this policy is unwise but that
it has not been successfully carried out in China. Regeneration has not kept
pace with logging. Of the 131 forestry bureaus established so far, 26 are
said to have exhausted their commercial timber reserves and 35 more are
on the verge of doing so (Forestry Development Section 1983). Ten of the
sixteen bureaus in the Yichun area of northern Heilongjiang, the center
of the forest industry, are reported to be at or near exhaustion. Not only
have timber reserves in the Yichun area fallen by almost 40 percent, from
415 million m^3 to 260 million m^3, but forested land has declined by 80,000
hectares. Stocking has deteriorated and less valuable hardwoods have in-
truded into the forest, reducing the proportion of conifers from almost 70
percent of reserves to barely 50 percent, and much less than that in second-
growth forests (Hu Zhengchang 1983: 16, Yin Jinghua 1983). Because the
need for workers has declined, the populace has been forced to rely more
and more on herb gathering and other sidelines for a livelihood (RR, Nov.
6, 1983; Liaoning Forestry Society et al. 1982: 147; Yang Zhanru 1982).
The Southwest, the second most important region in the state sector, has
a shorter history of large-scale commercial logging. But provinces such as
Sichuan and Yunnan have also suffered net declines in forest resources
that are due in part to imbalances in state logging (Wang Mingzhong 1983,
Bartholomew 1983a: 120 and 1983b: 11).

The situation certainly is not uniformly bleak, but there are many problems in the state sector. Why have planning and hierarchical authority
patterns been unable to prevent such problems? The answer lies in the
bureaucratic style of implementation that has ignored or distorted the valuation of resources, has failed to overcome bureaucratic rivalries, and has
been unable to escape the tragedy of the commons.

Prices. The first consideration is one of price or value. In a classical market
economy populated by numerous buyers and sellers with unrestricted entry, the forces of supply and demand would be expected to arrive at an
equilibrium price and output solution. Confronted with a commodity shortage, as in the case of the Chinese forest industry, prices would be expected
to rise to a level that would attract imports, fresh investment, and new

producers into the industry. Perfectly competitive markets do not of course exist in the real world, particularly for such semipublic goods as forestry. Consequently, some government intervention is justified to close the gap between the preference for public goods like conservation and the demand for private goods like wood. Forestry also is a long lead-time production process with many risks facing the producer, warranting a government role in terms of fire protection, research, and the like.

China's economy is centrally planned, permitting the state to raise commodity prices as high as it wishes to encourage production and resource renewal through replanting. But forest products are substantially underpriced in China. This underpricing arises from the characteristic tendency of centrally planned economies to keep the prices of agricultural products and other raw materials low, while raising the prices of manufactured goods to transfer wealth from the agricultural sector to industry and the urban areas (Lardy 1983). This scissors effect is magnified in the case of timber by special factors discussed below.

Because China is a closed economy and because there are inherent variations in species and quality, it is not easy to compare domestic prices with international prices. It is clear, however, that domestic timber has always been underpriced in comparison with world market prices. For example, China in 1980 imported hardwoods from Southeast Asia at about U.S. $150/$m^3$, while at the same time the procurement price for domestically produced timber was less than 100 yuan/m^3, and even factory or timber yard prices were on average less than 150 yuan/m^3 (at that time U.S. $1 equaled about 2 yuan, although subsequent devaluations of the yuan widened the differential to U.S. $1 equals 3.71 yuan by late 1986) (ZNN 1983: 383–86; list prices in Compendia of Forestry Laws and Decrees 13: 125–37).

The discrepancy between official prices and market value becomes even more glaring when the former are compared with the costs of production as well as with gray-market, or negotiated, prices. All accounts agree that timber is terribly underpriced, in some cases by three- to eightfold (Li Zhankui et al. 1982). In Heilongjiang, for example, the stumpage equivalent (*lin jia*) of timber for a long time was set at 56.8 yuan/m^3 at the harvest site. This figure barely exceeds officially acknowledged costs that are said to run 55.1 yuan/m^3, leaving little room for profit or a risk premium; nor does it discount the loss in value of capital while trees are growing on the stump (FBIS, Sept. 15, 1980: L6–7). A more revealing way to approach the problem is to compare official delivery prices with black-market prices, which run as high as 400 to 500 yuan/m^3 (Xu Wuchuan and Chen Daping 1982), although black-market prices would fall if production were increased.

There are several reasons why timber prices are so low even though calculations are nominally based on cost. Most fundamentally, the central planners deliberately set procurement prices below the average cost of production to encourage industrialization (Lardy 1983). In part, procure-

ment prices were based on low pre-1949 reference prices and actually declined in the 1950s before rising at a slow rate into the 1970s (Xu Wuchuan
and Chen Daping 1982). Moreover, not all costs are included in the Chinese
calculations. Most obvious is the cost of money; China does not discount
future revenues according to the present value of money. That may not
be very important in the case of annual farm crops, especially in a low-
inflation economy like China's, but it is an important consideration in forestry (Liao Shiyi et al. 1983) (table 7), and inflation is rising.

Still another wrinkle is associated with forestry. In the Soviet accounting
and planning systems adopted in China, no allowance is made for the costs
of reproducing naturally growing timber because there is no labor value
in a gift of nature. But even plantation forestry is handicapped by the long-
standing presumption that standing timber has no value because it is not
yet a commodity eligible for exchange. The only costs eligible for reimbursement involve logging and transportation. Milling and processing costs
also are eligible but are calculated separately because they belong to industry
rather than agriculture. China's only allowance for the cost of reproduction
is a silvicultural fee (*yulin fei*), which was intended to serve as a surrogate
for stumpage prices in state-owned forests. The fees were set too low,
however, and were administered in a highly inequitable fashion. They were
too low in the sense that in 1981 they amounted to only 19 percent of the
procurement price for timber in northeastern China, although leading
economists argued that they should have amounted to at least half the
procurement price to adequately finance regeneration. They really
amounted to a uniform surcharge assessed on all timber regardless of the
costs of production. This surcharge was particularly inequitable because
fee receipts were not earmarked for regeneration in the production areas
but were largely diverted to other purposes and jurisdictions (Liu Zhijie
1985). Indeed, for a long time fully 85 percent of *yulin fei* receipts were
treated as general government revenues rather than being reserved for
forestry use (Compendia of Forestry Laws and Regulations 5: 554, ZNN
1983: 383–86).

The *yulin fei* provided 38 percent of forest management funds in the
period 1949–81, rising to 48 percent in 1981, the other sources of funding
being state investment and revenue from operations (ZNN 1982: 323–24
and 332). The fee is generally set too low to cover the costs of regeneration.
Set at 15 yuan/m^3 in the Northeast, the fee has a perverse effect because
it stimulates the harvesting of easily accessible and high-quality timber while
discouraging a wider dispersion of logging since the price of timber on the
stump is uniform. Moreover, the fees, like other forms of capital investment
in forestry, are only applied to costs incurred in the first three years after
planting. That encourages planting, which the government monitors and
reports in banner headlines, but discourages postplantation management,
thereby lowering the quality of the next generation of trees (GR, Dec. 12,
1979; ZNN 1982: 331–32; Ministry of Finance 1985).

Table 7

Timber and Other Commodity Prices in China, 1950-1984

Year	Agricultural Procurement Prices	Grain	Tea	Timber	Timber Retail Prices (yuan/m^3)
1950	100.0	100.0	100.0		
1951					
1952	121.6	121.4	154.7	115.1	80
1953					80
1954					97
1955					100
1956					97
1957	146.2	141.4	241.6	105.9	100
1958					100
1959					100
1960					100
1961					100
1962					100
1963					100
1964					100
1965	185.1	190.0	304.1	141.7	100
1966					100
1967					100
1968					100
1969					100
1970					100
1971					100
1972					100
1973					107
1974					111
1975					106
1976					108
1977					108
1978	207.3	224.4	330.4	173.3	109
1979					120
1980	251.2	271.8	365.1	230.8	149
1981	257.2	283.5	371.3	293.1	197
1982	257.7	283.5	372.8	310.4	216
1983	259.8	283.8	370.9	310.4	215
1984	261.9	282.4	371.3	322.8	265

SOURCES: Chinese Statistical Yearbook 1985, 537 and 546. Data for some years taken from earlier editions.
NOTES: Timber procurement prices include logging and skidding costs and, in nonstate forests, stumpage prices. All data based on national averages.

The *yulin fei* system is widely believed to have deleterious effects on forest regeneration, but it was not until 1982, at a price research forum sponsored by the State Council, that the Ministry of Forestry proposed including the growth of raw materials as a production cost, even though this issue had been considered for decades and the Soviet Union had apparently enacted such a reform years earlier (Chen Peiyuan and Li Zhou 1984, Zhang Tong

1983, "Provisional Regulations" 1950, Compendia of Forestry Laws and Regulations 9: 62–67 and 11: 162–66, Deng Zihui 1957, Wang Zhangfu and Zhang Jianguo 1981). The ministry's tacit acceptance of the *yulin fei* system reflects the lack of influence held by economists and forest managers compared with planners and loggers. Even if this reform is eventually made, however, it is quite apparent that timber prices will still remain far below their scarcity value.

The planning and price systems not only discourage regeneration; they also encourage waste and overconsumption. Supplies are distributed to industrial consumers according to fixed allocations set in the plan rather than through a market process. This system requires that logs be shipped to Ministry of Forestry timber yards (*zong mu chang*) for sorting before being sent on to the sawmills. This procedure results in added handling costs and further timber deterioration (*Linye Gongzuo* 6: 12). Meanwhile, overly narrow price differentials in terms of species, quality, and size discourage loggers from producing timber in the most valuable dimensions (longer and wider logs), while perversely encouraging customers to requisition more valuable timber for lesser uses such as pulping (ZNN 1983: 383–86). Consumers thus have an incentive to request more and better quality timber than they need so that they can hoard the excess in the event of delivery shortfalls, or to dispose of the excess wood on the black market or for the personal use of their staff members. Timber yards at sawmills are consequently much larger than their counterparts in industrialized countries, and that increases the rate of timber deterioration (RR, June 28, 1984; FAO 1982: 174–78).

Perhaps more importantly, price and planning imperfections distort timber removal and milling decisions. Because timber delivered to the loading yard receives no premium based on quality, there is little incentive for loggers to deliver smaller pieces of wood that are harder to handle, or for the industry to invest in machinery to facilitate the handling of different sized pieces. Although most of the tree, including leaves and twigs, is eventually removed from the forest, the smaller pieces do not enter the state distribution system and instead are used for local construction and fuel needs. In fact, 87 percent of centrally allocated timber consists of logs; small pieces and branchwood account for less than 5 percent (ZNN 1982: 334). Although state forest farms are regularly criticized for burning high-quality timber as fuel, there seems to be no way to check this practice (JR, Oct. 18, 1985). The cost-plus pricing system also provides no incentive for the efficient location of processing plants, most of which are in urban areas far from the forests. The added burden of transporting bark and other low-value wood fiber strains the capacity of the railroads to move raw logs, creating a backup at rail heads and resulting in large losses from inadequate storage (RR, Apr. 21, 1984).

Prices for processed lumber also tend to be arbitrary. For example, because the centrally determined factory gate prices for some items, such as transmission poles and drilling platforms, are high, production exceeds demand by as much as a factor of five. By contrast, the equivalent prices for some items in heavy demand, such as railroad ties and bridge supports, are low. Consequently, the production of these items falls about 50 percent short of production quotas (Li Kaixin 1983).

Of course, forestry serves a conservation function in addition to providing wood products. To what extent does the cost-plus system of pricing make allowances for these public goods aspects of forestry? Apparently not at all. A handbook for forest enterprise managers occasionally enjoins them to place first priority on maintaining and enhancing the resource base but makes no provision for calculating the conservation benefits to society from forestry operations (Yang Furong et al. 1982).* China is no different than a capitalist society in this regard, of course, but the effect is aggravated by the underpricing of timber itself and thus helps to explain why the state sector often seems to ignore conservation. Indeed, the bulk of state forests (83 percent) is timber oriented, with only a small percentage classified as shelter or conservation in function (*Contemporary* 1985: 381).

Investment. Despite the distortions created by the pricing system, the planners could have increased investment in forestry to overcome the inefficiency occasioned by price imperfections. In fact, the state has invested significant sums of money in forestry, but the amounts seem to be far from sufficient to meet its expansive goals. This insufficiency largely arises from the regime's preference for industry over agriculture, a preference that appears to be a general characteristic of communist regimes. It was particularly true under Mao Zedong, when agriculture received only about 10 percent of state investment despite rhetorical insistence that agriculture was the "foundation" of the economy. Although agriculture's status has improved since Mao's death, investment still amounted to only 12 percent of the total in the 1970s and declined further in the Sixth Five-Year Plan (ZTN 1985: 423). As Premier Zhao Ziyang explained, the state expects to play only a supplementary role in the agricultural sector in contrast to its dominant role in the industrial sector (RR, June 1 and Sept. 20, 1983).

Investment and profit remission policies, however, have not served forestry well, even allowing for the bias in favor of industry. State investment on the forest management side in the period 1950–78 reportedly totaled 2,781 million yuan, an average of about 100 million yuan a year. By contrast, water conservancy received about 7,000 million yuan in investment during

*One study published in 1984 (Chen Yongmi 1984), relying on Japanese estimation procedures, concluded that the welfare or conservation benefits from forestry in Hunan alone amounted to over 535 billion yuan, about a hundred times greater than the annual gross output value of forest products for the country as a whole. This study's conclusions are wildly exaggerated but point up the fact that conservation benefits were not calculated at all in the past.

this same period. In other words, total investment in forest management since 1949 barely exceeds the amount invested in water conservancy in any given year in the late 1970s (Ministry of Finance 1985, Chi Weiyun 1982, Vermeer 1982: 825–26, ZTN 1985: 438–39).

It is unfair, of course, to equate forest management with water conservancy. Water conservancy typically involves more expensive engineering and construction. Nevertheless, both sectors fulfill conservation and flood protection functions. But this complementary relationship between forestry and water conservancy did not receive serious attention at the highest levels of leadership until after the Yangtze River floods of 1981. Alarmed by the magnitude of flood damage and warnings by ecologists of future catastrophes, the leadership decided to encourage a reallocation of funds from water conservancy to forestry. The sums involved are small, however, and will not alter the imbalance that handicaps forestry (Ross 1983b; China Agricultural Development 1983; FBIS, Feb. 11, 1982: Q1–2).

Investment on the industrial side of forestry has also been insufficient to meet the regime's goals in light of an acute resource shortage. Forest industry's share of total industrial investment actually fell from a peak of 3.3 percent in the early 1960s to 1.2 percent in the Sixth Five-Year Plan, 1981–85, although there was an increase in absolute numbers (ZTN 1985: 427). Lack of investment is a major reason why 60 percent of commercial forests have not yet been brought into production, causing older areas to be depleted. Within the areas being logged, management suffers from a lack of access because the road network averages only 0.7 m/hectare even in the Northeast—less than 10 percent of the density often found in developed countries—and many roads are unusable in bad weather. That is a major contributing factor to the scourge of forest fires (Li Zhankui et al. 1982, Forestry Development Section 1983, Liaoning Forestry Society et al. 1982: 448).

The peculiarities of the cost-plus system of accounting also affect investment patterns. In the period 1949–80, total investment in forestry (combining forestry per se and forest industry) totaled 1,330 million yuan, of which only 15 percent was devoted to forest management and regeneration (GR, Oct. 15, 1983; Chi Weiyun 1982). In a well-forested advanced industrialized country like the United States, the proportion devoted to management and regeneration is even lower, but China hardly falls in this category. More interesting is the fact that 90 percent of the remaining investment funds are devoted to logging and transportation of raw timber, leaving only 10 percent for processing. That helps to explain why the plywood and artificial board industries, which can use low-quality wood fiber and scrap, were badly neglected for thirty years. In 1979, the combined output of plywood, fiberboard, and particle board amounted to barely 6 percent of the production of sawn wood by volume, compared with 37 percent in the United States (Hou Zhizheng et al. 1982, ZNN 1982: 309–

11). Indeed, on average only 37 percent of the wood volume of harvested trees is ever converted into useful fiber (Zhong Xingfan 1982, Li Keliang 1982, Liu Zhuangfei 1982).

Forestry's lament extends even beyond prices and investment. Former minister of forestry Yong Wentao and others have complained that forestry actually suffers from disinvestment. Mandated profit remissions plus taxes substantially exceed state investment. Indeed, profit accumulated in the period 1949–80 in northeastern China alone totaled 6,450 million yuan, about 9 percent more than the state's aggregate investment, but most profits where remitted to the state for general budgetary purposes (Yong Wentao 1982; *Linye Gongzuo* 6: 29–30; Ministry of Forestry Technical 1983: 29; GR, Oct. 15, 1983; ZNN 1982: 320–23).

Bureaucratic Conflict. This analysis of the state sector so far has stressed how such economic considerations as prices and investment inhibit bureaucratic implementation. It appears that bureaus or agencies tend to maximize their own interests rather than the achievement of formal goals by following a mixed strategy of avoiding both conspicuous success and conspicuous failure. Performance that is too good attracts unrealistically high production norms in the next planning cycle, while abject failure draws criticism. In the long run, marginally successful performance is more likely to attract additional resources without entangling a bureau in politically risky relationships.

In principle, of course, the regime could simply command a subordinate organ to carry out assigned tasks regardless of the latter's preferences. In practice, the higher authorities' surveillance and command capabilities are limited in time, scope, and complexity. It is difficult to rely solely on commands for anything other than simple, unidimensional issues of the highest priority. Performance suffers whenever goals are in conflict or organizational structure does not correspond to the requirements of policy implementation.

A major problem in this instance concerns the chronic bureaucratic conflict between forestry or forest building (*linye* or *yinglin*) and forest industry (*senlin gongye*). The former is part of the agricultural system, while the latter chiefly belongs to heavy industry, although it also has a light industrial mission (Liu Zeng 1983). Each must satisfy production norms set by the state plan. Forestry is responsible for planting and managing forests while trees are on the stump. Forest industry is responsible for harvesting and tree removal. These two components of the forestry sector are clearly interdependent, but their relationship is sequential and therefore asymmetrical. Forest management depends on forest industry to harvest trees and clear slash in a manner that facilitates regeneration, but industry is not equally dependent on management. So long as there is a regional abundance of standing timber, industry can go from site to site without regard for replanting. Ultimately, of course, industry is dependent on new generations of trees to meet its delivery quotas, but many years may pass before the local supply of timber is exhausted—and even then industry has no reason to fear bankruptcy, while it does have to satisfy onerous production and profit-remission norms (RR, Nov. 7, 1985, and Mar. 14, 1986).* All the industry need do is to satisfy the same output, materials consumption, and other norms as the rest of Chinese industry, without regard to regeneration (Zhang Wenqi et al. 1982; RR, Jan. 7, 1980; GR, Feb. 12, 1980). Even more to the point, the next generation of trees takes years to mature, assuming they survive, and that reduces the incentive for industry to help management. One consequence is that 35 percent of standing timber by volume is left in the forest, hampering regeneration; another is the depletion of older logging areas (*Linye Gongzuo* 6: 30–35 and 7: 50–63).

Clearly, it is possible to manage this asymmetrical relationship better, but China is handicapped in this regard because enterprises do not own their plantations and only their harvesting expenses are reimbursable—a situation that discourages paying attention to management. Silviculture was not even part of enterprise evaluation until at least 1981 (Compendia of Forestry Laws and Decrees 15: 53–58). The state's response has been to tighten regulation, give management the authority to regulate industry, control timber production so that industry does not get too far ahead of management, and prescribe harvesting strategies to enhance regeneration. These measures have had a modest impact in terms of curtailing timber production, which has lagged behind virtually every other sector of industry, but the primary effect has been to further hobble forestry with unsound regulatory restrictions (Su Yuzhang 1984).

Despite the regulatory constraints, industry has still not provided sufficient help to management. A case in point is the choice of silvicultural systems. The PRC at first prescribed seed tree felling, a system intermediate between clear cutting and selection felling in which all trees are removed except for enough high-quality, well-spaced seed-bearing trees to support natural regeneration. The seed tree system soon was abandoned in the northeast because not enough trees were left standing while those trees that were preserved tended to be of low quality, vulnerable to windthrows, and frequently unable to disperse the heavy seeds of desirable species such as Korean pine (*P. koraiensis*) (Wei Zhenwu 1950, Mishima 1951).

Seed tree felling having been overextended and misapplied, the PRC in 1956 followed Soviet advice and adopted a new felling strategy for the Northeast. Under the strip shelterwood system, the stand is divided into strips parallel to the prevailing wind direction and then cut in an alternating pattern. The remaining strips provide seed and temporary shelter for re-

---

*There has been no provision for bankruptcy in the People's Republic because most enterprises are owned by the state and thus cannot be considered the actual owners of their assets. The post-Mao reforms led to the promulgation of a bankruptcy law in late 1986 that many consider an essential element in the effort to decentralize decision making down to the enterprise level, but its actual enforcement remains problematic.

growth before they themselves are cut several years later. Strip shelterwood also proved unsatisfactory because it was applied universally without regard to species or growing conditions. In addition, loggers opposed preserving the shelter strips and therefore tended to make the initial cutting strips too wide for the shelter strips to function effectively (Compendia of Laws of the PRC 1956: 348–60, Tang Polin 1957, Li Zhongxuan 1957).

As dissatisfaction with strip shelterwood increased, the Chinese tried more conservative management strategies to facilitate regeneration. New regulations were adopted in 1964 that placed first priority on selection felling, i.e., only removing designated trees while preserving the rest of the stand, or clear cutting of small patches no larger than five hectares (Compendia of Forestry Laws and Regulations 9: 86–93). Although some improvements were obtained, forest management still complained that selection felling was too intensive. Ranging up to 0.7 on a scale of 0 to 1, it impaired the prospects for natural regrowth. Loggers also were said to frequently practice high grading or creaming—removal of the best trees—often resulting in damage to the undergrowth. From a silvicultural perspective, however, less intrusive methods such as selection felling are not necessarily appropriate in old-growth stands or sites where the road network is inadequate, as is the case in China. Meanwhile, loggers complained that the restrictions placed on them were too onerous, often resulting in slower tree growth (RR, Jan. 23, and Dec. 18, 1964; Yang Zhanru 1982).

The basic problem appears to be not the choice of silvicultural strategy but rather the divergence in interests between forest management and forest industry. Management's interest lies in regulating logging so that regeneration is facilitated. Therefore, management demands that production from all sources not exceed growth, i.e., a nondeclining even-flow sustained-yield policy. This policy based on physical volume is the most conservative version of sustained yield. Because the state's artificial regeneration capacity is limited, management also favors the least intrusive logging methods, such as selection felling, even where it is inappropriate (FAO 1982: 144). Industry by contrast prefers the most efficient harvesting method regardless of its effect on future growth.

Management now has the nominal authority to regulate logging, particularly since the reabsorption of the Ministry of Forest Industry into the Ministry of Forestry in 1958, but has been unable to effectively exercise its power. That is because spending priority is determined at higher levels and is largely devoted to logging and removal rather than regeneration, and because industry is primarily evaluated in terms of production rather than regeneration. Although the two bureaucracies are joined together at the forestry bureau or administration level, there in fact appears to be a wide gulf between them. This split derives in large part from the fact that the state rather than industry or management holds ownership rights in forestry; that reduces the two bureaucracies' incentives to adopt a long-term perspective oriented toward future production. Although the higher leadership in principle could employ the instruments of dictatorship to compel the desired behavior, in practice the bureaucracies are left to administer themselves in accordance with their own organizational values.

Common Property Resource Aspects. Another reason for the shortcomings found in the state sector is encroachment by the local populace. As noted earlier, state ownership was asserted over most of the country's forests in the early 1950s regardless of local customs. Since the state often claimed the best standing timber, it is not surprising to learn that poaching and forest incursions are commonplace despite patrols by armed forest police (JPRS 83010 WWEQ, Mar. 4, 1983: 81–82). The best known case concerns the Ziwuling Mountains in eastern Gansu, home of the most extensive forests still standing in this arid, poverty-stricken northwestern province. Although Ziwuling is not a center of the logging industry, it is considered an important conservation asset in China's ambitious programs to establish protective windbreaks across northern China. Nevertheless, reports indicate that the forest there has retreated by more than six miles since the PRC was founded thanks to reclamation and the cutting of trees by peasants for fuel and other needs (RR, Nov. 1, 1978, and Oct. 9, 1983).

State forest ownership sometimes originated with the confiscation of landlord and temple woodlots and is closely intermixed with collective forests (Central People's Government 1951, Northwest Military and Political Commission 1951). In such cases, the local populace often regards state ownership as unjust and is predisposed to right long-standing grievances whenever state power weakens. To cite just two instances, peasants seem to have regarded state timber as common property free for the taking in Ruyuan County in the Yao Mountains of Guangdong, and to have plundered the Gaofeng state forest plantations in Guangxi with the connivance of cadres up to the county level (JPRS 82246 CRA 239, Nov. 26, 1982: 19, and 82547 CRA 244, Dec. 28, 1982: 176–77).

Such conflicts between the state forestry administration and the local populace are a worldwide phenomenon, but their high frequency in China is surprising because the regime is an often ruthless authoritarian state with a high degree of social organization that would seem relatively invulnerable to the theft of state property. Nevertheless, at least in periods when government authority has broken down, the government has appeared unable to deter illegal encroachments, due in part to a lack of sufficient concern by the relevant agencies.

The state's typical response has been to threaten severe sanctions, as it did in December 1980 at about the time that a more conservative tendency emerged in the central leadership. A State Council directive ordered strict controls on economic activity in the state forests and a shutdown of rural timber markets, and threatened severe sanctions against violators. Over the next several years, destructive behavior declined, although incidents continued to occur, thanks in part to a casual attitude by local officials and sometimes even conspiracy among them (RR, Aug. 6, 1979). Therefore,

Premier Zhao Ziyang in 1982 demanded that party leadership on this matter be tightened at all levels and that particular cases involving local officials be prosecuted as a warning to others (*Linye Gongzuo* 8: 6–9, ZNN 1983: 211–12). The ranks of the forestry police were increased to over 30,000, along with 5,000 procuratorial and judicial personnel (*Zhongguo Fazhi Bao*, Jan. 29, 1986). But of course law and order by itself can do little to enhance the resource base. Therefore, policy reformers have opened the system to market-oriented reforms. Before turning to market measures, however, I will examine the collective sector and campaigns.

The Collective Sector

The collective forestry sector in the PRC expanded rapidly, first by eliminating the private sector and then by afforestation. There are several reasons why the collective sector conducted 80 percent or more of afforestation until the 1980s. First, the Communist party has a preference for the collective sector within agriculture, in contrast to the Soviet and most Eastern European communist parties, which favor the state sector. With regard to forestry in China, the collective sector became dominant in the South as well as in other farming regions. In particular, windbreaks, the Four Arounds (along roadsides, along the banks of water bodies, around houses, and around villages), and special-use forests such as tung trees have been the province of the collective sector, but most timber plantations have also been established by collectives. The state sector has concentrated on more remote and difficult sites but has also suffered higher labor costs. Therefore, the government in many cases has preferred to support collective forestry—with modest subsidies, if necessary—instead of underwriting more expensive state forestry despite the Ministry of Forestry's preference for underwriting.

The collective sector is also believed to have many advantages in terms of harnessing the talent and energy of the rural populace. By centralizing the ownership of land and amassing savings for investment purposes, the collectives are able to arrange production and investments in a more comprehensive fashion than can private households operating tiny, widely separated plots of land. Moreover, for many years the collectives distributed income among households largely according to their work in behalf of the collective, establishing an apparent link between individual and group interests. By contrast, in a bureaucratic system, people are paid on a straight salary basis without any direct link between individual effort and compensation. Collectives are also small in comparison with a state bureaucracy, increasing the prospects for mutual exhortation and solidary incentives. States, especially in large countries, have found it expedient to capitalize on the size factor by dividing big amorphous goals into smaller, more comprehensible packages for the collectives to implement (Popkin 1981).

With its externalities and long lead-time production process, forestry would appear to be well suited to the collective sector. Indeed, the collectives have jointly mobilized hundreds of millions of people in seasonal afforestation campaigns. They have also organized their own forestry farms for year-round work and the provision of leadership for campaigns. By 1977 about 240,000 collective forestry farms had been formed, primarily at the brigade and commune levels, with a total work force of about 2.5 million. They managed almost 20 million hectares of land, of which about 12 million hectares were considered forested primarily as a result of post-1949 afforestation (Ministry of Forestry Afforestation 1983 I: 1).

Nevertheless, the performance of the collective sector has been highly uneven and disappointing on the whole. Although some areas have excelled, others have failed to show meaningful progress despite considerable expenditure of effort. Indeed, almost 65,000 collective forestry farms were dismantled in the first six years after Mao's death, during which time the total work force shrank by more than a third. Another 75,000 farms were in such desperate straits that their survival was in jeopardy, and many of them risked being dismantled or reorganized in ways that would greatly diminish their collective aspect (Ministry of Forestry Afforestation 1983 I: 1, ZNN 1983: 22). It is not even clear whether survival rates in the collective sector exceed the low levels encountered in the state sector. Moreover, one often finds reports of apparently successful plantations being wantonly cut down by the local populace, despite the institution of collective ownership and the long and difficult labor required to establish the woodlots. Why has the collective sector not been more successful? I begin my analysis with a focus on prices and marketing, then consider other factors germane to the collective sector.

Prices. Like grain, cotton, and other class I commodities, timber was subjected to a unified purchase and distribution system that was first used in 1951 and was largely in place by 1953. It enabled the regime to keep procurement prices artificially low through a compulsory and monopsonistic procurement process (Compendia of Forestry Laws and Regulations 5: 487, Kong Fanwen and He Naihui 1982: 9). Although this system enabled the state to tightly control much of the crop and assure distribution to priority consumers, it depressed production by keeping procurement prices artificially low, often below the cost of production. That reduced the prospects for forestry farms to ever become self-sufficient and meant poor living and working conditions and low morale for farm personnel.

Timber procurement prices were basically stabilized in 1953, with the stumpage price component (applicable only in nonstate forests) actually being fixed in 1956 while the other components—logging and skidding—were only allowed to rise modestly in response to cost increases, as table 7 showed. Because retail prices remained fixed for the entire 1954–72 period, any increases in procurement prices narrowed the margins enjoyed elsewhere in the distribution system and thus impaired service at other stages. Procurement prices were not raised across the board until 1973, and then by only a modest 10 yuan/m³ on average. A more substantial increase was instituted in 1979; it raised the average stumpage price by 30.6 percent, from 29.4 yuan/m³ to 38.4 yuan/m³. The stumpage price for the bellwether Chinese fir (*Cunninghamia lanceolata*) was boosted to between 14 and 17 yuan/m³ depending on quality and place of origin (Kong Fanwen and He Naihui 1982: 9–16), but it was still woefully inadequate. Taking into account the silvicultural fee (2 yuan/m³) as well as the inability to transport an average of 30 percent of the timber to the procurement station, one source calculated that the real return to a producer of *C. lanceolata* was only 9.79–11.89 yuan/m³ (Zhang Bo et al. 1983: 13).

Yet a survey conducted in Datian County in the mountains of central Fujian revealed even gloomier prospects for the collective forest operator. The costs of producing *Cunninghamia* averaged 10.8 yuan/m³ assuming a relatively fast 15–20-year rotation, exclusive of interest, risk, and a tax that averaged 1 yuan/m³, and without taking full account of labor costs (Chen Taishan et al. 1982). Similarly, the cost of a *Cunninghamia* plantation in a survey of Anhui collectives was said to average about 1,500 yuan/hectare for afforestation alone, excluding management, harvesting, and removal. If the procurement price structure in Anhui resembles Datian Xian, then a collective would need an exceptionally good yield for China of over 130 m³/hectare just to meet its afforestation expenses (Song Zongshui 1983b). Yet evidence from other countries indicates that harvesting expenses (which are typically disregarded in project design) comprise a large percentage—sometimes more than half—of the total costs of a forestry plantation (Hyman 1983). Were such expenses to be included, tree farming in southern China would appear to be even less viable on economic grounds.

Forestry prices for a long time lagged behind the rest of the agricultural economy as well as their true market value. Table 7 showed that timber procurement prices rose by only 73 percent in the period 1950–79, a slower rate than all other agricultural commodities except cotton, hemp, and tobacco, which are also industrial raw materials. The grain comparison is most important given the nature of the Chinese diet. Timber prices rose only three-quarters as fast as grain prices until the late 1970s, and some sources report that the timber:grain price ratio declined by half in comparison with the pre-1949 period (Chi Weiyun 1982; Kong Fanwen and He Naihui, 1982: 43–47, *Linye Gongzuo* 6: 15). The differential was even more stark with regard to tea, which competes with timber for land in the hills of South China. Tea prices rose over twice as fast as timber until the 1970s. Among the results of these price distortions was encouragement of poor logging and skidding practices because the state procurement stations would not accept below-grade timber, which could often be sold for higher prices for off-plan uses in local construction or even as fuelwood, since most rural households still ran short of fuel for months at a time in the early 1980s (*Linye Gongzuo* 6: 13–14).

Of course, there are countervailing influences. The woodsman can gather twigs and branches for fuel and leaves for fodder and collect herbs and fungi or hunt in the forest. Under some circumstances he can intercrop (practice agroforestry) while the trees are still young. He also enjoys some of the soil-conservation, wind-reduction, and water-conservancy benefits of forestry. None of these practices and benefits are reflected in the purchase price of timber and can no doubt be considerable. However, it is unclear whether the opportunity costs associated with the use of land for forestry rather than more profitable pursuits are outweighed by conservation and other nonmarketable benefits. In many cases, peasants were simply ordered to plant trees without regard to their economic rationality (Zhao Jie and Peng Yishang 1983).

Because of the problems confronting forestry, the central and provincial governments subsidize the collectives, particularly in the first few years before a plantation produces any income. Subsidies reportedly total 100 million yuan a year, but this figure amounts to less than 30 yuan per hectare afforested (FAO 1982: 118, ZNN 1984: 374). By contrast, the state spent almost 300 yuan per hectare, or ten times as much, for state afforestation in the late 1970s (ZNN 1982: 321). The subsidies are said to be insufficient by the Ministry of Forestry and are often haphazardly administered so that the collectives receive their subsidies even if the plantation fails (Yong Wentao 1982; RR, Sept. 20, 1983).

Low prices and inadequate subsidies reduce the collectives' interest in forestry as a productive investment. Many collective forest farms suffer from a lack of funding. Because collective forestry farms have poor economic prospects, they have difficulty recruiting and retaining a work force (RR, Mar. 14, 1980). Cultivation tends to be shortsighted and of low quality, with peasants more likely to abandon the plantations or to stunt tree growth by excessive pruning. To the extent that the peasants engage in forestry, they tend to favor tung, tea oil, and other special-use or economic forests rather than timber or shelter, because the former mature more quickly and are subject to fewer marketing restrictions.

The post-Mao regime has taken action to reverse the handicaps under which collective forestry operates. Most importantly, procurement prices were increased in the fall of 1979 by 30.6 percent on average and again by 36 percent in 1981, and by varying margins for other forest products (ZNN 1983: 383–86, Chen Taishan et al. 1982; the price lists are in Compendia of Forestry Laws and Decrees 13: 125–37 and 15: 77–100). These measures marked considerable progress but still left substantial gaps between costs and income and between list prices and gray-market or negotiated prices. The two rises taken together only boosted procurement prices for Chinese fir to 52.2 yuan/m^3, yet numerous sources indicate that producers could have obtained two to three times as much had price and marketing controls been removed (ZNN 1983: 432; RR, Nov. 4, 1985; JPRS 80514 CAG 198, Apr. 7, 1982: 34; Li Zhankui et al. 1982). Moreover, although stumpage prices for Chinese fir more than doubled in 1981, to

36–39 yuan—a long-overdue correction—allowances for logging and skidding costs actually decreased, nullifying some benefits of the price rise and discouraging specialization, which is particularly unfortunate since logging and skidding costs are generally quite substantial. Additional subsidies were also appropriated for hard-pressed mountainous regions, especially through new funds for economic development totaling 500 million yuan annually. But that was still not enough to compensate for the distorted prices (BR, May 30, 1983: VII).

Marketing restrictions were also briefly relaxed to improve commodity circulation by giving forest districts greater opportunity to exchange their produce for grain, and to give timber producers a fairer return by breaking the Ministry of Forestry's monopsony (FBIS, Apr. 16, 1980: T2, and Aug. 24, 1983: K1–3). However, the forestry authorities and central government became greatly alarmed over the increase in logging and marketing that ensued. Therefore a series of increasingly severe controls were reintroduced beginning in the winter of 1980 (RR, Dec. 6, 1980; FBIS, Aug. 24, 1983: K1–3), a topic to which I will devote more attention later. For now, I will note that the cost of trying to stamp out market exchanges is a dampening of producer incentives. For example, the Ministry of Forestry reacquired unified procurement and distribution power over forestry products in 1980. State procurement stations, however, are too few and too poorly situated, offer unfairly low prices, and are unable and unwilling to handle trade in small and irregular items and in the substandard timber that is used in handicrafts and for other purposes (*Linye Gongzuo* 8: 182–87). The ministry responds that intermediate and wholesale prices were not raised at the same time as procurement prices, squeezing its profit margins and preventing it from expanding its procurement operations (Kong Fanwen and He Naihui 1982). Although forestry departments were ordered in the spring of 1983 to improve their procurement and distribution operations, only 30 percent of revenue derived from collective forestry is ever returned to this sector (RR, Mar. 10 and Apr. 16, 1983; Forestry Development Section 1983).

Exhortation and Environmental Ethics. This analysis of the collective sector has so far stressed price and marketing issues or material incentives. The reader may wonder why more attention has not been directed to exhortation and environmental ethics. After all, several observers have argued that the equalitarianism and common property ownership characteristic of collectives enhances community action (Maxwell 1979). Some of the first Western foresters to visit the People's Republic of China noted with great admiration the high degree of "forest-consciousness" among the Chinese populace (Westoby 1979: 239–40). A major FAO study (1982) is replete with such observations as these: "the Chinese have successfully developed forest consciousness among the masses, by educating them on the material benefits of forestry" (26) and "since everybody is employed in productive work with a visible purpose, morale is high" (204–5).

It would be too easy and entirely unsatisfactory to simply note the near impossibility of accurately gauging popular culture in an authoritarian regime where freedom of thought is minimal at best. Nor will it do to argue that the state's policies, no matter how well absorbed by the people, are frequently self-defeating. Instead, one must analyze the shortcomings as well as the power of exhortation.

The collectives work best when they develop a sense of group cohesion and can establish direct, positive links between individual effort and group prosperity in the collective context (Chinn 1979). However, several factors inhibit collective performance in this regard. First, there is an asymmetrical relationship between group cohesion and the Communist party's original bias in favor of larger, more inclusive organizations. Cohesion is highest in small production teams that consist of about thirty households each and roughly correspond in many cases to natural villages. Teams have the advantages of small size, facilitating group supervision and neighborliness, as well as traditional cooperative social relations in some cases, and enabling them to operate on the basis of "conventions" or informal contracts rather than written rules and regulations. The CCP has tried to develop such conventions through such institutions as forest protection compacts in which the signatories pledge to protect the local forests and refrain from damaging them, but their consent is obtained as much through coercion as through voluntary agreement (Ross 1980a: 71, Lewis 1969).

No matter how successful the regime has been with regard to developing a sense of group consciousness in the countryside, the link between team cohesion and forestry is remote. That is because collective forestry, like rural industrial enterprises, is usually operated by the much larger brigades and communes (known as administrative villages, or *cun*, and townships, or *xiang*, respectively, in the aftermath of the decollectivization of farming, although forestry and many other enterprises often remain under collective management). These brigades and communes consist of hundreds and of thousands of households, respectively, whose leaders are subject to higher level approval and often are designated defacto by higher authorities. The larger collectives grew by expropriating the woodlots of the production teams, an action that created feelings of injustice among the victims. It also reduced the incentives for production teams to mobilize their members to engage in afforestation or to send their best workers to the forestry farms because of the free-rider effect inherent in brigade and commune enterprises whose profits are distributed among all production teams (*Summary of World Broadcasts* W954/A9, Dec. 12, 1973). Meanwhile, for reasons discussed earlier the forest farms are generally unprofitable, making them unattractive on their own merits. Thus collective forest farms were left vulnerable to breakup in the post-Mao era despite the economies of scale enjoyed by the larger units, except where all traces of natural village identity have been obliterated by changes in local administrative and economic geography designed to enhance the role of the brigade or administrative village (Sui Wenchang and He Zhuanjia 1983, Chen Wuyuan and Rong Yuyan 1983).

2)   A second factor inhibiting collective performance is that informal group cohesion is dependent on social stability, especially for a long lead-time production process like forestry, but the Chinese countryside has been marked by severe policy fluctuations based on conflicts within the leadership over the tradeoff between revolution and modernization. In the first years after the Communist takeover, the unit of organization in the countryside quickly moved upward from the household to the mutual aid team, the primary and then the advanced producers' collective, and ultimately the commune. The depression of the Great Leap Forward resulted in a devolution of authority back to the production team, which remained the unit of account in most parts of the country throughout the Maoist era, although there were persistent tendencies to advance from the production team to the brigade following the Dazhai model of communism. Not until December 1978, two years after Mao's death, did the pragmatists, or "managerial modernizers" in John Kautsky's terms (1969), emerge victorious over the radicals, or "revolutionary modernizers," and shift the basis of rural policy back to the household.

Regardless of the direction of change, it is important to stress that the process of change itself had a debilitating effect on forestry by muddying property rights and making them virtually unenforceable. Changes in property rights during land reform created unavoidable uncertainty, which only worsened during the several waves of collectivization. In each instance, the original owners often cut their trees down to forestall expropriation without fair compensation. Moreover, the new collective owners also increased logging to convey a misleading image of prosperity to their members (ZL, May 1956: 7–8; Liang Xi 1956).

Although the trend in the post-Mao period is away from collectivization, the problem of instability persists. During leftist upsurges, as in the 1975–76 jockeying to succeed Mao, production-team and household timber and special-use forests were cut down because they were considered "tails of capitalism" (RR, Feb. 12, 1978; FBIS, May 26, 1977: H3–4; Li Zhengke 1982: 172; Chan et al. 1984: 171–74 and 251–52). When privatization expanded in the post-Mao era, a topic to which I will soon turn, one consequence was a wave of logging by the new recipients of property rights, who feared that policy would change once again. As a result, many areas such as Yingshan County in the Dabie mountains of eastern Hubei reported massive deforestation beginning in the mid-1970s; some observers called 1979 the worst year since the starvation-wracked Great Leap Forward (RR, Sept. 24, 1980, and May 25, 1983). Foresters sadly appealed for simple continuity in policy to let the collectives plant and manage their trees without fear of interruption—a critical factor in the case of plants that need years to mature (Yang Furong et al. 1982: 11–12, Ministry of Forestry Policy 1981).

A third factor inhibiting collective performance is that the collectives fail ⟨3 to establish sufficiently close links between individual effort and reward. Households are compensated from the collective's income (after taxes, reinvestment, and other deductions) on the basis of the work points they have accumulated. This arrangement creates a potential for free riding since household income can only rise modestly in response to additional effort, encouraging households to slack off or channel their energies into private plots and sidelines. The Chinese call this syndrome the "big rice pot," and it seems to be more serious in forestry than in agriculture as a whole because the production process is long term and forest products are more severely underpriced. A collective therefore has an incentive to undervalue forestry so long as it is an economic drain on the rest of the collective, and often requires that tree planting be performed in campaigns without pay. Indeed, no more than a quarter of all collective afforestation was ever conducted by the forest farms themselves, with the remainder being done by ordinary peasants during campaigns. The low wages earned by collective forestry workers were a major reason why so many forest farms were abandoned after Mao's death, a situation that eventually forced other farms to raise wages in order to stop the flight (Chi Weiyun 1982, ZNN 1983: 373, *Linye Gongzuo* 6: 27, Ministry of Forestry Afforestation 1983 I: 1).

Science, Campaigns, and Leadership. Forestry performance in the collective sector also suffers from other drawbacks. The low level of scientific research and technical extension work is one of the most important. The Chinese leadership's rhetoric has been vigorous in support of such scientific and technical advances as the development of trees that provide *susheng fengchan* (fast growth and high yield) (ZL 1959 7: 7–10), the "comprehensive utilization" of wood fiber, the artificial board industry, and biological pest control. Nevertheless, science and technology have lagged far behind the country's needs and international advances. Meanwhile, well-intended slogans were reduced to meaningless shibboleths; the second half of *susheng fengchan*, for example, was often forgotten in a single-minded pursuit of rapid growth regardless of timber quality, while afforestation was in general overemphasized at the expense of the management of existing forests (*Linye Gongzuo* 6: 27 and 184).

There are two reasons for this kind of distortion. First is the CCP's jealousy of independent modes of inquiry and autonomous elites (intellectuals) who might challenge its power. Not until the early 1960s did the party and the scientific establishment reach a modus vivendi under which the scientists were encouraged to pursue their own interests so long as they accepted the party's political primacy. Then everything was thrown into chaos by the Cultural Revolution, which led to the closing of universities and research institutes and the celebration of pseudo-scientific "science for the people" (Suttmeier 1974).

The second reason for the distortion is that forestry operators often lack the logistics and incentives to improve forestry production with scientific advances. Fewer than half of the one million secondary and tertiary graduates in agriculture and forestry that the country has produced since 1949 actually work in the fields for which they were trained. On average, there is barely one trained extension specialist per commune or township in agriculture as a whole, let alone forestry (RR, May 5, 1983).

The consequence of these two factors has been the spread of untested, half-baked concepts while proven technology has been wasted (RR, Nov. 14, 1983). For example, Mao Zedong endorsed an eight-item charter to advance farming that included deep plowing and close planting. Each item was estimable under certain conditions, but taken together without regard for crop or climate they amounted to a prescription for agronomic disaster. Foresters responded with their own six-point charter (proper species selection, careful site preparation, healthy planting stock, close planting, tending and protection, and improved technology) that was similarly imprecise and unrealistic (Li Fang 1961, Compendia of Forestry Laws and Regulations 8: 8–10). Meanwhile, the funds needed to establish genuinely superior plantations, almost 3,500 yuan per hectare according to one source, have frequently not been available (Liaoning Forestry Society 1982: 238–39; Hu Jushun 1983).

Similarly, China has invested great efforts in biological pest control, particularly through the propagation and release of parasitic wasps (*Trichogramma dendrolimae*) and the entomophagous fungus *Beauvaria bassiana*. Biological controls are receiving increased attention worldwide for integrated pest management because they cause less environmental damage and are sometimes cheaper than chemical pesticides. Biological controls, the application of which is labor intensive, may also be particularly suitable for developing countries, which have low labor costs but lack experience with chemicals. No matter how well intentioned, however, there has been an unfortunate tendency in China to promote biological controls without adequate experimental evidence or statistical procedures. The consequence was to overestimate the effectiveness of biological controls, in part because *Trichogramma* has a high mortality rate. Statistical reanalysis now shows that the parasites have had no significant effect on the timing, range, or severity of larch caterpillar outbreaks, which are a major problem in the Northeast and have their counterparts elsewhere in the country (Shen Ji 1984, Yu Yongzhi and Sun An 1984). Meanwhile, of course, other measures were neglected.

A far broader problem is the diffusion through emulation in campaigns of model experiences that may or may not be exaggerated but often have only local or pilot project significance. Under the logic of point and plane, an advanced area develops a new technique (the point) that other areas (the plane) are invited to witness and urged to apply. This approach ideally facilitates innovation through pilot testing and extension work that directly involves the farmer (Zhongguo Linye Gongyuehui 1973). In practice, however, the results overwhelm the procedure. New technologies are disseminated under political pressure before testing has been completed in the home locality and without regard for their viability in the absence of special government assistance. Nevertheless, cadres in other areas may rush to adopt the new ideas lest they be labeled politically passive (Travers 1982). A case in point is the tendency to plant the same species (Chinese fir in the South, poplars in the North) over wide areas regardless of their suitability to local conditions or vulnerability to disease (RR, May 7, 1984; Liu Mingxu 1984; *Dili Xuebao* 38, 4: 414). Without competition, the nurseries have no incentive to diversify their output.

Sometimes, of course, the issue primarily involves disputes among scientists and bureaucratic agencies. For example, driven by well-founded concern about erosion, afforestation is promoted around the country under the slogan "Greenification of the motherland." Nevertheless, there are areas such as the northwestern loess plateau and the red hills of southern China that may be too dry and poverty-ridden for forestry to succeed. Many botanists and animal science specialists argue that grass seeding and livestock raising are economically superior and ecologically acceptable options in such cases, although this sector of the economy is also subject to shortcomings in terms of pricing and incentives (RR, Oct. 21, 1983; Hou Xueyu 1982; Song Zongshui 1983a; Zhu Bangchang 1983; BR, Oct. 21, 1985: 10–11). Not until the spring of 1984 did the political elite endorse animal husbandry for the southern hills (GR, Mar. 18, 1984). Enderton (1984: 270–80) discusses a similar problem with regard to the rubber vs. forestry debate on Hainan.

Clearly, it is possible to devise site-specific, ecologically sound, and economically oriented choices among trees, shrubs, grasses, and flowers as the widely cited slogan *yin di zhi yi* advises. An example is the great progress made in extending forest cover in the North China plain in the 1970s and 1980s as a result of the introduction of more tolerant varieties such as *Populus tomentosa* to replace the less adaptable *P. cathayana*. But doing so is much harder when campaigns are surging. As the reform-minded party general secretary Hu Yaobang said in the mid-1980s:

> The principal defect in our leadership at present is a lack of thoroughness in our work or, if we are thorough, we neglect the details; we pay attention to the details once and consider proceeding on a "one knife cuts all" basis. As a result, we encounter new difficulties and obstacles. I hope that you will resolve to develop a set of complete forestry work procedures in the next few years. This will make a great contribution to solving one of our country's big problems: the forestry issue. . . . You must implement central directives in an innovative fashion. Add a creative touch when carrying out central directives. This is not some kind of routine work—the mechanical administration of central instructions or waiting for orders. . . . Central policies emerge from nationwide conditions but, because China is very big, these policies cannot stipulate all issues precisely and in detail. This requires all localities to act in accordance with local conditions . . . on one hand con-

duct[ing] detailed research, on the other seek[ing] truth from facts. (LJ 1986
4: 3–4)

Leadership. Some problems affecting collectives could be solved by effective leadership. As Frohlich et al. (1971) and Olson (1965) argued, leaders
or political entrepreneurs can overcome divisive tendencies by committing
their own resources and ambitions to the success of the organization. Leaders can articulate visions of the future in a way that encourages altruism
in place of personal interests and can supply the energy and supervision
needed to overcome free-rider effects. For example, they may obtain funds
from external sources to meet the up-front costs of producing collective
goods, or they may convince the rank and file that the local benefits from
national projects outweigh the costs.

Leadership is regarded by the CCP as an indispensable element in every
public endeavor. One rarely encounters an official policy statement that
fails to include the need for strengthening leadership, frequently in conjunction with ideological work. This kind of exhortation is understandable
in a one-party, mobilizing dictatorship, although it is more common when
radicals are in power. Unfortunately, it does not help much to explain
variations in performance given the difficulty of measuring leadership
quality. Ordinarily, one would presume that leadership talent is distributed
normally except in unrepresentative model units that generally have better-
qualified, or at least more politically powerful, personnel.

Leadership at the grass roots, however, may have weakened over time.
Bernstein (1967) and others have stressed how effective local leadership
was in the early years of the People's Republic when the party's prestige
was high, goals were less complicated and infused with a revolutionary aura,
and there was plenty of opportunity for career advancement within the
party. Over time, however, the party committed major blunders and lost
much esteem, while career mobility has been sluggish, with most rural
cadres in the 1980s still without a middle-school education. Cadres also
often fear to emerge from the crowd lest they become subjects of criticism
after some future policy reversal. An additional factor introduced in the
post-Mao era was the allure of private wealth, which reduced the attractions
of public service.

But there is yet another aspect to the issue of leadership: the compatibility
between the performance requirements for specific policies and the criteria
by which cadres are evaluated. The answer is decidedly negative with regard
to forestry, which for years was dominated by one key criterion: grain
output. The primary economic standard until the late 1970s was grain
output under such slogans as "Dig tunnels deep and store grain everywhere." Although the most prominent slogan, "Take grain as the key link
and develop a diversified economy," stressed balance, in practice it was
operationalized as "Take grain as the only link," encouraging ecologically
abusive agricultural reclamation in Gansu and other fragile steppelands

(FBIS, July 5, 1977: E17–18, and Oct. 12, 1978: M1–2) and in semitropical areas, including Xishuangbanna (Hu Tongwen 1983) and Hainan (JPRS 82405 CEA 290, Dec. 7, 1982: 24–36).

The damage that ensued not only signals problems in policy formulation and implementation but also suggests that the party has difficulty evaluating performance along more than one dimension at a time. With a distinct preference for local self-sufficiency and in the absence of a universal standard of performance such as net profit, there is a tendency to overstress some commodities regardless of the economic imbalances that ensue. "*Nong, lin, mu-que yi bu ke*" (Farming, forestry, and animal husbandry are all indispensable) and similar Maoist slogans are operationally meaningless.

The post-Mao regime has shown an awareness of the consequences arising from neglect of ecological conditions and has placed great stress on the principle of local suitability (*yin di zhi yi*). Much of the arid Northwest, populated by pastoral peoples, has been instructed to stress forestry—either singly or in conjunction with animal husbandry—rather than grain (FBIS, Mar. 16, 1979: K2–3). This policy reform has been impeded, however, by barriers to the shipment of grain from other parts of the country to those areas no longer expected to produce all their own food. It has also been obstructed by political opposition from Chen Yun and other conservatives who insist that grain must always enjoy first priority for social and strategic reasons (Yang Rongshen 1983: 17; CD, Sept. 24, 1985). The central government has responded with grain subsidies to Hainan and other critical areas; in addition, international assistance is being directed to fragile, erosion-prone areas in southern Ningxia (FBIS, Oct. 18, 1982: K14–15; NYT, Feb. 7, 1983).

Beijing's options in this regard are limited, however, because the state procured only 20 percent of the nation's grain harvest as of the early 1980s—a smaller proportion than in the 1950s. Less than 1 percent of the harvest is available for consumption outside the province of origin (Lardy 1983: 46; BR, Jan. 10, 1983: 15). Grain is sufficiently scarce in some parts of the country for black-market channels to operate (RR, Jan. 19, 1984; BR, Jan. 30, 1984: 10). Thus, for example, Gansu, one of the poorest and most arid provinces in the country, must increase grain procurement from indigenous sources to meet the needs of poor highland areas despite the danger of aggravating soil erosion. It is questionable whether the Hexi Corridor can meet the added demands placed on it by the province (Qu Yaoguang 1983). Other provinces have also increased grain subsidies out of their own resources, but there is considerable pressure to tighten the eligibility requirements—a move that would lead to deforestation if subsidies were reduced (RR, Aug. 20, 1983). Faced with political opposition from conservatives and limits on its resources, the central government in 1982 decided to halt calls for the conversion of farmland to forestry and other less intensive uses and instead to urge an increase in afforestation and erosion control only on condition that the area devoted to grain be maintained at current levels (Jing Ping 1983, Li Yuanzhu 1983). Cadres, presented with such conflicting signals but aware of the abiding necessity of feeding their growing populations, can be expected to place less emphasis on afforestation than the regime demands, even though farmland actually devoted to grain production continued to decline into the mid-1980s.

Another problem involves the single-minded emphasis on afforestation. In the past, the number of trees planted was so strongly emphasized that quality was often ignored, warranting such complaints as "Why is it that every year we plant trees but none ever seem to grow?" and "Trees dot the hills in the spring but half are gone by summer, the rest are dying by autumn, and none are to be seen in winter" (Liaoning Forestry Society et al. 1982: 760–62, Wang Zhangfu 1983). During the Great Leap Forward the situation was so bad that escalating state plans called for planting far more trees than there were seedlings available (ZL, February 1958: 12).

Even in less radical periods, planting campaigns are prone to excesses: acting in a rush without preparation (*yi hong er qi*) and uprooting existing trees for replanting elsewhere (RR, Feb. 22, 1982). Despite early post-Mao efforts to limit annual afforestation to some 4 million hectares (itself an ambitious volume), during the Sixth Five-Year Plan, 1981–85, the reported pace soon accelerated to over 6 million hectares. This surge was in part simply a matter of fabrication by subordinates anxious to please their superiors (RR, Jan. 31, 1985). The real problem is that the instrumental goal of planting trees subverts the real policy goal of improving the resource base. While massive effort is devoted to planting trees, the actual cultivation of young trees is neglected because management is much harder to implement in a sudden burst of activity. Since the cultivators have no material interest at stake in tree survival, the tendency is to follow a brief flurry of activity in the spring by inaction, frequently leading to plantation failure (RR, Mar. 26, 1980, and Mar. 23, 1985; *People's University Agricultural Economics Reprint Series* 1982 23: 115–24; Zhang Kexia 1957). This tendency suggests that campaigns, which are intermittent organizations, have limited value for ongoing policy programs. One of the most dramatic examples of that is the Obligatory Tree Planting campaign, begun in 1981 with great fanfare, which requires that everybody between the ages of eleven and sixty-five participate in forestry without compensation. Organizational and common property resource problems have proven particularly acute in this case, and the program has since been relegated to peripheral status (Ross 1987; RR, Mar. 1, 1986).

On the whole, there is no reason to assume that local leadership alone is able to overcome the structural weaknesses that hamper collective forestry. Major reforms are needed. Some improvement may result from the separation of political and economic functions in the collective sector associated with the dismantling of the communes (BR, Jan. 30, 1984: 9–10). Of greater importance would be a conversion from the coercive and collective (*jiti*) farm to a more voluntary, democratic, and production-oriented "cooperative" (*hezuo*) in which the members would voluntarily decide which programs to undertake (Huang Daoxia 1983). But it will not be easy to effect such a transition. One idea is to treat forests and other collective assets as a form of community property in which everyone owns shares (*gu tiao*). Shares would be distributed on an equal per capita basis according to the value of standing timber, while new shares would be acquired through labor, cash investment, or purchase from others. A shareholders' committee would be responsible for governance. This idea has been tried in the Fujian Mountains (GR, Feb. 27, 1984; ZL, Dec. 1984: 23–24). In general, however, problems in the collective sector drove the regime to reemphasize the private sector.

The Private Sector

Private forestry was virtually eliminated in the 1950s. Occasional efforts were made to revive the private sector, especially in the aftermath of the Great Leap Forward, but they were largely abortive (*Nanfang Ribao*, Apr. 27, 1961, and Jan. 7, 1962). For example, during the mid-1970s, many private orchards and small woodlots were destroyed as "capitalist tails" (Li Zhengke 1982: 172; RR, Feb. 12, 1978; JPRS 73022 CAG 27, Mar. 19, 1979; 28–40). With the exception of small numbers of trees planted around houses that enjoyed tenacious legitimacy as one category of the Four Arounds (RR, Feb. 17, 1983; *Zhongguo Xinwen*, Apr. 15, 1972: 1), private forestry generally disappeared.

The situation changed dramatically in the post-Mao era thanks to the reforms sponsored by Deng Xiaoping. Private forestry enjoyed a remarkable renaissance in two forms beginning in 1978: the extension of private plots to forestry and the development of the contract responsibility system.

The highly productive private plots had been a rather constant feature of the rural economy except during the Great Leap Forward but were regarded suspiciously by party officials because they competed with the collective for labor and other factors of production. Private plots had never been as common in forestry because of the PRC's bias toward public ownership of natural resources such as forests and because the Ministry of Forestry believed that privatization and small-scale operations were incompatible with sound forest management. Dissatisfied with the slow pace of collective afforestation and with the inefficiency and high costs of state forestry, the post-Mao leadership decided to extend the concept of private plots to forestry. As in farming, the collective retained ownership of the land, but households were granted the right to cultivate the land for their own needs or, within limits, to market the produce. The land consisted largely of sloped wasteland (*huang shan*) rather than more valuable forested land and was distributed on an equal per capita basis. Certificates of possession, which were subject to cancellation in the event of abuse or neglect, were issued by the local authorities with the expectation that the plots would not be disturbed.

The original scope of private plots for forestry was limited to 1 to 10 *mu* per household (15 *mu* equals 1 hectare), or 5 percent of total wasteland in poor, mountainous areas of the country. But this ceiling proved to be short-lived. Party general secretary Hu Yaobang, a committed reformer who was impressed by the contribution private plots were making in farming and wished to encourage vegetative approaches to flood control following the severe floods that struck China in the summer of 1981, took a personal hand in broadening the application of private plots to forestry. While visiting Yixian County in the Taihang Mountains of Hebei in the spring of 1982, he endorsed afforestation as a flood control measure. He specifically favored expanding private plots to 15–20 percent of wasteland, larger even than the 15 percent norm adopted for farming in 1979 (FBIS, July 8, 1982: R2; ZL, June 1982: 2). In so doing, Hu overrode the objections of foresters and opposition from left-leaning officials (Ross 1983: 226–27). As a follow-up measure, collective authority over the private plots was greatly reduced in 1983–84 when the right of inheritance was granted.

Private plots have become much more widespread in forestry. By 1985, 50 million households had over 30 million hectares of private hills, an average of over half a hectare per household, making private plots responsible for almost a third of all land considered afforestable (RR, Mar. 12, 1986). For example, Guangxi allowed private hills on 20–30 percent of collectively owned wasteland (JPRS 82782 CAG 248, Feb. 1, 1983: 78–79), while in poverty-stricken Guizhou private plots averaged six hectares (He Tingxian 1983).

Nevertheless, private plots are only the lesser of two forms of privatization that developed in the post-Mao era. The larger is the contract responsibility system under which collectives and some state farms retain full or part ownership but contract with households to manage forests. The aim is clear: by establishing direct links between responsibilities (*ze*), rights (*quan*), and rewards (*li*), it is hoped that households will acquire a strong, direct interest in developing forestry. The contracts can be task-specific, such as contracts to deliver seedlings, plant trees, or protect forests. In such cases, which are referred to as *huang shan zaolin chengbao dao hu* (contracting the afforestation of wasteland to households) and other such terms, the household is promised a fixed payment to be made after the task is completed in accordance with quality norms. Bonus payments are usually provided if the contractor's performance exceeds the terms of the contract, while a nursery contractor may be permitted to sell for his own account any excess seedlings he produces. Conversely, a failure to satisfy the terms of the contract calls for reduced payment, with the contractor obligated to make up the deficiency.

The more popular form of contracting involves the assignment of an entire site to a household or group of households for management. By

1986, over 40 million hectares had come under responsibility contracting for forestry (RR, Mar. 12, 1986). Under *huangshan da baogan* (the big contracting of wasteland), the collective provides the site and often the seedlings and other material inputs. In return, the contractor agrees to perform all labor involved in afforesting and managing the site. The contractor in principle has the autonomy to make all decisions regarding management, but his discretion is limited in several respects. The collective retains land ownership and must approve all logging by the contractor. Land use is restricted to forestry, although intercropping may be allowed. The type of forest to be planted must also be approved by the collective, frequently on the basis of the state plan. The contractor's reward is a share of the income obtained from harvesting, as much as 80–90 percent, as well as all incidental income such as firewood.

Although contracting was originally intended for wasteland only, in practice many sites have at least some second-growth forest, a situation that has led many cadres to limit the scope of responsibility forestry. To overcome this objection, the collectives were directed to determine the standing value of the timber at the beginning of the contract period and then either exclude this amount from the future distribution of dividends or treat the management of such wood on a strictly task-based responsibility basis. This directive aims to protect the interests of the other members of the collective and to discourage the immediate logging of all trees by the contractor. Should the contractor neglect forestry or otherwise fail to perform as expected, the collective may terminate the contract after a three- to five-year probationary period (RR, Apr. 21, 1983; Yang Furong et al. 1982; JPRS 83357 CAG 250, Apr. 28, 1983, 125–32, and 84770 CAG 279, Nov. 17, 1983: 56–60; Yang Yu and Wang Shikuei 1983a).

As in the case of private plots, this reform began in farming before it was extended to forestry. Therefore, the contract term originally was for a season or a year as might be appropriate for farming. One unfortunate consequence of short-term leases was to discourage cultivators from investing in permanent improvements to the land (BR, Aug. 8, 1983: 26–27). This factor was of greater concern in forestry, where the collective might repossess or transfer the trees before maturity, unilaterally depriving the cultivator of a share in future income (JPRS 76200 CAG 95, Aug. 8, 1980: 26–30; FBIS, May 26, 1983: O6). Therefore, the regime found it necessary to issue certificates specifying the contractor's rights of cultivation and to extend the lease term for up to fifty years (RR, June 6 and July 22, 1983; Wang Jianzheng 1983). This move preceded the party's decision in 1984 (Central Directive No. 1) to extend farming contracts to as long as fifteen years, and in 1987 to fifty years.

The post-Mao reforms embraced markets as well as ownership and management. In addition to raising the official procurement price for timber, producers were allowed greater freedom to sell their above-norm output to the highest bidder. Rural timber markets opened in logging areas, attracting purchasing agents from factories across the country. The prices offered generally exceeded even the recently increased procurement prices.

It is important to note that these changes were not entirely orchestrated in advance by the higher leadership and remained vulnerable to political opposition, especially since privatization was carried further than the reformers had originally authorized (FBIS, Mar. 29, 1985: W13). The critical decisions on rural policy taken at the Third Plenum in December 1978 had only loosely defined the terms and extent of privatization, which were then carried forward in the course of implementation (RR, July 14, 1983, and Mar. 1, 1984; ZNB, July 19 and Aug. 25, 1983; FBIS, Jan. 31, 1984).

This phenomenon of implementation outrunning formal policy can also be observed in the history of the Forestry Law. Adopted in provisional form by the Standing Committee of the National People's Congress on February 26, 1979 (FBIS, Mar. 2, 1979: E1–10), it was one of the first items of formal legislation enacted as part of the post-Mao regime's broad effort to restore order and a legal foundation to society. The PRC's newfound faith in the power of law to specify proper behavior was somewhat disingenuous in light of the Communist party's claim to supremacy as expressed in the Four Cardinal Principles. But it was part of a major effort to alter the Chinese tradition of governance by conformity to standards of propriety (*li*) rather than rule by law. Restoration of a legal structure was a critical element in building a foundation for the more decentralized, property-rights-oriented regime being created after Mao's death, and it appears to have had broad appeal to a society that yearned for stability after more than a decade of turmoil.

For present purposes, the key point is that the Forestry Law did not anticipate the extent of privatization that was soon to follow, even though the law was intended to serve as the organic basis for forestry policy. The law was soon eclipsed by events. For example, the law's primary emphasis was on the indivisibility of state and collective property. The contract responsibility system was not mentioned at all, and in fact the assignment of collective forests to individuals was virtually prohibited (article 3).

The delay in specifying the details of privatization was due to political opposition as well as inexperience. The opposition emanated from party officials who were opposed to ideological heresy, from local administrators fearful that separating management and ownership would leave the collectives with power in name only, and from the central bureaucracies (JPRS 83642 CAG 260, June 9, 1983: 21; *Zhongguo Nongmin Bao*, Mar. 8, 1983). Central planners and procurement officials complained that decentralization and the accompanying liberalization of marketing jeopardized fulfillment of the state economic plan. The Ministry of Forestry shared these views; it also objected to responsibility forestry and to any encroachment on state land to expand private plots ("the two hills"). These objections in part reflected the ministry's long-standing position that household management is inherently inefficient (Liu Zhijie 1983; RR, June 25, 1980; GR,

Mar. 4, 1981; Yang Yu and Wang Shikuei 1983a; Ministry of Forestry 1981).

The opponents focused on the great wave of deforestation that took place in 1979, reportedly the worst such episode since the Great Leap Forward, when ill-conceived "backyard steel furnaces" and communal cooking campaigns led to wholesale mining of the forests; the effects are still visible in parts of southern China. The critics blamed the problem on the reforms, arguing that the loosening of controls created a climate in which socially harmful behavior could take place. They pointed to the fact that purchasing agents for industrial enterprises were flocking to forestry centers and bidding up the prices for timber, which producers were only too happy to supply regardless of the ecological consequences. The state also suffered because timber was being surreptitiously diverted from official distribution channels to the gray market (Shen Guansheng 1982; JPRS 75186 CAG 71, Feb. 22, 1980: 22–24; GR, Oct. 20 and Nov. 26, 1980).

The rise in concern over deforestation and runaway markets coincided with a shift in the balance of opinion within the higher leadership to the "readjusters," or planners, after a heady two years of reform. The principal consequence for forestry was a strong emphasis on law and order. Stringent controls were reimposed on logging and marketing in a series of State Council directives beginning in December 1980—earlier decrees, dating back to January 1979, having proven ineffective. The forestry bureaucracy was ordered to regulate all logging by issuing permits to ensure that production did not exceed growth. Private markets for timber and bamboo were ordered to close, and the Ministry of Forestry was granted total authority to procure and distribute wood products (RR, Dec. 6, 1980, and Mar. 12, 1981; Compendia of Forestry Laws and Decrees 14: 25–27). These restrictions were incorporated into the Sixth Five-Year Plan (1981–85), which was adopted in December 1982. Ultimately, timber and cotton became the only remaining commodities for which it was prohibited to sell above-norm production through negotiated prices or through the market (FBIS, Dec. 5, 1983: P3–4).

The opponents of reform seemingly hoped to reverse the tide of change once and for all. Their activities encouraged officials in some areas of the country to stall the extension of private and responsibility systems (Li Zhankui et al. 1984), while necessary clarifications were kept in abeyance on such key issues as the inheritability of private plots, the duration of responsibility contracts, and the treatment of standing timber. Yunnan in particular is said to have resisted the introduction of the responsibility system for two years, a notable contrast to this frontier province's accustomed leadership role in the reforms (JPRS 82241 WWEQ 377, Nov. 16, 1982: 117–18, and An Pingsheng 1983; on Yunnan in general, see Domes 1985: 166 and Shambaugh 1984).

Other officials, led by Premier Zhao Ziyang, acknowledged that a deforestation problem existed and agreed that it warranted a law-and-order

crackdown (*Linye Gongzuo* 8: 6–9). As Zhang Jingfu, the head of the State
Economic Commission, ruefully explained, the gap between the official
price and timber's true market value had grown so wide that there was no
alternative to tighter controls in the short run (ZL, August 1982: 2–7). For
the most part, however, officials sympathetic to reform reasoned that the
ultimate cause of deforestation was not privatization but rather excessive
and irrational controls, which dampened entrepreneurship. Although they
conceded that the pace of reform had to be slowed until regulatory authority was reestablished, it was critical that the momentum of defining and
demarcating property rights be continued.

Thus, some elements of the reform process continued to advance even
during the readjustment phase of 1980–82. That was made apparent in
the Central Committee–State Council joint directive on forestry development and forest conservation, "Decision on Some Problems Regarding Forest Conservation and Forestry Development," issued in the spring of 1981.
This important document identified conflicting and unstable property
rights as the primary cause of deforestation. In other words, the problem
was defined as one of transition toward clearer, more enforceable property
rights. The directive explicitly endorsed private plots and responsibility
systems, the leadership evidently realizing that forestry's problems ante-
dated the introduction of the responsibility system. Instead of ordering a
return to collectivization, this directive ordered that property rights continue to be decentralized but on a firmer, less conflictual basis during the
period of readjustment (Ross and Silk 1987).

The chosen instrument was the Three Fixes, which began in 1981 and
was to be basically completed by the end of 1984. The Three Fixes were
prompt and equitable resolution of all property rights conflicts, demar-
cation of private hills for afforestation, and establishment of production
responsibility systems for collective forests, usually on a household basis,
all for the purpose of stabilizing newly privatized forestry (*People's Procuracy*
1983: 303–6; FBIS, June 22, 1982: K13–14; Zhang Jingfu 1982). Nevertheless, there is some reason to question how effectively the nearly two
million property rights cases were handled by local officials and temporary
work teams consisting of cadres drawn from other jurisdictions, who were
explicitly ordered to disregard all suits based on pre-land-reform property
claims, presumably a source of many grievances. Nor is it clear how well
newly assigned rights will be defended in the future against challenges by
other parties, especially the state and collectives, since disputes are almost
always resolved through politically colored discussion and mediation processes rather than by an effective and independent judicial system (ZL,
December 1982: 2; *Linye Gongzuo* 7: 95). There are, in fact, numerous
reports of newly privatized forests being chopped down by neighbors of
the new owners; such cutting obviously jeopardizes the entire policy (e.g.,
RR, Apr. 24, 1985; JPRS 84549 CAG 275, Oct. 17, 1983: 44, and 84689
CAG 277, Nov. 7, 1983: 42–43). Indeed, only 1,781 counties and munici-

palities had resolved all their disputes by the end of 1985, indicating that nearly a thousand still had disputes outstanding (RR, Mar. 12, 1986).

Nevertheless, there was enough support from within the higher leadership to keep the momentum of privatization going despite opposition. By the middle of 1982, General Secretary Hu Yaobang personally endorsed the expansion of private plots. As the readjustment phase diminished, the pace of privatization picked up. Central directives in 1983 and 1984 (No. 1 in both cases), which were finalized at National Rural Work Conferences, did not order retractions; instead, they called for further perfecting and expanding responsibility systems (FBIS, Apr. 13, 1983: K1–13; RR, Dec. 29, 1983, and Jan. 23, 1984; Commentator 1984). Newly prosperous peasants were commended as activist elements rather than being persecuted as reactionaries (FBIS, Jan. 24, 1984: 10), although there was new emphasis in 1984 on the need to balance specialization (*fen*) and privatization with unified (*tong*) marketing and jointly supplied infrastructural services (Jing Ping 1984, Lu Rizhou and Du Zhuangye 1984).

With regard to forestry in particular, privatization, including the widespread extension of responsibility systems to state and collective forestry farms and greater freedom for private households, was approved in the Party Center and State Council's annual greenification directive in 1984 (RR, Mar. 1, 1984; Jin Qi 1984b). Most collectives and state forest farms had established some form of responsibility system by late 1984, involving almost 4 million specialized households and 70 million hectares in private and responsibility forestry (RR, Dec. 31, 1984). Foresters and economists met to consider how economic instruments could assist forestry (RR, Mar. 29, 1984). The new minister of forestry, in his 1983 annual address to provincial forestry bureau chiefs, explicitly rejected charges that privatization was a cause of deforestation. Instead Yang Zhong, who had been promoted from a Sichuan provincial post by the pragmatists, demanded further privatization. His use of the phrase *yi fang er bao* (first, policy relaxation; second, production guarantees) was a slap at leftists who had proudly trumpeted the slogan *yi da er gong* (first, big; second, public) to justify communization during the Great Leap Forward. Of course, Yang conceded the need for certain modifications; for example, established stands of timber would need more stringent regulation than wasteland and might be unsuitable for household management. Similarly, Yang insisted that ownership and inheritance applied only to private plots and not to responsibility forests. On the whole, however, Yang's support for privatization was pronounced and represented a major evolution from the ministry's traditional qualms about privatization (Yang Zhong 1983b).

Privatization advanced further in late 1984 and early 1985, after the conservative tendency within the higher leadership suffered a setback during the Combat Spiritual Pollution campaign of the previous winter. The process of revising the Forestry Law was completed, making this statute permanent after nearly six years of provisional status. The new law (article

23) formally authorized contract-guarantee forest management, thereby reversing the absolute prohibition on the transfer of state and collective forests found in the 1979 draft law. General Secretary Hu endorsed the merger of private and responsibility forests, eliminating a distinction that was already in the process of disappearing (FBIS, Dec. 17, 1984: K3). The new law also further emphasized the principle of "ownership to the planter" and allowed individual households to cut trees around their own houses without first having to obtain permission from local government. At the same time, the law reaffirmed past policy with regard to strict control over all other logging via a permit system to ensure that logging did not exceed growth and cited specific provisions within the Criminal Law that pertained to violation of this and other policies. In sum, the new Forestry Law solidified the legal foundation for private and enterprise management under the broad rubric of regulatory controls (RR, July 5 and Dec. 31, 1984; ZL 1984: 3–4; ZRGGYG 444, Oct. 10, 1984: 771–78).

Possibly of greater importance were the changes made in 1985 with regard to regulatory policy. As part of a general relaxation of agricultural policy announced in Central Directive No. 1, the regime announced a relaxation of the agricultural procurement system. Although compulsory delivery quotas would remain in place for forestry as well as grain and a small number of other key commodities, prices would be greatly relaxed for above-quota production as the regime shifted from a fixed-price policy to a price-stabilization policy (RR, Feb. 15 and Mar. 25, 1985). To spur development in poorer mountainous areas, 225 counties were relieved of timber procurement and delivery quotas altogether to enable them to obtain higher prices on the market, although their overall logging volume would continue to be regulated to ensure that logging did not exceed growth (ZRGGYG 446, Oct. 30, 1984: 866–69). These actions were taken chiefly to raise income in collective forestry areas, but indirectly to accelerate resource development in the southern region of the country, where growing conditions are more favorable (Liu Chengdong 1957; *Linye Gongzuo* 6: 86–97; Wang Youchen 1984; JPRS 81644 CEA 261, Aug. 27, 1982: 90–95).

The legal and regulatory changes made in 1984–85 combined more precise definition and enforcement of property rights with greater autonomy in marketing. Logging itself would be regulated even more tightly by bringing even off-plan production under the "single-ledger" permit system to prevent deforestation, but marketing would be liberalized to provide the producer with a larger return and a bigger incentive to reinvest in forestry. This policy was summed up in the phrase *shan shang guan yan, shan xia fang kai* (stringent regulation in the mountains, relaxation in the lowlands). In this fashion, it was hoped that the basic thrust of reform policy would survive the transition from bureaucratic planning to market exchange without an epidemic of forest destruction.

The reforms enhanced private forestry and spurred participation in afforestation and forest management. Afforestation increased by 25 percent in 1983 and by 10 percent in 1984. It is impossible to say how much is genuine rather than a product of false reporting, but it is clear that the increases were due in large part to household effort. Households were responsible for 38 percent of afforestation in 1984 and over 50 percent in 1985. The higher percentages came in the remote hilly provinces of Guizhou, Gansu, and Shanxi, where, because they are largely ill suited to farming, the central government decided to promote forestry and animal husbandry in contrast to the Maoist emphasis on grain production (Zhang Zhida 1985; RR, Jan. 23, 1984, and Mar. 12, 1985; He Yanxian 1984; GR, Mar. 11, 1983; FBIS, June 28, 1983: R6). Indeed, the regime has further spurred privatization in the badly eroded loess plateau by including gully control within the scope of responsibility forestry by households, in units as large as ten hectares or more with major implications for soil conservation. Initial success has been reported since decentralized management predicated upon more fully articulated property rights became the policy in 1983 at the National Water Conservancy Work Conference. By the mid-1980s over one-third of rural households had contracted to manage over 50,000 square kilometers in all. That requires subsidies by the central and local governments totaling several hundred yuan per square kilometer but appears to be better suited for harnessing the energies of the local work force than campaigns (RR, July 5 and 8, 1985; CD, Sept. 11, 1985; ZNN 1984: 20; Wang Wende and Qiao Zhangbao 1983; "Regulations on Water and Soil Conservation Work," in Ross and Silk 1987).

Moreover, prosperous suburban areas have seen many private nurseries spring up to supply a suddenly profitable market (Liu Pufeng 1983, Zweig 1983). This development indicates that households, in accordance with classical economic expectations, are responding positively to favorable entrepreneurial opportunities. Therefore, entrepreneurship has been further encouraged by permission to establish larger and unequally sized responsibility contracts on a voluntary basis in place of equal per capita allotments, thus improving the prospects for genuine household forest farms (Yan Anyun 1984; FBIS, Sept. 12, 1983: K16–17; RR, June 3, 1983).

Li Jinyao and Private Forestry Problems. To get a more human perspective on privatization, it is instructive to take a look at China's most famous household woodlot operator, Li Jinyao. Li, like any model, is unrepresentative of the country as a whole, but his story nevertheless is revealing. Li is a member of Lianjiang Brigade in Gaiwei Commune, Xianyu County, in the coastal hills of Fujian. His brigade assigned six peasants to establish a collective forest farm in 1969. They planted about seventy hectares of Masson's pine (*Pinus massoniana*)—a hardy and fast-growing conifer that unfortunately is characterized by poor form and low-quality wood—and other crops in exchange for annual stipends totaling 900 yuan and 600 catties of grain. The plantation developed slowly and unsatisfactorily. After ten years, tree height averaged less than one meter. Under the impetus of the reform-oriented Third Plenum, the brigade in July 1979 negotiated a responsibility contract with Li and three others to manage the plantation. The brigade retained ownership and pledged to supply most of the capital, while Li and his partners committed themselves to perform the work.

Income was to be divided according to its origin. The brigade would keep all revenue from harvesting the pine. Income from woody oils would be divided evenly between the brigade and the operators. Any income obtained from Chinese fir (*Cunninghamia lanceolata*) and eucalyptus to be planted later would be shared on a 10:90 and 40:60 basis, respectively, with the larger share in favor of the brigade. In other words, the collective's share of revenue was higher for timber than for other forest products. The costs for planting stock would be split according to ownership share, provided that all brigade funds were used on the plantation itself rather than on adjoining private hills assigned to Li and the others. The brigade also pledged to construct and maintain housing and other elements of the infrastructure and to make 0.8 hectare of farmland available for the contractors to raise their own grain.

Despite the changes, the terms continued to be unappealing to three of the four contractors, who soon asked to be relieved of their obligations. As the only remaining contractor, Li was able to negotiate better terms. He secured a new contract to manage a tea grove, promising to supply the brigade with 100 catties of tea leaves a year within seven years in exchange for the right to all additional production. Li also obtained a quarrying permit for six years under which he kept all the revenue in exchange for building a three-kilometer access road to his plantations that would be made available for public use.

Li began with five workers and within three years he was managing 200,000 pines and had planted 70,000 firs, 70,000 eucalypts, and 5,000 tung trees. He had also established a 4.3-hectare fruit orchard, planted over 150,000 herbaceous plants as well as some banana trees and sugar cane, built his three-kilometer public road, and constructed buildings with twenty-eight rooms. His trees averaged 2.5 meters in height, or 2.3 times the growth of the previous ten years. His work force expanded to thirty, and Li hired tractor drivers and other free-lancers for more specialized tasks such as hauling stone.

The burgeoning operations led to criticism that Li was an antisocialist exploiter of labor. Intervention by officials at the county level, at the behest of provincial party first secretary Xiang Nan, was needed to clear Li. The responsibility system now officially was said to be socialist because land ownership remained with the collective, which defined the terms of management. Although the earnings of Li and his workers averaged between 1 and 2.5 yuan daily, far higher than the average peasant income at the time, they were considered acceptable because they were based on labor (FBIS, Aug. 26, 1983: O2).

Moreover, it was explained that Li was actually operating at a loss. Because his trees were still immature, his income was derived largely from farming and sidelines. During the first 2.5 years, revenue reportedly totaled only about 19,000 yuan, over 30,000 yuan less than costs, which amounted to 49,000 yuan. How could Li sustain such large losses? To meet the short-fall, Li borrowed 270,000 yuan from overseas relatives and obtained a 27,800-yuan bank loan through his brigade.

Li's family was becoming rich in accordance with the new, post-Mao ideal. Over the first 2.5 years, his own family earned 5,292 yuan, a very large sum even for a household with as many as two to five members in the work force at different times. When not working on the household forest farm, family members engaged in sideline businesses that earned them an additional 6,230 yuan. They reinvested over 4,100 yuan in the farm, but that still left them with a handsome income by Chinese rural standards. Their income promised to rise substantially as their trees matured (table 8), although unfortunately no cost projections are available. The first profits were realized in 1983 and totaled over 4,800 yuan (Yang Tao 1982; RR, Dec. 8, 1981, Feb. 2, 1982, and June 9, 1983; GR, Apr. 30, 1983).

Li's case ended happily. Not only were his entrepreneurial ambitions given the stamp of approval but in an extraordinary ideological twist Li was admitted into the Communist party. Others in Xianyu Xian allegedly were reassured. Soon over 10,000 households were managing over 20,000 hectares of wasteland for their collectives, and Li himself applied for an additional 400 hectares (GR, Apr. 30, 1983; RR, Apr. 22 and Nov. 11, 1983; Li Jinyao 1982; Yang Tao 1984a).

Nevertheless, even Li's remarkably positive case history reveals some problems facing private forestry, particularly lack of capital. Without a

Table 8

Li Jinyao Household's Forestry Income--A 20-Year Projection

Species	Yield	Value Per Unit Output (yuan)	Revenue (yuan) Brigade Share	Contractor Share	Total
Masson's pine					
Timber	100,000 m^3	50.0	500,000	0	500,000
Fuelwood	30,000 piculs	2.0	60,000	0	60,000
Chinese fir	250 m^3	100.0	40,500	4,500	45,000[a]
Eucalyptus	10,000 m^3	17.5	118,000	77,000	195,000[b]
Branches, leaves	12,000 piculs	2.0	0	24,000	24,000
Total timber				105,500	824,000
Fruits and oils	No data available				

SOURCE: Yang Tao (1982).
[a]Includes 20,000 yuan from sale of thins.
[b]Includes 20,000 yuan from sale of thins at 1 yuan per tree.

source of overseas capital, Li's operation never could have grown so fast or so large, yet few Chinese have such favorable connections. Credit was made available by the bank, a noticeable change from practice in the past, when bank lending was less extensive and rarely available to forestry. A low-interest revolving credit was provided to Liu Hongjie, the largest contract guarantee forestry operator in Zhejiang, who is reported to enjoy similar success (RR, Apr. 25, 1984).

It is impossible for most rural households to manage forests without credit or subsidies (Zhao Mingguang 1985). Some provinces have responded to this need by borrowing money from the Agricultural Bank for use by forestry households. Guangxi set up a 100-million-yuan fund in this fashion, with the loans to be repaid in timber at the end of the harvest cycle. Some officials, including Premier Zhao Ziyang, have recommended that this concept be applied nationwide by converting annual governmental subsidies to collective afforestation, which total 170 million yuan, into a credit fund. That would expand the pool of credit by creating an off-budget source of capital that would eventually be replenished by loan repayments (Liu Jinkai and Shi Xizhai 1984; RR, Apr. 6 and 8, 1981; ZL, March 1983: 19; BR, Apr. 11, 1983: 27), although inflation-conscious officials and the Ministry of Finance greeted this proposal warily.

Other problems also arose after marketing was liberalized in the fall of 1984. While price increases were anticipated and even considered desirable by the reformers, the size of the increases and the disruptions in distribution patterns for timber, steel, and other commodities were deemed too precipitous for a society still scarred by the memory of the hyperinflation of the 1940s, and long coddled by the artificial price stability imposed by central planning. Indeed, China suffered its highest rate of inflation in over thirty years in 1985. As inflation and overheating of the economy became political issues for the conservatives, the regime brought a temporary halt to price reform in the spring of 1985 by such measures as the imposition of a relatively narrow pricing band to govern all timber transactions. That succeeded in stabilizing prices for the time being after an increase of about 30 percent (CD, Nov. 11 and 29, 1985).

In terms of implementation, the major problem was that local officials and the state bureaucracies retained substantial power over contracts, permits, services, and taxes and used it to increase their own revenue and to hamstring entrepreneurs. Even in Li Jinyao's case, the brigade demanded the lion's share of revenue from timber plantations, and that appears to be a common occurrence even when the contractor does the planting himself. When it comes time to harvest, it is up to the local government to issue logging permits under the *yi ben zhang* (single-ledger) system introduced in 1983 in order to ensure that the total volume of production does not exceed growth. This power could obviously be used to punish recalcitrant producers by withholding permits.

With regard to marketing itself, the reforms threatened the Ministry of

Forestry and the State Commodities Supply General Administration. These two agencies had never been able to completely control timber distribution even under the unified purchase and supply system when most planned and unplanned timber moved through other channels. However, the new market liberalization policy represented an enormous challenge to the existing system. Therefore, the Commodities Pricing Bureau responded by defining reform in terms of carefully monitored markets operating under its own auspices, thereby increasing its span of authority and negating part of the purpose behind the reforms. This response involved such measures as the organization of municipal timber markets under the control of local commodities supply bureaus and the addition of plywood and other processed wood products to their system of distribution (China Timber Company 1984, Han Gangli 1985).

In the logging areas, termination of the Ministry of Forestry's monopsony over procurement led to intensified competition among purchasing agents from factories and mills all over the country who flocked to the forests to buy timber and other raw materials. This increased business benefited producers but aroused the ire of local factories, who were dependent on secure and low-cost local sources of raw materials. In some cases, officials in producing areas effectively squelched competition by forcing producers to sell their products at below-market prices to the local, government-owned factories (JR, Aug. 19, 1985). Other officials welcomed the arrival of outside purchasing agents but tried to monopolize the local timber trade to ensure their control over the additional revenue resulting from higher prices (LJ 1985 3: 22–26; Lu Weiguo and Wang Mingshui 1985). More often, they tacked on a series of taxes and charges for road use, general governmental purposes, and support of the county forestry bureaucracy. That typically left the woodsman with as little as 10 percent of the actual "forest gate" price to show for his efforts—despite the price rises—and had negative implications for entrepreneurship (Zhang Zhida 1985; RR, Feb. 27, 1985; JPRS 84244 CAG 378, Sept. 1, 1983: 62).

Local officials were not the only ones to get into the act. Where the railroads enjoyed a virtual monopoly over transport, they practiced extortion of their own, refusing to load timber on the grounds that timber no longer enjoyed the priority of a state-planned commodity. Timber would still be shipped, after the usual delays, but only after the payment of additional fees and the awarding of co-ownership to the local railway bureau (RR, Feb. 27 and Aug. 20, 1985).

The regime responded to these problems in the manner favored by the reformers, forcing prices down to solve the immediate problem and relieve political pressure without abandoning the ultimate goals of the reforms (CD, Nov. 4 and 29, 1985). Indeed, Central Directive No. 1 of 1986 announced that the rural reforms would basically continue despite the need for backfilling. In this sense, the steady but discontinuous reform process would go on. At the same time, the regime moved to outlaw excessive local taxes and administrative charges that were threatening to cripple the reforms ("Circular on Halting the Imposition of Chaotic Levies and Fees on the Peasants," in RR, Nov. 1, 1985; RR, Nov. 23, 1985; CD, Aug. 17, 1985). However, this can at best be a slow and uneven process given the conflict of interests between conservatives and reformers in Beijing and entrepreneurs and local officials striving to maximize their budgets in an economy no longer under their direct control.

An additional issue involves the overall setting of land-use priorities. Although household management and the other reforms provided long overdue recognition of the need for more efficient management, they did not mark a sufficient break from the long-standing pattern of favoring the planting of trees (or grasses) everywhere without regard for economic wisdom. In other words, many sites being offered to contractors are of marginal productivity with no assurance that they will be profitable, although their lack of viability may not be apparent until some years down the road. That is particularly likely if the regime cannot resist the temptation to suppress timber prices. Ironically, success may aggravate the problem because the arrival of large additional volumes of timber may strain market demand in a country that has discouraged timber consumption for years. The risk faced by forestry entrepreneurs under such a scenario can only be alleviated by continuing government subsidies, which may be justified in any event as recompense for forestry's social benefits such as soil conservation. It would be preferable, however, to relax the requirement that such lands be used only for forestry (or grass) to enable the land to be devoted to its most efficient use, subject only to a conservation easement where necessary.

Conclusions

I have analyzed forestry policy in terms of three distinct categories: state, collective, and private. These categories closely correspond to the three implementation strategies identified earlier (bureaucratic-administrative, campaign-exhortation, and market-exchange). Each form of ownership-management has advantages and drawbacks related to common property resource management, incentives, and free-rider effects.

In general, the state or bureaucratic sector did poorly in terms of resource management, regeneration, productivity, and other criteria (ZNN 1982: 311–13). That is somewhat surprising because a long lead-time production process like forestry is naturally conducive to planning. Moreover, the state sector enjoyed economies of scale, favored access to investment, and the most highly skilled work force.

These advantages proved illusory in practice. Administration was hamstrung by bureaucratic rivalries between growers and loggers, while the planning process operated only by excluding fuelwood and locally consumed timber, the largest categories of demand, from material balances equations. China is not unique in this regard, but the emphasis on industrial wood in the plan was so extreme that it aggravated existing distortions. Because only 3 percent of China's forest area was designated for fuelwood use, the rural populace suffered great hardships while deforestation intensified. The problem was so severe that former minister of forestry Yong Wentao (1982) conceded that the failure to account for fuelwood in the state plan was forestry's greatest misfortune (Li Keliang 1982).* Even timber production and resource conservation were hamstrung by artificially low and inconsistent prices and taxes that discouraged reinvestment in plantations, sawmill technology, and the development of an artificial board industry.

The collective sector also suffered from many of the same problems that affected the state sector, such as producer prices set below the cost of production. Rather than securing broad-based voluntary cooperation from its members, it resorted to coercion, which often proved incapable of generating a sustained effort. While trees would be planted in large numbers at the height of a campaign, little attention would be paid as they withered over the coming months.

The private sector was long suppressed but enjoyed a broad resurgence beginning in 1978, taking charge of almost 70 million hectares in private plots and responsibility contracts. This development recalls the visions of some early twentieth-century foresters who favored agroforestry homesteading as a way to harness individualism to national purposes (Lin and Yule 1916). Private forestry can be more productive and less costly and there are numerous highly positive reports of model rural entrepreneurs like Li Jinyao who have thrived under the new policies. Serious problems such as overcutting and disputes over property rights also have arisen, but the reformers argue that they are due to the traumas of policy transition and uncertainty over the stability of the new policies. While cracking down on violations of law and order, the reformers have also moved to reassure cultivators that the reforms are permanent by punishing local officials who suppress successful individuals (Lin Wenshan 1983; RR, Mar. 1, 1986).

Although households are efficient producers for certain purposes such as small woodlots and orchards, they may be deficient in terms of economies of scale and sometimes in terms of an economic or production orientation (e.g., Zivnuska 1974, Dana and Fairfax 1980: 282–86). Nor can it be said that public ownership is always inferior to private ownership (Krutilla et al. 1983). The question is only in part one of unleashing households. What

---

*Fuelwood's share of the rural energy budget is declining as the standard of living rises with increased development of coal, hydro, and other renewable energy sources. Such development is necessary because unmet energy demands require a severalfold increase in fuelwood production, yet many wood-producing areas are so far from population centers that transportation is very costly (Li Baihang 1984). Failure to provide other energy sources will have dire consequences in terms of human hardship and declining soil fertility.

is ultimately more important is the opportunity and incentives for individual households to expand their holdings or to voluntarily combine into production cooperatives (*hezuo*) for silvicultural, marketing, protection, and other purposes that exceed the capabilities of the individual. This change was endorsed in September 1984 at the annual provincial forestry administrators' conference. At the same time, state forestry can also benefit from an enterprise, profit-and-loss orientation in place of the accustomed bureaucratic structure (Yang Tao 1984a; ZL, October 1984: 7–10).

In other words, although privately run operations may have the strongest incentive structure, the orientation and autonomy of the unit are also important variables. Under the bureaucratic planning system, producers had little reason to improve their performance. Although Marxist economic principles involving land rents and values might appear to benefit forestry by encouraging plantations on land otherwise suited for higher uses, the actual result was to encourage overlogging of the most accessible areas while remote wasteland continued to suffer from inattention. While the Ministry of Forestry traditionally regarded the profit drive as incompatible with conservation (JR, Apr. 26, 1984), its absence slowed resource development and aggravated deforestation. Therefore, a regime whose policy is more profit oriented and based on incentives is likely to benefit not only timber production but also conservation.

For improvements to occur, however, the state must provide improved infrastructural supports. Such supports include continued policy stability; a greater pool of capital for investment credits made available on attractive terms (Zhao Mingguang 1985, Liu Jinkai and Shi Xizhai 1984, Wang Yijun 1984); assured access to grain for areas specializing in forestry, including subsidies where necessary; higher producer prices and freer markets; improved technical services; fire and pest protection; crop insurance (LJ 1985 4: 22–32; ZL, June 1985: 22–23); and security against rapacious local governments that threaten to tax the profit out of forestry (Wen Quan 1984). A high level of imports is also highly desirable to meet demand, at least until domestic production comes on line (FBIS, Apr. 18, 1985: K6–7). As in the past, imports are greater when the moderates are in power than under the autarkic Maoists, and were newly promoted in a small way by Chinese investments overseas in North America, Brazil, the South Pacific, and elsewhere under the auspices of the China Corporation for International Cooperation in the Forestry Industry (BR, Apr. 15, 1985: 30–31). Without these supports, economic reform will remain incomplete and may actually worsen conditions by legitimating cut-and-run behavior without providing sufficient stimulus for reinvestment.

Progress is visible in all respects, but it remains unclear how consistent the regime's backing will be, how strong the regime's leverage is vis-à-vis revenue-hungry local governments, or whether enough timber can be made available to satisfy increasing economic demand when the forestry budget is growing by only 2 percent annually (JPRS CST-84–004, Feb. 14, 1984:

27) and the number of reserves established for conservation purposes has increased to nearly 300 covering almost two million hectares. Moreover, the trend in the state sector continues to be one of merely administrative decentralization down to the prefectural and county levels (RR, Oct. 13, 1984; Song Zuowen 1985), which, based on past experience, is likely to aggravate control problems without improving management incentives (RR, Nov. 13, 1979, and Feb. 10, 1980; *Zhongguo Fazhi Bao*, Feb. 22, 1986). Such promising experiments as extending the responsibility system to workers in the state forestry system, may be stifled at the local level.

One thing above all else should be clear. Any future reversals in policy, such as the confiscation of newly awarded property rights, will greatly impair forestry development by reducing trust in government and producer incentives. Many Chinese officials, including Vice-Premier Wan Li, already recognize that fear of policy instability is the most critical obstacle to improving China's forestry resource base. While conceding the need for some restrictions on logging, they argue that regulation must be applied with a light hand and with respect for recently distributed property rights (Zhu Zanping 1984; RR, Mar. 1, 1986). Otherwise, the populace's worst fears will be realized and forest decline will only worsen.

III.

WATER POLICY AND NATURAL HAZARDS

In the last chapter, it was found that bureaucratic and campaign methods resulted in inefficiency and enjoyed only limited success with regard to forestry. I concluded that the market-exchange method, which involves the devolution of property rights and decision-making autonomy to self-interested individuals or firms, generated the most positive performance. But is this finding of general significance, or is forestry an exception? After all, forests are immobile, renewable, commodity-type resources and thus are particularly suited to market methods, even though the resource also has externality or public goods characteristics. Are market methods also appropriate for other policy sectors?

Our attention now turns to water, a closed system resource without which life could not exist. Additional sources of water can be discovered and used but, with the exception of such exotic and expensive technologies as cloud seeding and desalinization to convert water vapor and brine into freshwater, the resource cannot be expanded, although cyclical variations occur naturally. Like oil, copper, or any other exhaustible resource, water of course can be recycled or reused to expand the usable potential. Thus, the issues that affect water resources largely concern management and distribution within a steady state rather than an expanding state. In practice, the distinction only becomes salient when the economic or physical resource limits are approached.

Water also has more public goods features than forestry. It exists in large pools or streams for the most part and therefore comes under public or joint ownership more frequently. It is physically more difficult to exclude outsiders from enjoyment of the resource, particularly with regard to in-stream uses such as recreation and fishing. Water also differs from forestry because too much as well as too little can be dangerous. There is no counterpart in forestry to flooding or waterlogging except to the extent that other land uses are diminished. Indeed, expanding the forest resource base can exert a positive impact on problems as diverse as soil erosion and the greenhouse effect in the atmosphere caused by buildups of carbon dioxide.

Because of differences between water and forestry, it is important to determine whether policy performance follows the same pattern. To what extent is water resources management also affected by externalities, free riders, and the tragedy of the commons? Is policy performance influenced by the choice of implementation instrument, i.e., state direction, appeals to collective interests, or encouraging individuals to pursue their own interests? Can property rights to water be assigned to individuals and can water be priced according to its scarcity? Is a community's susceptibility to floods or other natural disasters influenced by public policy? These are the questions to be examined in this chapter, but first I will outline China's situation with regard to water.

Water: A Critical Resource

Water would be reasonably plentiful in China were it not for the effects of regional and cyclical variation and population pressure. Precipitation averages about 630 millimeters a year, about 80 percent of the world average. Precipitation totals 6 trillion m^3 annually, of which a little less than half, or 2.6 trillion m^3, is converted to surface flow and is theoretically available for use. In keeping with its geographical size, China ranks fifth in the world in this regard, behind Brazil, the Soviet Union, Canada, and the United States.

The rest of the precipitation is returned to the atmosphere through evapo-transpiration or seeps into the ground. Some of the latter becomes groundwater, some of which can eventually be pumped to the surface for use. China officially estimates that it has total groundwater resources of 800 billion m^3, amounting to about 30 percent of annual stream flow. After allowing for groundwater recharge, China considers that a net of 70 billion m^3 of groundwater is available for use, i.e., about 10 percent of the groundwater resource. That leaves China with a resource base of about 2.7 trillion m^3 in any given year, which is enough water to cover the entire country to a depth of eleven inches (Yang Qicheng 1982; Ferguson et al. 1982).*

The resource base becomes less impressive when China's enormous population is considered. One billion people lower the per capita resource base to only 2,700 m^3, about one quarter of the world average. This figure may seem ample until one realizes that it barely exceeds per capita withdrawals in the United States, which were estimated to total over 2,400 m^3 per capita in the mid-1970s according to the Water Resources Council (Frederick 1982: 219–20; U.S. Water Resources Council 1978). Such figures are of course based on considerable guesswork. Nevertheless, the fact

---

*These figures may not be completely accurate. For example, the volume of the groundwater resource may ultimately prove considerably larger. Nonetheless, much of the surface water theoretically available for use ultimately flows into the sea for lack of sufficient reservoir capacity and to preserve the estuarine ecology.

that water already has become a critical issue even at China's currently low level of economic development makes it quite apparent that water policy will become more important as modernization proceeds.

Moreover, China has an uneven geographical distribution of water. Fifty-three percent of the country is considered arid or semiarid, i.e., precipitation averages less than 500 mm (20 inches) a year. In general, precipitation increases as one goes southward and eastward, with the 1,000-mm isohyet running roughly from Sichuan in the West to Jiangsu along the east coast. Eighty-two percent of surface water and 70 percent of groundwater is found in the South. Because the North is drier, it relies more heavily on irrigation, an important element of China's agricultural infrastructure. Two-thirds of irrigated farmland is in the North, increasing the burden on an already inadequate resource base (RR, Oct. 5, 1983; GR, Aug. 22, 1983).

Another way of grasping the geographical imbalance is to compare major river systems. Most of China's rivers run west to east. Streamflow in the great rivers of Central and South China, the Yangtze and the Pearl, is many times greater than that of the Yellow River and other major northern river systems (table 9). Even the small rivers of Zhejiang and Fujian, including the Min and the Jiulong, which empty into the East China Sea, have a combined flow over three times greater than that of the Yellow River. The

Table 9

China's Major Rivers

River	Length (km)	Silt Load (kg/m^3)	Average Annual Runoff (10^6 m^3)	Drainage Area (km^2)	Runoff/ Drainage Area (m^3/km^2)
Zhujiang (Pearl)	2,210		341,000	442,585	770,000
Rivers in Zhejiang and Fujian			200,100		
Changjiang (Yangtze)	6,300	1	979,000	1,808,500	541,000
Huai	1,000		50,000	269,150	186,000
Huanghe (Yellow)	5,464	37	56,000	752,443	74,000
Hai	1,090		29,200	264,617	110,000
Liao	1,390		15,700	228,960	69,000
Songhua			76,000	528,000	144,000
Rivers in Tibet			359,000		

Table 9

China's Major Rivers
(Part 2)

River	Cultivated Land (10³ ha)	Runoff Cultivated Land (m³/ha)	Irrigated Land (10³ ha)	Irrigated/ Cultivated Land (%)
Zhujiang (Pearl)	5,200	66,000	2,700	51
Rivers in Zhejiang and Fujian	3,100	65,000		
Changjiang (Yangtze)	24,700	40,000	15,000	61
Huai	12,600	4,000	7,300	58
Huanghe (Yellow)	13,100	4,300	4,300	33
Hai	11,300	2,600	6,400	56
Liao	4,700	2,900	1,300	27
Songhua	11,700	6,500	1,300	11
Rivers in Tibet	200	1,795,000		

discrepancy is even greater on an area basis because the northern rivers drain sizable expanses of territory. Such wide imbalances build pressure for policy intervention in the form of interbasin water transfers from the South to the North, a redistribution of population from the North to the South, or a greater conservation effort in the North.

The problem is particularly acute in the Beijing-Tianjin area, also known as the Jinglu region. This area, the national government center, is home to millions of people and the scene of a great deal of economic activity. Greater Beijing's population has grown to nine million and that of Tianjin to nearly eight million, with additional millions living in the neighboring prefectures of Hebei. Beijing's residential water usage is reported to have increased at an annual rate of 15 percent from 1949 to 1979 (He Weicheng 1982). Major water-intensive industrial complexes, including the Capital Iron and Steel Works and the Beijing General Petrochemical Works, have been established since 1949, while older industries have expanded. Meanwhile, agriculture remains a major element in the local economy of the northeastern corner of the North China Plain.

Economic development in this vital region is increasingly jeopardized by water shortages. Beijing's circumstances are particularly precarious. Consumption increased from 7.8 million tons in 1950 to 550 million tons in

Table 9

China's Major Rivers
(Part 3)

River	Population (thousands)	Per Capita Runoff (m^3)	Reservoir Storage Capacity (10^6 m^3)	Reservoir Storage Capacity/ Runoff (%)
Zhujiang (Pearl)	74,110	4,601	38,800	11.0
Rivers in Zhejiang and Fujian	62,800	3,186		
Changjiang (Yangtze)	345,800	2,831	92,000	9.4
Huai	124,790	401	35,800	71.0
Huanghe (Yellow)	81,670	686	53,600	95.0
Hai	88,360	330	24,700	85.0
Liao	28,330	554	12,900	82.0
Songhua	46,520	1,634	18,500	24.0
Rivers in Tibet		1,830	196,000	

SOURCES: Data on length, drainage area, and cultivated land drawn largely from Chinese Statistical Yearbook 1985, 4-5. Data on runoff, irrigated land, population, and reservoir capacity drawn largely from Chinese Economic Yearbook 1985, IV-17. Other sources: Yao Bangyi and Chen Qinglian, "South-North Water Transfer Project Plans," in Biswas et al. (1983): 133; Perkins (1976), 605; Sigurdson (1977a), 70-71; Gregory (1978); GR (Dec. 25, 1981); Shen (1979); and BR 26, 2 (Jan. 10, 1983): 27. Population figures based on national population of 970 million.

1984 (Beijing Water Company 1984; CD, Nov. 15, 1984). Precipitation is said to average 635 mm annually, although the real figure may be as much as 15 percent lower (FBIS, Mar. 22, 1982: R1). Since 1949, aqueducts have been extended to the surrounding area, increasing the surface water supply by over 40 percent, and more than a score of reservoirs have been built. Although published figures vary, under ordinary circumstances there would be a slight margin of supply over use (tables 10 and 11).

This positive margin is established only at considerable hardship. Residential or municipal use in Beijing averages about 140 liters daily per person, barely 70 percent of the official norm of 192 liters and only about one-quarter the average in American cities, although it is nevertheless higher than the overall urban standard of 120 liters (ZRGGYG 1982 18: 795–99, Wei Zhongyi and Ren Hongzun 1983: 2). More importantly, over

Table 10

Water Supply in Beijing

Source	Volume (million m^3)
Surface	
Local	2,572
Outside	1,915
Ground	<u>2,500</u>
Total	6,987
Recoverable	
Surface	3,000
Ground	<u>2,500</u>
Total	5,500

SOURCES: RR, Nov. 28,
1981, and Feb. 2, 1982;
JPRS 79347 CRA 171 (Nov.
2, 1981): 49-52.

Table 11

Water Usage in Beijing, 1978

Sector	Volume (million m^3)
Agriculture	3,000
Industry	1,350
Residential	<u>280</u>
Total	4,630

SOURCES: RR, Nov. 28, 1981,
and Feb. 2, 1982; JPRS 79347
CRA 171 (Nov. 2, 1981): 49-
52.

80 percent of surface water and groundwater recharge is already committed. In several areas, the groundwater aquifers are being rapidly depleted and water quality is declining. The water table has fallen by up to 30 m in a 1,000 km^2 area (BR, May 3, 1982: 29). If the economy develops as projected, with the gross value of output quadrupling between 1980 and 2000, water demand is expected to more than double under the best of circumstances (State Council 1984a).

The problem in Bejing becomes more serious during a drought, such as the one experienced in the early 1980s. Rainfall dropped below 400 mm annually from 1980 to 1982, drying up reservoirs, increasing withdrawals of groundwater, and forcing reductions in deliveries. By 1982 the shortage reportedly amounted to 1.2–1.4 billion m^3 annually (FBIS, Apr. 12, 1982: R1; He Weicheng 1982). New reservoirs, including Dianjinfeng, with sev-

eral hundred million m³ capacity are planned or under way, but because
of the sedimentation of existing reservoirs, not to mention pollution, no
net increase in storage capacity is anticipated (He Weicheng 1982).

Tianjin's situation is even more difficult than Beijing's because precipitation is lower, averaging only 560 mm annually, and the city is located at
the mouth of the Hai River, leaving it vulnerable to upstream diversions.
Tianjin has been denied access to Miyun and four other major reservoirs
upstream that now serve Beijing exclusively. Residential usage in normal
times is only half that of Beijing, placing the city far below already inadequate official standards. During the drought of 1982, daily usage was reduced by two-thirds, leading to the diversion of low-quality Yellow River
water to the city on an emergency basis (Zhang Nan 1982; RR, June 14,
1982; FBIS, Nov. 6, 1981: R6). Because of the drought, Tianjin's already
pending application to divert water from the Luanhe River northeast of
the city was expedited and the project rushed to completion (RR, July 18,
1982; Wei Zhongyi and Ren Hongzun 1983; BR, June 14, 1982: 8–9).
Other provinces in North China, including Shanxi (FBIS, Jan. 8, 1982: R6–
7, and Feb. 22, 1983: R3; JPRS 83576 CAG 289, May 31, 1983: 35–39)
and Shandong (FBIS, Feb. 22, 1983: O2), also suffer from water shortages
that are aggravated by irrigation and other diversions.

The geographical imbalance is paralleled by uneven precipitation on both
a seasonal and an annual basis. China has a monsoon continental climate
in which 70 percent of precipitation falls in a three- to four-month period
from June to September, especially the two middle months. Unfortunately,
this pattern does not correspond to the needs of agriculture, by far the
largest consumer of water. Agriculture's demand tends to be greatest in
the spring and early summer, but rainfall is heaviest in mid- to late summer,
when temperatures and evapo-transpiration rates are highest. The seasonal
imbalance, coupled with frequent droughts arising from wide annual
swings in precipitation, creates a large need for water storage.

The fluctuations in precipitation also increase the danger of flooding,
which has always been a major hazard in China. Severe floods such as those
that occurred in the Yangtze and Yellow River valleys in 1981 are caused
by heavy and prolonged monsoonal storms, sometimes exacerbated by
snowmelt. Floods in coastal areas of the Southeast are typically caused by
typhoons. Other contributing factors are the soil structure, slope, and land-
use patterns. Sediment from the easily erodible loess plateau washes into
rivers, leading to streambed aggradation and indirectly to flooding in the
Yellow River basin. The steep hills of southern and southwestern China
accelerate streamflow and aggravate the flood danger. Land-use patterns,
including deforestation, cultivation of sloped land, buildup of human settlements in floodplains, and dumping in river channels, all increase the
flood danger (Wang Mingzhong 1983, Ross 1983b).

Throughout China's long history, government has assumed extensive
responsibility for water resource management. As the balance between de-

mand and supply has grown more critical and as the number of people vulnerable to natural disaster has risen, the need for wise public policy has grown. How has the People's Republic of China responded to this need?

Water Supply and Demand

As noted, China's water resource base is very small on a per capita basis and is subject to substantial cyclical fluctuations. Consumption in 1978 is estimated to have totaled 477 billion m³, about 17 percent of the resource. Consumption by one estimate is projected to increase to between 640 and 740 billion m³ by the end of the century, still only about one-quarter of the resource (table 12). This projection is almost certainly too modest, however, since it anticipates a rate of increase in usage of less than 2 percent annually over a twenty-year period in which economic output is expected to quadruple and living standards to rise substantially. Since consumption during the PRC's first thirty years grew at approximately the same rate as the economy as a whole, the 0.63:1 coefficient for water consumption per unit economic growth accepted by the State Council may be too conservative. It would, however, project consumption of about 1,300 billion m³ in the year 2000 if the economy meets its overall growth target (JPRS 83286 CAG 254, Apr. 18, 1983: 21–33, and 80717 CAG 203, May 3, 1982: 1–4; State Council 1984a).

Looking at individual sectors, agriculture not surprisingly is the largest user of water, accounting for 420 billion m³, or 88 percent of total consumption. Agriculture uses water principally for irrigation. China increased irrigation very rapidly in the 1960s and 1970s until over 44 million hectares, or about 45 percent of all farmland, was irrigated, a much larger percentage

Table 12

China's Projected Water Needs

Sector	1978 Usage (billion m³)	2000 Usage (billion m³)	Average Increase (% per year)
Agriculture			
Irrigation	400.5	492.0–558.0	1.03–1.67
People, livestock	13.7	24.3	2.91
Animal husbandry	5.3	13.0	4.59
Total	419.5	529.3–595.3	1.17–1.76
General industry	26.3	66.7– 96.5	4.70–6.70
Thermal power	26.0	40.0	2.10
Municipal	4.9	11.0	4.10
Total	476.7	647.0–742.8	1.54–2.24

SOURCES: Li Boning (1983): 3; ZNN (1983): 229.

than in the United States (JPRS 84111 CAG 371, Aug. 12, 1983: 67). Irrigated land generally is more productive, generating two-thirds of the nation's agricultural output value (Yang Qicheng 1982). Only about three-quarters of presently irrigated land is considered reliable, however, and less than half is drought resistant or capable of withstanding all but the most extraordinary droughts. Some Chinese officials therefore stress that even currently irrigated farmland requires more water and that the irrigation system must be further extended if China is to double its agricultural output value by the year 2000 as anticipated in the Four Modernizations. In other words, the projected rate of increase in agricultural usage of 1.17–1.76 percent is unrealistically low (Li Boning 1983).

The other categories of usage by contrast are much smaller than agriculture, yet they are projected to increase at much faster rates. Industry currently consumes 50–60 billion m³, or 11 percent of total usage, about half of which is accounted for by thermal power generation. Official projections anticipate an annual increase in usage of 3.5–4.6 percent through the end of the century, about half the rate of increase expected in industrial output (ibid.). This projection is very ambitious when one considers the inefficiency of industrial water usage. *People's Daily* (May 19, 1983) reported that 573 m³ of water is required for every 10,000 yuan of industrial output value, one-third the efficiency obtained in Japan a decade earlier. The steel industry consumes water at ten times the rate of advanced industrialized countries, while pulp production uses five times as much water as the leading countries (Wang Baozhen 1984). Although some savings can be expected as modern technology is introduced and as light industry expands at a faster rate than heavy industry, industry's demand for water is still likely to grow at a considerable rate.

Municipal or residential usage by contrast is a minor component of nationwide demand at present, totaling only 5 billion m³, or just 1 percent of total usage (RR, Oct. 5, 1983). Nonetheless, residential demand is proportionately much greater in the politically and economically significant cities and is likely to grow rapidly even if China continues to suppress urban population growth. As noted earlier, current levels of consumption are low, with an official norm of only 120 liters per person daily. At such low levels, it is clear that water will show high positive elasticity with respect to income, i.e., demand for water will rise very fast as income rises and, indeed, current economic policy anticipates a sharp rise in the standard of living. In Beijing, for example, per capita consumption exceeds 300 liters daily in the better districts of the city and reaches as much as 2,000 liters a day in first-class hotels, far higher than the citywide average of 140 liters (Ma 1981: 5).

Not only are water withdrawals likely to increase at a substantial rate for quite some time to come, but China also faces substantial and growing demand for instream or nonconsumptive uses that often involve ecological values and water quality. Thus, some portion of streamflow must be left in the rivers to dilute wastes and prevent saline intrusion where rivers empty into the sea. Over one-third of the Yellow River's precious streamflow must be released into the sea to minimize a silt buildup at its mouth (FBIS, June 30, 1983: K16–17). Other instream uses such as hydroelectric power, navigation, and fishing are of direct economic importance and are targeted for major expansion in China's modernization plans. Recreational uses and habitat preservation are also likely to grow in importance as the standard of living and leisure time rise.

Implementation Strategies

This brief sketch indicates that demand for water is likely to rise quite rapidly. Yet China already operates on a tight resource base because of its large population and other factors. Under such circumstances, how did inefficient consumption patterns become so widespread? To what extent can present shortages be attributed to past policies, and how can the policy mix be improved in years to come? For answers I turn to the three implementation strategies introduced in chapter 1.

Bureaucratic-Authoritative Implementation

Shortly after winning power in 1949, the central government laid claim to ownership of all rivers and other bodies of water in China, an edict that has been enshrined in all of the PRC's constitutions. Together with the establishment of a Soviet-style planned economy, the table was set for a tightly administered, centrally directed policy process. Under such a regime, user needs could have been closely scrutinized on a material balances basis for their compatibility with the broader strategy of economic development and the adequacy of water resources. Water would still have been used as wastefully as any other resource in a centrally planned economy, but more attention would have been paid to balancing supply and demand and to calculating technical coefficients.

In practice, water policy has been incidental to the planning process, resulting in even lower efficiency. The two coordinating commissions with overall charge of the economy, the State Planning and State Economic commissions, did not exercise their potential influence over water. Their reluctance was due in part to the general incapacity of the planning process when confronted with a large, diverse, and often fragmented economy, and also to occasional Maoist assaults on planners. The planners were also ideologically inhibited from including water in their calculations because it was not regarded as a product of human labor in the Marxist sense but rather as a gift of nature or a free good. So long as water supply appeared ample to satisfy the needs of favored economic sectors, especially heavy industry, there was no need to plan water consumption.

Therefore, the bureaucratic-authoritative approach has tended to emphasize satisfaction of the supply side of the equation without regard to the regulation of demand. New sources of supply are continually added to accommodate the rising needs of the economy. Users are either charged on a flat-rate basis or permitted to withdraw water without charge rather than according to the volume of water they consume. Moreover, when a fee is imposed, the price of water is predicated not upon its scarcity but rather according to the allowable costs incurred in the distribution system, and even the latter tend to be calculated on an unrealistically low basis.

In agriculture, by far the largest consumer of water, farm operators are assessed a flat fee based on the acreage irrigated rather than on the volume of water consumed (Yang Qicheng 1982, Nickum 1974: 104–8). With regard to residential usage, either no charges are imposed or flat-rate fees are assessed, sometimes according to the number of people served. In most cases, usage is not metered and households do not pay their own bills. Instead, their unit (*danwei*) pays the charges for all residents (Ross 1983a). Industrial users are charged for water in a more varied fashion but often on a flat-rate basis as well. All of the above refer to centrally delivered water, e.g., water supplied by rural irrigation districts or by municipal water companies. Self-supplied well water or river water is free (JPRS 80845 CREA 233, May 18, 1982: 28–29).

When demand rises, the bureaucratic response is to increase the supply. Indeed, there is a built-in incentive for water companies to accommodate demand because, under a fixed price structure, their bonus funds are predicated upon the volume of delivery rather than profits (Wang Changsheng 1983, ZRGGYG 392 1982: 795–99). Large additional increments to the supply necessarily involve new construction to store or divert more surface water or to pump more groundwater. Among the largest projects in recent years are the Luanhe diversion to supply Tianjin with as much as a billion tons of water annually and the diversion of water from the Bilue River to serve Dalian (FBIS, Aug. 22, 1983: S2). However, both of these projects pale in comparison with the South-North (*nan shui bei diao*) project, the first stage of which is under construction. It will transfer as much as 15 billion m^3 from the wetter regions of the South to drier regions more than 1,000 kilometers to the north (Biswas et al. 1983, Liu and Ma 1983).

As noted earlier, there is still considerable potential for expanding supply, since only 17 percent of the resource is being consumed. Groundwater usage in particular amounts to only 7 percent of reserves and probably could be safely increased in many areas, with such exceptions as Shanghai, where problems of surface subsidence and degradation of water quality have forced reductions in groundwater pumping (BR, Aug. 15, 1983: 20–21; JPRS CST-84-029, Sept. 27, 1984: 145–52). Moreover, China may be very conservative when estimating accessible groundwater resources. Some hydrologists maintain that arid Shanxi, for example, has a high likelihood of substantial groundwater resources within a thousand meters of the surface (JPRS 83642 CAG 260, June 9, 1983: 68), although it is unclear who would pay the high pumping costs associated with deep subsurface water.

Although additional water is physically available, supply has lagged behind demand for several reasons. Most obviously, funding is limited. That is not to say that water conservancy has been starved of funds. In fact, water conservancy generally has enjoyed the lion's share of funding within the broader agriculture–water conservancy–meteorology sector. In 1979, for example, investment in water conservancy totaled 3.29 billion yuan, about three-quarters of total investment within the sector as a whole (ZNN 1982: 320–22). In the period 1950–81, the state spent 76.3 billion yuan in all on water conservancy, helping to finance the construction of over 86,000 reservoirs with 420 billion m³ of storage capacity (up from 30 billion m³ in 1952), 28,000 dams, and 168,000 kilometers of dikes (Zhang Nan 1982; ZNN 1982: 77; JPRS 79630 CAG 177, Dec. 9, 1981: 4–11; RR, Aug. 23, 1983; BR, Aug. 13, 1984: 17). This expenditure was well in excess of revenues from water conservancy.

Most capital investment has been for flood control, however, and even it has been underfunded (Oksenberg 1969). Although water resources projects now are more frequently designed with multiple functions in mind, they are not always fully compatible. For example, flood control may require the emptying of reservoirs in advance of the rainy season, disrupting irrigation, navigation, and hydroelectricity schedules. Similarly, inland water shipping has shrunk by one-third since 1965, in part because of a failure to consider the requirements for navigation in terms of unimpeded channels and the flushing of sediment when designing dams (BR, Aug. 27, 1984: 4–5).

Still, the amounts provided for agriculture–water conservancy–meteorology pale in comparison with the amount lavished on industry. The agricultural sector has never received more than 18 percent of the capital investment budget, and this abnormally high percentage was recorded only in the early 1960s, when the country was recovering from the Great Leap Forward. Agriculture's share hovered around 10–11 percent in the 1970s before falling to 6 percent in the early 1980s. By contrast, industry's share is around 50 percent. Some spending for water resources may be included under other categories such as communications, but it seems apparent that water, like agriculture and other elements of the infrastructure, has not enjoyed the planners' favor (JPRS 84111 CEA 371, Aug. 12, 1983: 121).

The problem doubtless has become more severe since 1980 as a result of the post-Mao regime's drive to trim public spending and capital investment and to substitute bank loans for government appropriations as the state's principal investment instrument. For example, major projects such as the Luanhe diversion might not have survived the construction cutback had it not been for North China's terrible drought, which the political leadership could hardly overlook. However, its multibillion-dollar cost delays the full approval of the huge South-North transfer.

Nor has the water supply system been self-supporting. Indeed, receipts are said to be too low to finance the maintenance of existing facilities, let alone to finance expansion. That does not mean, of course, that all elements of the system are unprofitable. Urban water companies generally operate in the black, but that is due in large part to the failure to fully account for maintenance and depreciation expenses (Wang Yanxiang n.d.: II-20). Nonetheless, they are less profitable than most other industries, and their overall level of profitability has declined rather steadily from .046 yuan/ton of water in 1972 to .036 yuan/ton in 1983. More importantly, as is true with state enterprises in other sectors, most of the profit that the waterworks earn is siphoned off by the state in the form of mandatory profit remissions, which exceeded total state investment during the period 1973–82 by 24 percent (Wang Hongzhu 1984: 6, State Statistical Bureau 1985c: 157).

A study of large reservoirs and irrigation districts showed that the average cost of water should be 22 li/m^3 for operating expenses alone, excluding capital and interest expenses (1 li equals .001 yuan). However, charges actually averaged only 1–2 li/m^3, or less than 10 percent of real costs. Agriculture pays the lowest rates (1.1 li/m^3 on average in large irrigation districts), with industry second and urban residents paying the highest charges; but even the latter paid no more than 8 li/m^3. In the area served by the Guanting and Miyun reservoirs near Beijing, the theoretical cost was said to have been a much higher 48.3 li/m^3, presumably reflecting the dry conditions, sedimentation, and urban congestion in the area. Nevertheless, the charges are only 1 li for agriculture, 1.5 li for industry, and 5 li for urban residential users. This creates tremendous deficits that lead to the deterioration of facilities. One high-ranking water resources official estimated that by 1990 from 5 to 7 percent of facilities will have to be replaced annually as they wear out (Li Boning 1983: 3; ZS April 1985: 29). It hardly seems possible that the water supply system under such arrangements can finance maintenance, let alone essential replacements and additions to the system.

A second problem is political. Analysts generally regard the river valley as the appropriate institutional level for water policy in order to coordinate the interests of all users, both upstream and downstream. Such a setup requires a transfer of power from the central and local governments to the valley or basin authority and involves the sharing of power among neighboring territorial units, especially on an interprovincial basis. Of course, delivery systems and other disaggregable functions can still be performed at the local level. A river valley approach also forces increased coordination among bureaucracies with diverse but related responsibilities. It is clear that any effort to introduce a river valley authority in a decentralized polity can arouse great opposition—which helps to explain why the Tennessee Valley Authority model was never replicated in the United States. And the United States is not necessarily an exception, as indicated by Maass and Anderson (1978: 366–68), who discovered that local control of irrigation systems is far more prevalent than centralized control by higher levels of government.

China is more authoritarian and seemingly more centralized than the

United States. As Donnithorne (1972 and 1981) and others have observed, however, China is actually remarkably decentralized in many respects, with bureaucracies and localities functioning as "independent kingdoms" with which the central government must vie for control of scarce resources through both formal and informal measures. Water policy is no exception. Authority over most aspects of water resource management and hydro-electric power is centralized in the Ministry of Water Resources and Electric Power, although the two functions have sometimes been housed in separate agencies. Exceptions to this ministry's mandate include navigation, which is under the Ministry of Communications, and fisheries, which are the responsibility of the Bureau of Aquatic Products, part of the Ministry of Agriculture, Animal Husbandry, and Fisheries since 1982. Coordination between the Ministry of Water Resources, other agencies with water-related missions, and especially consumer agencies such as agriculture and the industrial ministries can in principle be provided by the State Council and the state's planning and other commissions. However, parochial rivalries have proven hard to overcome, and little coordination actually occurs; consequently, navigation and other instream functions have been impaired (Lampton 1983; *Sichuan Ribao*, May 29, 1984; Lu Qinzhi et al. 1983). The establishment of a unified water resource management regime has been recommended (FBIS, Oct. 26, 1979: L4), but it is unclear whether it would have the authority needed to overcome parochial rivalries.

Coordination at the river valley level is nominally provided by supra-provincial interagency planning offices, of which the oldest was set up in 1955 for the Yellow River on the foundations of the pre-1949 Yellow River Water Conservancy Commission. The Yellow River commission could not have been an especially popular model for the rest of the country if one looks at its rate of diffusion. Its counterparts for the Pearl and Songhua rivers, in particular, were not established until the post-Mao era (ZBN 1981: 309, ZRGGYG 1982 13: 584–85). In some cases coordination has been virtually absent, with navigation and pollution control functions divided between the central government along the main stem and the provinces in charge of the tributaries. In any event, the planning offices cannot always prevail over the provinces, whose more narrow geographical interests they are expected to override, and are regarded as mere appendages to the Ministry of Water Resources both by their own personnel and by the other ministries (Greer 1979: 73–77, Lampton 1983, Nickum 1981: 30). When provincial opposition is encountered, as in the case of Sichuan's objections to the proposed Three Gorges project along the Yangtze, the Yangtze River commission has had to mobilize strong support from downstream beneficiaries, especially in Hubei, and to rely largely on central government and even foreign funds to circumvent the local opponents.

The weakness of river valley authority results in a failure to adequately balance competing needs. It is made worse by the lack of cost-benefit analysis for project evaluation (Baark 1981). Cost-benefit analysis did not receive high-level recognition until the National Water Resources Research Conference of November 1980; it was not made mandatory for large-scale projects until 1985 (SD 139–85, "Economic Analysis Standards for Water Resources," *Shuili Shuidian Jishu* 1985, 6: 1–21). With regard to water, the principal consequence is that riparian parties, i.e., users whose property adjoins water bodies, enjoy the unstated right to make withdrawals without limit. Indeed, the common property phenomenon created by state ownership gives upstream users an incentive to use as much water as they can to preclude downstream users from increasing their own consumption, thus creating a de facto right of first use, which can later be formalized in official policy. Thus Tianjin, China's third largest city, which is located near the mouth of the Hai River, found itself with a progressively smaller share of the river's flow. Upstream diversions of the outflow from five of six major reservoirs built after 1949 reduced the city's surface water; streamflow fell by over 70 percent between the early 1960s and 1982 (FBIS, Apr. 12, 1982: N3; RR, July 18, 1982; JPRS 83716 CEA 352, June 20, 1983: 35–39). A similar logic prevails for groundwater. Each property owner has the right to pump water through wells drilled on his own property regardless of the consequences for his neighbor. Thus, a common property resource regime perversely leads to overconsumption even in an environment of water shortages.

Another consequence is a bias in favor of small projects that lie within jurisdictional boundaries to minimize conflicts with neighboring jurisdictions and to obviate the need for approval from higher levels of authority. This bias was widespread during the Maoist era, when institutional tendencies were reinforced by an ideological preference for local self-sufficiency (Oksenberg 1969). To be sure, small-scale hydroelectric projects built largely with local labor and funding are one of China's most renowned accomplishments. Nevertheless, such projects may preempt larger, more efficient waterworks, with negative consequences for navigation and other functions.

One other way to overcome interjurisdictional conflict is to expand the spatial jurisdiction of selected localities to internalize authority over the resource. Local coordination has always been part of the dual (vertical and horizontal) authority system of administration. This aspect of governance has increased in the post-Mao era, with many large cities acquiring direct authority over the surrounding hinterland on some economic matters (DZ, November 1983: 9; JG, September 1983: 27–37; RR, Apr. 15 and Aug. 26, 1984). This may affect water resources—although it still does not eliminate the tendency to tailor resource development according to political boundaries.

These practices may expedite river basin development but provide no assurance of efficient outcomes or sound management after the project has been completed—a particularly serious issue on the Luanhe River—or the pacification of upstream areas opposed to condemnation of their land and the forced relocation necessitated by the construction of dams and the filling of reservoirs. There have been many instances in which work was obstructed by local residents, who sometimes practice extortion before they agree to move. In practice, residents have good reason to object to the construction of water resource projects and other public works in their vicinity. Following the Soviet practice that regarded land as a free good, no compensation was paid to the displaced parties. Replacement farmland was often inferior. Moreover, reservoir management regulations deprived remaining residents of the opportunity to fish or make other use of the new flatwater resource. The consequence often was severe poverty. For example, residents in the vicinity of the Wangkuai Reservoir in Fuping County, Hebei, were said to be barely surviving on rations of 116 catties of grain a year in 1982 while the reservoir, with its fishery potential, remained off limits to them (Li Zhankui et al. 1984; FBIS, Sept. 23, 1983: P1–3, and Sept. 29 1983: K8–9).

Resistance to resettlement can pose problems even in an authoritarian regime. In the case of the Luanhe diversion, personal intervention by the mayor of Tianjin and the minister of water resources was needed on numerous occasions to overcome bottlenecks, particularly objections by the people scheduled to be displaced (BR, Sept. 26, 1983: 23; JPRS 84600 CRA 276, Oct. 24, 1983: 76–77; Lu Yun 1984: 22–23). New awareness of the immense resettlement burden involved has slowed approval of the Three Gorges project along the Yangtze River even though it is greatly favored by navigation and hydropower interests as well as downstream areas in Hubei. Depending on the dam's height, it would force the relocation of up to two million people and flood 45,000 hectares of farmland (Huang Faruo 1985; Li Weiwu 1984: 23–24; JPRS CST-84-054, July 9, 1984: 64–65; LaBounty 1982).

Although such conflicts of interest are inevitable, they are aggravated by the absence of a market for land to determine its value and by the weakness of institutions to adjudicate disputes (CD, Nov. 11, 1985). However, new regulations issued since 1982 will reduce some of the friction involved in acquisition of land by the state. The new regulations mandate compensation for several categories of loss, including the productive value of land, the value of crops already in the ground, the cost of new construction, and moving expenses (Land Management Law 1986, in Ross and Silk 1987). In the Tianjin suburbs the average payment is said to run over 300 yuan per hectare. Subsequently, on the eve of the thirty-fifth anniversary of the founding of the PRC in 1984, a joint party-state directive on economic development in distressed rural areas pledged that a portion of all electricity- and water-related revenues derived from reservoirs would be paid to the displaced population as a form of compensation (Chang Chunyin and Kong Min 1984; GR, Oct. 1, 1984; State Planning Commission et al. 1983; JPRS CST-84-004, Feb. 14, 1984: 136–49). Although that represents considerable progress, an indication of how much remains to be done came when *People's Daily* actually praised a Shandong prefecture for breaking with past patterns by taking steps to resettle those displaced by reservoir construction. The editors considered such behavior by public officials to be long overdue and commended this innovation to the country as a whole. However, *People's Daily* also acknowledged that government funds for relocation would remain very limited (RR, Apr. 29, 1984).

In recent years, environmental questions also have affected expansion of the water supply system. Heightened concern for the environment is surely in order, but one consequence is construction delays. Questions regarding seawater intrusion at the mouth of the Yangtze and other impacts have tempered enthusiasm for the South-North project, the biggest interbasin transfer of them all. After having approved the project in principle in 1978, the central government so far has only authorized a modest transfer along the largely preexisting eastern or Grand Canal route, in part because of environmental considerations (Biswas et al. 1983, Liu and Ma 1983). This may be contrasted with the mood at the height of the Great Leap Forward. At that time not only was environmental concern absent, even engineering feasibility typically was disregarded, resulting in a high project failure rate (Oksenberg 1969).

Although planning and river basin coordination have been limited, the government has exercised influence in two respects. All interbasin water transfers require prior approval, by the central government in the case of interprovincial arrangements or by provincial governments for intraprovincial transfers. As noted earlier, Tianjin's long-standing proposal to divert water south from the Luanhe River required central government approval because the river runs through the surrounding province of Hebei. Were it not for the drought of the early 1980s, it is unclear whether approval by the central government would have been so swiftly obtained, enabling opposition from Hebei and elsewhere to be circumvented.

The government's control of funds and supplies also is an important lever of influence, since lower levels of government and economic entities may be unable or unwilling to assume the full cost of projects even if there are no legal or political impediments to construction. The Luanhe diversion, for example, was rushed to completion at a reported cost of 1.5 billion yuan after being raised to the status of a high-priority state project. This figure may well understate the project's true cost, and yet it still would have strained Tianjin's budget had the central government not provided direct subsidies and a low-cost military labor force (Zhang Nan 1982; BR, Sept. 26, 1983: 20–23). Unfortunately, government subsidies often underwrite such wasteful projects as the canal built in the 1970s to irrigate Xiyang Xian, home of the erstwhile Maoist model Dazhai Brigade. However, the central government's leverage in this regard has declined in the post-Mao era as a result of economic decentralization and liberalization, with many localities now more reliant on self-financing of public works.

Although funding shortfalls and political considerations may constrain expansion of the supply system, the fundamental factor is the inexorable rise in demand, which threatens to swamp all increases in supply. To be sure, the PRC in 1949 began with only two dozen reservoirs of consequence and lacked a modern infrastructure outside some urban quarters, while in the rural areas irrigation networks were antiquated and underdeveloped (ZNN 1980: 25). Moreover, economic and population growth has been rapid, annually averaging 5–6 percent for the former and 2 percent for the latter since the late 1950s (Ashbrook 1982: 105). Enormous expansions in the supply system obviously were inevitable and desirable.

Consumption, however, has risen in tandem with economic growth and far outpaced the growth in population because conservation was neglected. For example, the irrigated area has more than tripled since the early 1950s and total agricultural usage is believed to have increased by over 460 percent, or over 5 percent annually, between the early 1950s and 1979 (JPRS 83286 CAG 254, Apr. 18, 1983: 21–33). Increases of such magnitude would strain any delivery system, let alone one subject to the physical limitations and institutional weaknesses already described. The most troubling question for the future is how to curtail the rate of increase in demand, which is becoming harder and harder to satisfy.

What then is the bureaucratic-authoritative solution to the supply bottlenecks that could no longer be ignored by the early 1980s? In addition to increasing deliveries, the principal step has been to extend planning down to the enterprise level and issue sterner and more frequent commands to conserve. For example, enterprises in centrally planned economies typically devote greater effort to satisfying their physical output norms than to minimizing their consumption of raw materials. Therefore, the bureaucratic response has been to formulate specific consumption norms for inputs such as energy or water as the supply situation becomes critical. The norms govern the volume of water available to producers, although it is unclear how the norms are formulated. Are they based on the most efficient producers, the average producer, an idealized consumption:output coefficient, a projected margin of improvement, or some other norm?

In any event, the purpose is clear: by the threat to curtail supplies, less efficient producers will be forced to shape up. Therefore, enterprises were directed to designate supervisors to take personal responsibility for conservation measures. Ultimately, of course, the issue can be taken out of the hands of consumers by shutting the valves for hours or days at a time, a common occurrence during the drought of the early 1980s in North China. For example, Tianjin mandated a 30 percent reduction in residential and urban consumption in 1980 that was to be achieved as much through shutdowns as by raising efficiency (Zhu Laidong 1981).

Such measures obviously can be effective in reducing consumption, but their success is likely to be limited to emergencies when the salience of the issue is extremely high. At other times, consumption norms are frequently ignored to attain more compelling output and profit targets (RR, Aug. 12,

1981; JPRS 79324 CAG 170, Oct. 28, 1981: 1–2). Moreover, strict consumption norms and shutoffs tend to be employed indiscriminately without regard for variations among factories; neither do they provide the information needed to determine how to improve efficiency. Set too high, they excuse inefficiency; set too low, they force irrational shutdowns and other ill-considered responses. The bureaucratic approach thus is subject to severe limitations. For alternatives, I turn first to campaign-exhortation.

Campaign-Exhortation Implementation

Campaigns essentially summon the populace to solve their problems voluntarily through joint action under local direction. Although the use of coercion always is possible in the event of noncompliance, the hope is to avoid direct commands and instead rely on persuasion. Voluntary compliance may reduce the political costs associated with the imposition of drastic, often unequal sacrifices by a distant authority. Campaigns can be mobilized either to increase supply or to reduce demand, but presumably they are more acceptable if the sacrifice is of direct benefit to participants. Thus, campaigns seek to convince people to do what would be in their own interest anyway, although that is easier to accomplish when there is a high degree of correspondence between contributors and beneficiaries.*

Supply-oriented campaigns operate primarily through slack-season farmland construction, a rather constant feature in the countryside. These campaigns to build dams, ditches, and other projects, often without benefit of modern equipment, were a prominent element in the PRC's water conservancy infrastructure during its first three decades. Participants receive an additional ration of grain and often earn work points, but the normative incentive aspect is strong. Aggregate investment by localities and the masses, possibly based on imputed labor costs, is said to have totaled 380 billion yuan in the period 1949–81 out of total state investment of 460 billion yuan. Although not all of this total can be considered truly "campaign" in nature because it consists in part of locally planned construction performed by year-round farmland capital construction teams, it nevertheless is over five times larger than state investment during the same period (RR, Aug. 23, 1983; Vermeer 1977: 65–77; ZNN 1982: 77).

The two most famous supply-oriented campaigns were the mass irrigation campaign of 1957–58 and the tube-well-drilling effort in the North China Plain in the 1970s. The 1957–58 campaign involved the reported mobilization of over 100 million people for the construction of ditches, reservoirs, and irrigation works. As noted earlier, there was a bias in favor of small-scale projects and against technical standards that contributed to

---

*It can be hypothesized that conservation-oriented campaigns will be more successful downstream than upstream because downstream residents know that any water they save can be used for local benefit. Unfortunately, data are not available to test this hypothesis.

the natural disasters suffered later during the Great Leap Forward. The worst mistake was to overemphasize storage at the expense of drainage so that new reservoirs often aggravated salinization and waterlogging by raising water tables (Nickum 1974: 111–12). In general, great waste occurred over the years due to the neglect of technical considerations and such ancillary functions as watershed vegetation. Many facilities were prone to sedimentation, contamination, or breakdown, which aggravated flood danger (JPRS 79528 CAG 175, Nov. 25, 1981: 8; GR, May 8, 1982). Nevertheless, the mobilization embodied in the waterworks campaign was so vast and seemingly successful that it ignited the Great Leap and the organization of the rural populace into large communes (Oksenberg 1969).

The second major instance of the campaign approach to supply augmentation involved the drilling of hundreds of thousands of tube wells in the 1970s, especially in the North China Plain. The wells played a major role in the expansion of irrigation. For example, paddy area increased from 21,000 hectares in 1973 to 102,000 hectares in 1980 in the municipalities of Beijing and Tianjin, which include substantial tracts of farmland in suburban counties. In all, 60 percent of the Jinglu region's 984,000 hectares of irrigated farmland were served by wells by the early 1980s (Wei Zhongyi and Ren Hongzun 1983, Yang Qicheng 1982). Ground water has been a big help to agriculture in this dry region where surface water is less plentiful, and much of the surface streamflow had already been appropriated for other uses. The wells can also reduce drainage and salinization problems by lowering the water table and vacating subsurface water shortage capacity. Although benefiting from some government assistance, the tube wells differed substantially from the centralized bureaucratic approach in terms of policy. Unlike reservoirs and canals, which require at least some form of joint management, wells can be individually sunk and thus are extremely difficult to register, let alone monitor or regulate (Nicholson 1981: 29–30).

Problems arose, however, because wells were sunk without sufficient knowledge of the size or other physical properties of the groundwater resource and because there was inadequate account of the pooled nature of the resource. Well operators, who were usually collectives rather than individuals, were free to pump as much water as they needed without regard for the needs of others. Not surprisingly, many wells were drilled too close to one another, depleting the aquifers, accelerating the decline of water tables, and even causing surface subsidence. Many wells were unsuccessful or soon fell into disuse. Ironically, the application of excessive volumes of water not only flooded fields but also aggravated drainage and salinization problems, negating one of the wells' benefits in some areas (Nickum 1974: 246–48, 270, 319–25; Wei Zhongyi and Ren Hongzun 1983; GR, Aug. 22, 1983).

Campaigns also have been employed as conservation measures. Propaganda is increased during droughts to urge people to reduce their consumption and stretch supplies so that higher-priority needs can be met.

During the drought of the early 1980s, water conservation campaigns were prominent, although in most areas they remained subordinate to energy conservation drives. Rallies to conserve water were held in Beijing on August 28, 1981, and in November after the summer rains failed to appear. Substantial reductions in consumption were reported as a result of emergency measures, although no clear effort was made to distinguish between bureaucratic and exhortational measures. Dalian and Shanghai actually claimed small increases in industrial output despite reductions in water consumption (RR, Jan. 8, 1982). Qingdao claimed to have cut consumption in half while minimizing service interruptions through a mixture of conservation, the drilling of additional wells, and the use of seawater for cooling and certain other purposes (RR, Apr. 7, 1982). In all, 910 million tons of water were said to have been conserved in 1982. However, that amounted to less than 3 percent of urban consumption nationwide, although the savings were greater in the drought-stricken areas (FBIS, Oct. 11, 1983: K9–11).

There is no doubt that exhortation can be effective as an emergency measure. In a major study of drought response in California, Berk et al. (1981: 148–49) found that conservation frequently generated reductions in usage of as much as 30 percent, although success was concentrated in the more flexible residential and governmental sectors rather than industry. This study identified several factors that influence consumer response to exhortation: whether consumers believe that a real shortage exists and affects an important reference group, that the appeal is predicated upon moral principles and stresses fair contributions to the welfare of the group, that individual participation can make a difference, that the cost and inconvenience are modest, and that all members of the group are participating.

Without reliable data on Chinese public opinion it is impossible to speak with confidence of attitudinal responses to emergencies or any other situation. It would appear that the government is well positioned to communicate information in this highly organized society and has experience in making moral appeals and closely supervising compliance. Nevertheless, the free-rider effects arising from common property ownership and the absence of meters or individual billing may overwhelm these advantages. In any event, it must be stressed that the effects of exhortation tend to be short term. The California study did not incorporate long-term observations but nevertheless revealed that a partial retreat in conservation practices had begun even before the end of the drought.

Thus, campaign exhortation is able to mobilize substantial effort in behalf of adding new supplies or conserving existing resources, at least when the government enjoys popular trust. Technical feasibility, however, must be ensured or the result is likely to be wasted effort, as in the Great Leap Forward. Technical considerations tend to be ignored during the height of campaigns because campaigns artificially stimulate enthusiasm toward a single task and tend to override the voice of caution and the role of experts. This is a serious drawback because a preoccupation with increasing water deliveries results in neglect of essential management and agronomic techniques (Skogerboe 1983: 42–44). Campaigns also show limited ability at best to avoid the deficiencies encountered in common property resource management as shown during the rush to drill wells during the 1970s. Whatever effectiveness campaigns muster also tends to be evanescent rather than permanent, and even the short-term effect may be harder to achieve since the party's prestige plummeted in the Cultural Revolution. Although prestige can be rebuilt, it is not surprising that, faced with these limitations, the post-Mao leadership was willing to entertain new market-oriented ideas to cope with increasingly severe water shortages.

Market-Exchange Implementation

Market exchange had been only a minor factor in water policy for years because of the party's ideological aversion to letting markets and prices dictate outcomes, an aversion that was stronger with regard to natural resources than for the economy as a whole. To be sure, water companies and irrigation districts by law were expected to collect service fees, which were to be earmarked for use within the water supply system rather than as general revenues. Such fees were introduced in the early 1950s to serve as the primary source of revenues for system maintenance and management (Ministry of Water Conservancy 1957 and 1965, in Nickum 1981: 245–62). Fees were not calculated on a volumetric or usage basis, however, and frequently were not systematically collected because of management shortcomings, political turmoil, and evasion by ratepayers.

The problem was aggravated by the lack of democratic control over irrigation districts and other institutions. That alienated peasants and other consumers from the resource management authority. Most decisions were made at the production brigade level on up, yet peasants only had the right to directly elect officials at the lowest level, the production team. Higher levels controlled both political and economic power, and thus were able to impose their preferences without due regard for the peasants' wishes concerning water resources or other issues (Zhou Zishi 1983). Although water resource management institutions could continue to operate without the direct support of the people, the absence of usage-based rate schedules restricted their ability to regulate consumption. In leftist periods, water usage fees were actually condemned for encouraging the people to become cunning protectors of their own interests with regard to their fair share of deliveries rather than willing defenders of the collective interest. Therefore, fees were either disregarded or collected on a flat-rate or area-served basis (Huanggang Prefecture 1974: 148–51). Peasants derided the system with such slogans as "If you pay the water charges you will suffer a loss; if you don't you will gain an advantage" (JPRS 84257 CAG 270, Sept. 2, 1983: 24–29).

Attention to market-exchange methods increased dramatically in the post-Mao era for several reasons. Most importantly, the new leadership was much more determined to pursue economic development at the expense of wornout dogma, although the first impulse under Hua Guofeng was to expand production bureaucratically through a huge construction drive, as revealed in the Ten-Year Plan 1976–85, which included some water projects (Hua Guofeng 1978: 18–26). It was not until the party's Third Plenum in December 1978, when Hua's power was trimmed, that economic development became closely linked to economic reform involving a quest for greater efficiency. Market-exchange methods were more promising in this regard than the other implementation alternatives.

Two other factors also favored a greater role for markets in water policy. The pragmatists liberalized the scope of intellectual and personal freedom, increasing the opportunity for intellectuals to influence public policy. Economists in particular enjoyed a renewal of prestige that encouraged them to analyze public policy in accordance with the dictum "Seek truth from facts." They vigorously advocated the wider application of economic methods in water policy as well as the rest of the economy. Nevertheless, the pace of change in water policy also appears to have accelerated as a result of the drought of the early 1980s which forced factory closures and reductions in residential consumption, making economical use of water a much more salient consideration (JPRS CAG 1, Jan. 12, 1984: 67–68).

The advocates of market-exchange methods dissected the inefficiency of existing patterns of water use and showed how management and pricing reforms could ease shortages at much lower cost than through new construction. As the largest sector of consumption, agriculture received a great deal of attention. Analysts estimated that 57 percent of the water theoretically available for irrigation was lost in conveyance or storage through evapo-transpiration, seepage, and other factors. That left only 43 percent of irrigation water available for field application, although some of the missing water may have been surreptitiously diverted by upstream farmers (Liu and Ma 1983: 259; JPRS 84257 CAG 270, Sept. 2, 1983: 24–29). The water that was delivered was rarely applied efficiently because farm operators lacked incentives and technology. For example, only 100,000 people were assigned to water conservancy work in 1982—an average of just two per commune—and many of them were considered unqualified (RR, July 3, 1982).

Because fees were assessed on the basis of area irrigated rather than volume consumed, operators tended to apply water indiscriminately, even though this practice washed away soil and fertilizer and exacerbated drainage and salinization problems (RR, Aug. 23, 1983; Yang Qicheng 1982). Under the prevailing system of area charges in China, farmers failed to take even such elementary, labor-intensive waste-reduction measures as leveling their fields and irrigating in the cool of the day (*People's University Agricultural Economics Reprint Series* 1982 16: 60–62; JPRS 83576 CAG 259, May 31, 1983: 35–59). As a result, it is estimated that only 25–40 percent of irrigation water was used effectively, which is significantly worse than other notoriously wasteful areas such as the Colorado River basin in the United States (RR, May 19 and Oct. 5, 1983; JPRS 84770 CAG 279, Nov. 17, 1983: 42–43; *People's University Industrial Economics Reprint Series* 1982 21: 82–84; ZNB, August 1983; Rogers 1983: 90). Even this figure fails to fully convey the severity of the problem because some irrigation is for the questionable purpose of farming thirsty crops in arid areas (Yang Qicheng 1982). By contrast, studies of irrigation patterns in India and elsewhere indicate that volumetric charges provide decision makers with a rough indicator of the marginal value of water and encourage more sparing use of water by irrigators, although efficient outcomes remain dependent on reliable water supplies and improved techniques (Reidinger 1980: 285).

Industrial and municipal users also came in for criticism. Paper, steel, and other major industries consume five to ten times as much water per unit output as their counterparts in developed countries (Wang Baozhen 1984; State Economic Commission et al. 1981; FBIS, Oct. 11, 1983: K9–11; RR, Oct. 5, 1983). As for recycling, although Chinese farmers have traditionally relied heavily on human wastes to fertilize their fields, recycling of water in aggregate is very modest. Industrial reuse of wastewater is less than 20 per cent in most instances, and the volume of sewage discharges is rising as fast as industrial production (RR, May 19 and Oct. 5, 1983; Wang Baozhen 1984).

Inefficient water use is due in part to inferior technology as well as the singleminded pursuit of physical output at the expense of other goals. Poor management and institutional distortions are also factors, since low flat-rate prices reward waste. One source estimated that consumption under the prevailing flat-rate system was up to three times as great as it would be under a metered-usage, progressive fee system (RR, June 3, 1982).

Critics of the existing system also noted the high cost of increasing supply, which could be lowered by more efficient use of existing sources. For example, China is able to use less than 50 percent of its water storage capacity—substantially below the world average (Smil 1984: 80). The cost of adding an additional cubic meter of water reportedly averages 0.5 yuan and rises to 0.6 yuan or higher in Beijing and other arid areas (Li Boning 1983; *People's University Agricultural Economics Reprint Series* 1982 18: 75–83). It is estimated that China would have to spend 85–140 billion yuan in the period 1978–2000 to meet the conservative demand projections shown in table 12. In the cities, for example, construction costs for centrally supplied running water are said to total 150–200 yuan and 0.35 kwh in electricity per ton of water. The same volume of water if not recycled costs an additional 300 yuan plus 0.06 kwh in capital expenditures for sewage treatment. By contrast, conservation and recycling are said to cost only 30 yuan and 0.1 kwh of electricity per ton of water, with the added benefit of reducing water pollution (RR, June 3, 1982; FBIS, Oct. 11, 1983: K9–11). In agriculture, although the capital costs associated with irrigation are lower than elsewhere in Asia, they are still said to run 1,500–3,000 yuan/hectare excluding the cost of the waterworks itself and the interconnections between fields (Li Boning 1983, Pannell 1982: 326, Lardy 1983: 139).

Although these numbers are imprecise, the critics' recommendations to the leadership were not: accurately assess the size and quality of the resource, register all withdrawals, and then meter consumption, institute charges for all water users based on their volume of consumption, improve the management of water resources, and reduce the state's investment in new water supply by forcing beneficiaries to bear a larger share of the costs (Ministry of Water Conservancy 1980).

These recommendations were in line with the leadership's own determination to increase efficiency and reduce capital expenditures. Therefore, market-exchange methods were given increased prominence at a series of conferences convened in the early 1980s. The most notable was the national water conservancy meeting held in Beijing in May 1981, which endorsed a shift in emphasis from the construction of new facilities to the improved management of existing installations. That involved setting fees according to volume of usage and reallocation of water in time of scarcity from less valuable agricultural uses to industry. These changes were reflected in the water management regulations approved in draft form by the State Council the following month (JPRS 79630 CAG 177, Dec. 9, 1981: 4–11; ZNN 1983: 376–78). The preparations for these decisions began in 1980 while the reformers were dominant, but they were not taken until after the Central Work Conference of December 1980, when more conservative officials led by Chen Yun had temporarily gained the upper hand over reform elements. The fact that market methods continued to be advanced in 1981 indicates that they had significant momentum and that planning enthusiasts such as Chen were also willing to employ market methods to cool down an overheating economy characterized by runaway construction expenditures.

A series of conferences was subsequently convened on urban water use. The first, held in November 1981 in Dalian, involved delegates from fifteen northern cities (ZRGGYG 1982 1: 20–21) and was soon followed by a similar conference in Anhui for southern cities (RR, Dec. 22, 1981). Both gatherings decried the great waste exhibited in existing consumption patterns and agreed that conservation must precede future expansion of supply, although many of those present at the latter conference conceded that public support was lower in the more humid South. Two larger follow-up conferences on urban water conservation were held in 1982 and 1983, providing evidence of continuing concern about this problem. Stressing the fact that 80 percent of China's larger cities suffered from water shortages to varying degrees, these conferences strongly endorsed breaking the "big water pitcher" mindset under which water was provided without regard to need and with no incentive for efficiency (ZRGGYG 1982 18: 795–99; RR, Oct. 5, 1983).*

The outcome of this flurry of activity was a series of policy reforms that amounted to a mixed bureaucratic-market approach. Equal emphasis was to be placed on the development of new sources and on conservation. All consumption of water was to be closely regulated. Residential and urban consumption was to be metered, often for the first time, and flat-rate pricing was to be replaced by volume-based pricing. Even wells were to be registered, and new wells in critical areas would not be approved if they threatened to impair the functioning of existing wells in the vicinity. Consumption norms were ordered for major consumers, especially economic enterprises, the threshold being variously set at 10,000 tons or 50,000 tons a month depending on the locality. Enterprises were ordered to assign ranking engineers or other officials to take charge of water usage in order to raise the issue's priority, and these managers were made eligible for bonuses or penalties based on their unit's performance (FBIS, Aug. 28, 1981: R1–2; RR, Jan. 8, 1982; ZRGGYG 1981 2: 57–60; for Beijing, JPRS 80026 WWEQ 336, Feb. 4, 1982: 43–50).

The usage norms are intended to encourage prudent consumption by inducing enterprises to use internal funds and, if necessary, bank credits to raise their efficiency. Consumption above the norm is to be priced from two to five times the rate of below-norm consumption. Even well water is included, with the charge doubling for above-norm consumption (RR, Oct. 4, 1980; ZRGGYG 1981 2: 57–60). This incremental block pricing rate schedule is intended to encourage conservation and recycling while assuring social fairness by retaining low flat rates for basic needs. Nevertheless, the regime is not willing to allow price alone to influence consumption. Rather than allow consumers to decide how much water they wish to purchase, persistent violators of usage norms are threatened with supply cutoffs and sharply higher incremental rates.

Some progress has been reported in carrying out the new policy. In drought-affected Tianjin, the local authorities imposed a package of usage norms, administrative controls, and incremental block pricing. The Railroad Construction Bureau residential compound reported that usage declined by 75 percent and that average service charges actually fell as a result of conservation (RR, Oct. 25, 1981; FBIS, Sept. 2, 1981: R3). Although the bureau is an unrepresentative model, its results do not lie much outside the elasticity range of -0.2 to -0.7 applicable to residential customers in the United States (Morgan 1980: 942).

In Shanghai, where excessive groundwater withdrawals since 1921 had caused measurable surface subsidence, floods, and structural damage, dor-

Big water pitcher is an adaptation to water policy of the term *big rice pot*, which signifies the sloth inherent in socialist economies.

mant regulations to regulate the drilling of wells were reissued in 1979. In 1982 they were supplemented by volume-based usage charges and fines for violators of usage norms. Together with the stepped-up recharge of wastewater, these measures have led to a decrease in groundwater withdrawals, a rise in the water table, and an end to subsidence in the city proper, although the problem persists in suburban districts (JPRS CST-84-029, Sept. 27, 1984: 145–52).

Looking at the nation as a whole, the fifteen largest cities stated their commitment to eliminate the practice of having the *danwei* (unit) paying a single utility bill for all their members by the end of 1983. A year earlier, 58 percent of households in these cities were reported to be served by individual water meters, although presumably that refers only to households served by the central distribution system (FBIS, Apr. 13, 1983: K23). The state has also vowed to withhold funds for water supply expansion projects unless cities first increase their industrial recycling rates.

In 1984 the State Council confirmed the policy trend of the past several years in a directive that placed equal emphasis on conservation and supply expansion (*kai yuan jie liu bing zhong*). It was the first time that the State Council had ever issued a directive focusing specifically on urban water conservation. All large and medium-sized municipalities were ordered to abolish existing flat-rate systems in favor of progressive rate schedules by the end of 1985. New construction projects were to incorporate household meters, while existing housing would make do with meters for each gate (*men*). In addition, water supply companies or utilities were directed to cease their exclusive emphasis on increasing sales and profits by also stressing conservation through the formulation of consumer usage norms and the diffusion of conservation techniques. Industrial users were told they would find water consumption written into their production plans on an economic responsibility basis linked to rewards and sanctions (State Council 1984; RR, June 26, 1984).

The State Council put this policy into operation a year later in an important set of regulations on water utility rates (State Council 1985). This document stressed that water must be regarded as a commodity rather than as a gift of nature and clearly attributed wasteful consumption and the imbalance between supply and demand to irrationally low water charges. While recognizing the impossibility of fully rationalizing prices in the near term, the regulations ordered that water rates be recalculated to include delivery costs, management expenses, and maintenance and depreciation charges, as well as an allowable profit margin for industrial consumption. The regulations applied to all categories of consumption, even including hydroelectric projects, which were to be assessed on the basis of a percentage of electricity sales. This latter application of economic instruments to an essentially instream use of water, which was facilitated by the parent Ministry of Water Resources and Electric Power's having responsibility for both functions, promised substantially higher revenues for the system as a whole as China's hydroelectric potential is harnessed, although the basis for setting the charges is unclear. The regulations allowed favorable rates for agriculture in general and especially for grain farming to reduce the impact on that sector of the economy and provided exceptions for farmer-built facilities and recycled industrial wastewater.

On the whole, these reforms aim to shift water resources policy in the direction of scarcity pricing and away from the older zero- or low-cost, plan-dominated policy structure. Indeed, the regulations for water rates go further with regard to price reform than the economy as a whole. There, price reform had already slowed down by the spring of 1985, after an upsurge in inflation following the State Council's October 1984 directive on urban reform.

It will not be easy to carry out the new policies in light of the inadequate managerial and technical capacity in urban utilities and rural irrigation management districts. Rates may have to be raised to politically disquieting levels to have the desired impact. Because water charges at present are extremely low and most enterprises lack economic autonomy, the price elasticity for water is generally no better than -0.1, far less than in market economies, although the pattern in unrepresentative model units may be more favorable (Wang Yanxiang n.d.). Nor is it clear that the higher charges will be sufficient to finance construction, maintenance, and other expenses while preventing receipts from being diverted to unapproved purposes.

Ratepayers are also limited in their capacity to conserve water. Industry lacks full freedom to change product lines in response to higher costs or changes in demand, making it difficult to adjust to higher utility rates. Older housing cannot be individually metered where there are communal cooking and washing facilities. Nevertheless, decentralized decision making and more realistic pricing should generally exert a positive financial incentive for water conservation.

Agriculture

Agriculture is by far the largest consumer of water and one of the most inefficient. For China to make progress on conservation, it is clear that agriculture must play a major role. Two aspects of agricultural water use are relevant here. One involves the extension of irrigation to new areas without sufficient regard for economic costs or the availability of water, while the second concerns more efficient use of existing irrigation systems. In the former case, Chinese agricultural policy has been strongly biased toward expanding irrigation despite often prohibitive economic and environmental costs. The regime's tendency in this regard was based on the perceived political need to become self-sufficient in agricultural production and was bolstered by the Ministry of Water Conservancy (an antecedent of the Ministry of Water Resources and Electric Power) whose mission was predicated in part on increasing the demand for water. The tendency was welcomed by local officials, especially in dry regions that needed irrigation to boost agricultural output. Most of the labor was provided by farmers in low-cost off-season waterworks construction campaigns, which made these projects more feasible but often aroused resentment among farmers when the burden they bore outweighed whatever benefits they expected to receive.

The state moved more slowly on the agricultural front than it had with regard to urban water consumption, in contrast to the prevailing pattern of post-Mao economic and political reforms in which change began in the rural areas. Water resources management was an exception because it often raised costs to farmers in the short run, unlike the reforms, which in general brought the peasants higher procurement prices and other material incentives. With regard to the extension of irrigation, the regime did not take decisive action until 1983. The geographical focus was the Northwest, a huge, arid, windswept region bordering Mongolia and the Soviet Union that is of considerable strategic importance. Its economic potential rests on rich mineral and coal deposits, but its remoteness and harsh climate make it China's poorest region. The region's strategic importance is related to its high proportion of minority nationalities, mostly Moslems and Mongols (RR, Sept. 21 and Dec. 28, 1983; Lardy 1983: 173 and 180–83).

In 1983 the Politburo suddenly designated the Northwest as the region of the future, raising its priority for future development. With leadership interest now high enough to warrant several visits by the country's highest officials (Zeng Jianhui 1983; BR, Nov. 28, 1983: 4–5), one might have expected a renewed commitment to water resource development to relieve the region's most intractable handicap. Such was not the case. Instead, the emphasis was on local solutions and conservation of water. In part that was because economic strategy now stressed reducing overall state investment while concentrating remaining funds on the coastal regions, where existing facilities, a better trained work force, and superior access to the outside world promised faster development for the country as a whole. In other words, the Northwest's newly won status was more symbolic than real, with genuine improvements to be introduced only gradually. In addition, regional policy for the Northwest was shifting away from the inappropriate recent emphasis on grain production toward ecologically balanced development, with increased attention to soil conservation, grasslands management, and forestry.

Premier Zhao Ziyang used his March 1983 visit to the Northwest to stress that agriculture needed to become more efficient, especially with regard to water. Zhao acknowledged the benefits of irrigation but insisted that water was in short supply and could not be made available in substantially increased volumes except at prohibitive cost to the economy as a whole. He advised farmers in the Northwest to practice dryland farming, even if that meant having to suffer through droughts as often as one year in seven (and presumably more often in many areas). Zhao also demanded that farmers pay more for the water they used by replacing flat-rate pricing based on the area irrigated with volume-based rate schedules. He implied that industry's priority was higher than agriculture's, so that some water actually would have to be reassigned from farming to other uses, as had already occurred in the Beijing area during the recent drought (RR, Apr. 10, 1981, and June 1 and 3, 1983; NJJ 1983 7: 1–3; FBIS, Apr. 6, 1983: 1–2, and June 3, 1983: K5–8). The industrial needs that Zhao had in mind included hydroelectricity and mining, particularly for slurries to transport coal from water-short Shanxi and Inner Mongolia to the big cities of the East and to the coast for export (RR, Dec. 19, 1983; JPRS 83376 CAG 259, May 31, 1983: 35–39; *People's University Industrial Economics Reprint Series* 1981 15: 63–64; FBIS, June 20, 1983: K24–25; Weil 1983).

Zhao's message could not have been very popular in the Northwest. It amounted to a reversal of the party's heroic image of persevering in struggle against all obstacles, as in the parable of the foolish old man who removed the mountain (Mao Zedong 1945). The new policy restated the central government's long-standing position that water and soil conservation are primarily local responsibilities (Vermeer 1977: 293–94) but implied that henceforth central government assistance would focus on raising efficiency rather than augmenting the water supply. This change would further reduce the need for central government funding.

The new policy represented a challenge not only to the Northwest but also to the Ministry of Water Resources and Electric Power whose sense of mission or organizational purpose was challenged in two respects. On one hand, the ministry was proudest of its flood control success, which had greatly reduced the threat of catastrophe along the Yellow River and elsewhere. On the other hand, the ministry was mindful of the need to be continuously on guard against flooding, particularly in the case of the heavily silted Yellow River, whose dikes had to be raised annually. Vice-Minister Li Boning (1983) explained that the principal focus of river management must be flood control, and he invoked the dean of the conservatives, Politburo member Chen Yun, to bolster his case.

In response, the reformers argued that the flood control problem had largely been solved, at least in terms of what engineering measures could hope to accomplish. Flood control would naturally continue to be a top priority but henceforth would have to share its billing with the need to increase water supplies in parched northern China, a point stressed when Politburo member and senior Vice-Premier Wan Li led a high-level inspection tour of the Yellow River valley in the summer of 1984 in the company of the minister of water resources and electric power. Increasing the water supply would inevitably involve some new construction in order to expand reservoir storage of rainy season runoff for use the following spring and in dry periods (ZS, September 1984: 2–6). This division over water policy closely paralleled the split between Chen Yun and the reformers over farm policy, with Chen insisting that grain production must come first ("grain shortages can cause social disorder ... we cannot afford to underestimate this matter"), in contrast to the reformers' efforts to diversify the rural economy and make it more market responsive (RR, Sept. 24 and Oct. 13, 1985).

The reformers' concern about water supply brought them into conflict with the ministry's traditional views in another respect as well. As noted earlier, the reformers saw little need to expand irrigation and agreed with Chen Yun on the need to keep the growth in capital construction from overheating the economy, although they differed on ways to manage the economy. That led the reformers to place more priority on the efficient use of water, in part to free some irrigation water for diversion to industrial and municipal use. By contrast, the ministry's bias was toward engineering or hard solutions involving new construction projects. The ministry's long-standing outlook was expressed by veteran vice-minister Li Boning (1983), who conceded the need for improved policy and modest price reforms but argued that dryland farming could never satisfy China's needs for agricultural produce. More irrigation was a necessity from his perspective, although there were others who defended dryland farming (Tong Pingya 1984, Liu Xunhao 1983, Zhang Qinwen 1983, Liu Zhanjiu 1983). Resistance from the ministry and regional interests may explain the three-month lag in publishing Zhao's March 1983 remarks until a national conference on water resources was convened (NJJ 1983 7: 1–3). The conference was held shortly after the convening of the new National People's Congress, during which Premier Zhao, in his report on the work of the government, stressed the need for economic readjustment and reform and the replacement of elderly officials who were out of step with the times. The water resources conference discussed new regulations on water resources and hydroelectric projects, prepared by the ministry in the interim, that mandated increased user charges to cover costs plus prescribed profit (JPRS 84737 CEA 398, Nov. 14, 1983: 10–11).

As of the mid-1980s the higher leadership's commitment to more efficient management seemed to be sufficient to maintain the reform momentum. The Ministry of Agriculture organized a conference in the summer of 1983 in Yanan, the party's hallowed wartime capital, to promote dryland farming and livestock raising (NJJ 1983 9: 8). The experiences of several model units were publicized to demonstrate the advantages of improved management under a responsibility system coupled with volume-based prices. The goal was to establish management responsibility systems in 80 percent of small-scale water conservancy projects by the end of 1984 (JPRS 84689 CAG 277, Nov. 7, 1983: 24–26). Thus, institutions would be set up to run an essential infrastructural element even while agriculture was becoming increasingly privatized; simultaneously, these institutions would provide management with the authority, incentives, and revenues to run an efficient operation.

Huangxian County, in the lee of the Shandong Peninsula, was a widely praised example. Huangxian reportedly had suffered chronic breakdowns in its irrigation facilities. The county established an irrigation service company to contract with farm operators to provide fixed volumes of water in exchange for increased fees. Such management companies, operating on a contract responsibility basis, had been authorized by the ministry in 1981, although apparently many had not functioned smoothly at the outset. They were instituted to replace the inefficient commune and brigade management structures that were dissolving in the traumatic transition from collectivized agriculture to the household-based contract responsibility system (ZNN 1982: 408–10).

The basic charge in Huangxian was set at 0.005 yuan/m^3, which was higher than under the commune system, but this figure was halved if the client had to lift his own water from the point of delivery. The farmer reportedly benefited from an assured supply, even though his costs were higher. Moreover, the charges still totaled less than 3 percent of the gross value of agricultural output on average, or only 7 percent of the net benefit derived from irrigation. In other words, farmers could be persuaded to tolerate higher fees because irrigation remained a low-cost bargain (RR, Aug. 23, 1983; GR, Oct. 2, 1983). Other models stressed the economic advantages of dryland farming and lower applications of water when the appropriate agronomic techniques were used (Wu Yicai 1983; GR, Sept. 2, 1983; Jia Bangjie 1983; Zhou Zishi 1983).

The scope for more efficient water use is even broader elsewhere. The general approach is to impose charges on all water used in agriculture in order to provide a stronger incentive for conservation, while establishing enterprise-oriented resource management units to operate the irrigation systems more economically and scientifically. The aforementioned 1985 State Council regulations on water fees set the rules in this regard on the heels of the National Water Resources Reform Symposium held in December 1984 (ZS, February 1985: 26). Water rates are to be set in accordance with the costs borne by the delivery system to reflect conditions of resource availability with an allowance for seasonal variations, although the government continues to subsidize the construction of other types and phases of resource development projects. An additional profit margin is assessed for the irrigation of cash crops, thus providing a small incentive to maintain grain production, which is considered very important by many conservative leaders. These fees, together with ancillary income, would help the management units become self-supporting, freeing them from the status of bureaucratic appendages. Flood control and other water resource functions with broader social benefits would continue to be financed out of general government revenues.

Several problems arose. In many areas the existing management structure broke down before the new enterprise-oriented units could take their place. Meanwhile, state investment in water resources as a proportion of overall state investment fell sharply, from as high as 5 per cent in the 1950s to only 2.7 per cent in 1984 (ZTN 1985: 431–39), and local government funding fell particularly sharply. Farm households, suddenly freed from the confines of the collectives, sometimes used their new freedom to cart collective property home for their own use, including pipes and machinery. The number of reservoirs declined slightly, from 86,900 in 1982 to 84,998 in 1984, while irrigated area declined by about 3 per cent (ZTN 1985 and earlier; RR, Sept. 11, 1985). Much of the reduction was probably due to the abandonment of marginal sites, but the decline may have contributed to flooding and other problems in some areas (RR, Oct. 26, 1985).

It was also unrealistic to expect ill-managed, politically influenced irrigation districts to transform themselves into self-supporting, professionally run enterprises overnight. Farmers were bound to resist paying higher bills, and they were often abetted by local officials who ordered the sluice gates to be opened even when farmers were in arrears (ZS, March 1985: 3). Poor management, an expensive maintenance backlog, and untrained workers were also chronic problems that could not be expected to vanish merely upon the announcement of a change in policy.

These shortcomings appear to have been due more to the sequence in which the reforms were introduced than to their content. That is to say, the reduction in investment and the collapse of some administrative structures occurred because the return to household-based agriculture preceded the management changes instituted in 1985, helping to bring about a vacuum of authority that aggravated the problems of transition to a new system. These problems could have been minimized had the management and rate changes come first or coincided with the changes in land-use patterns.

As a short-term solution, the regime has resorted to the familiar expedient of stepped-up farmland capital construction campaigns, albeit with more attention paid to equity considerations in the campaigns, with workers who are brought in from other areas receiving additional compensation (RR, Feb. 18, 1986). In the long run, however, substantial gains are to be had from a more market-oriented approach in which incentives are more closely matched to benefits. The Ministry of Water Resources' 1985 "Report on the Strengthening of Farmland Water Resources Management Work" marked some progress in this regard by approving the contracting of management on a long-term basis down to the household level where appropriate and by putting more emphasis on improved material incentives and fringe benefits for full-time personnel (RR, Nov. 2, 1985).

Even William Hinton (1983: 12–16), who writes about the Chinese countryside and is a severe skeptic with regard to markets and household-based agriculture, found not only that Fengyang Xian in the North Anhui Plain had prospered in agriculture as a result of price, marketing, and other reforms but also that its water resources management had improved. Farmers were persuaded to use water more economically by strict requirements for advance payment.

Moreover, increased revenues were obtained for system maintenance and expansion through a conversion from flat-rate schedules to volumetric or progressive rate schedules, and because the newly prosperous farm households could afford special assessments for construction projects that were genuinely beneficial. In other words, economic development actually fostered cooperation to a greater degree than poor, inward-looking agricultural communities had previously been able to muster.

Many political as well as technical obstacles remain to be overcome if the mixed market-bureaucratic approach is to succeed with regard to water policy in the agricultural sector. The state must continue to subsidize water resources, albeit at somewhat lower levels, or permit further substantial increases in farm gate prices for agricultural produce. Otherwise it will be extremely difficult to raise irrigation charges high enough to cover costs. For example, even the rate schedule in Huangxian County, the new model, raised charges to barely 10 percent of the average national replacement cost. The regime is hesitant, however, to allow farm gate prices to rise in the near future lest budget deficits rise (Lu Baifu and Yuan Zhenyu 1983), although the price and marketing reforms that began in 1985 partially alleviated this problem. State investment in agriculture will rise in the Seventh Five-Year Plan (1986–90) after actually declining in the early 1980s, when the regime apparently believed that rising rural prosperity would relieve it of most of its former responsibilities. But the increase will be relatively modest (JPRS 84111 CEA 371, Aug. 12, 1983: 121). Consequently, the water delivery network may be starved of funds, making local cadres reluctant to abandon campaign-style mobilization unless farmers agree to support mutually beneficial projects.

Within the water resources sector, however, the state can reallocate some of its investment funds from expanding supplies to the introduction of more efficient technologies such as sprinkler and drip irrigation. There is vast potential in this regard. Drip irrigation was used on just 10,000 hectares nationwide in the early 1980s, although it promises to at least triple the efficiency of water use (RR, July 18, 1982; Liu Yunfa and Wang Wanxin 1983). Moreover, the state could allow local water companies to seek investment from other areas of the country by floating bonds or other financial instruments to raise startup funds and spread the risk. The rise of interprovincial investments in the post-Mao period suggests that this option has promise.

Another problem involves interregional equity. The Northwest and other arid areas are poorer than the rest of the country and already rely on the state's limited grain subsidies to satisfy part of their food needs. Although existing irrigation systems are inefficient, improved irrigation and dryland farming cannot reasonably be expected to meet the food requirements of a population that is growing at a faster rate than the country as a whole yet is not permitted to migrate elsewhere. A case in point is the Shiyanghe River valley in Gansu, which is expected not only to achieve self-sufficiency but also to satisfy grain shortfalls elsewhere in the province. Yet the valley is straining to satisfy the needs of its own residents, thanks in large part to a doubling of population since the early 1950s (JPRS 82203 WWEQ 376, Nov. 9, 1982: 15–16 and 33–47; Qu Yaoguang 1983). Not until 1983 did the regime acknowledge that some desolate areas would never be able to escape poverty because of their low and steadily declining arable land, water, and other resources. By the fall of 1985, over 130,000 people had been moved from the Dingxi Perfecture and Hexi Corridor in Gansu, southern Ningxia, and elsewhere in western China to more favorable sites in the same region, with plans to increase that number to 800,000 by 1990 (CD, Nov. 20, 1985; RR, Oct. 1 and Nov. 4 and 20, 1985).

Migration to areas better able to support economic growth is clearly desirable. However, this new policy seems to be based more on coercion to compel the relocation of entire communities than on freedom of choice, despite protestations that participation is "entirely voluntary." To the extent that coercion is involved, the participants' plight may actually worsen if they respond sullenly to their new homes. It would be far better to allow additional freedom of movement, which would permit people to move to more favorable locations on a genuinely voluntary basis.

Because of unfavorable conditions in the arid Northwest, local officials realize that they cannot come close to self-sufficiency without substantial increases in water and other inputs. Consequently, Xinjiang and other provinces still favor new construction over conservation, even in their revised water management regulations, despite the central government's policy (FBIS, Dec. 8, 1983: T4). Needless to say, the Ministry of Water Resources also is likely to continue to have reservations about the new policy if its budget is impaired. These problems promise continuing controversy.

Natural Hazards Policy

Before proceeding further, I wish to examine the PRC's natural hazards policy to see whether the categories of analysis that I have been using with regard to water policy are also applicable here.

China has a long and calamitous history of natural disasters. In the past two millennia, over 1,000 major floods, a like number of droughts, and over 3,000 earthquakes were recorded in dynastic histories and other sources. These figures undoubtedly understate the frequency of catastrophes in remote regions beyond the central government's effective control and in periods for which the historical records are incomplete. In many instances the death toll was truly enormous. It is estimated that 830,000 people were killed in the great earthquake of 1556 centered in Huaxian, Shaanxi. Over 100,000 were killed in the Gansu earthquake of 1920. Like numbers were killed in the Yangtze River flood of 1931 and the Han and Yangtze floods of 1935. Almost a million died in 1938 when the Republican government opened the Yellow River ditches in a desperate effort to halt the Japanese advance (Ross 1984, ZNN 1980: 25). Even more severe losses were recorded in droughts and famines.

In some cases, the PRC enjoys an enviable record in minimizing the toll arising from natural disasters. For example, the 1981 Yangtze River floods are reported to have been comparable to the most severe such catastrophe ever recorded in Sichuan province, yet fewer than 2,000 people were killed and economic recovery began soon afterward (Ross 1983b: 212, ZNN 1982: 296). In other instances the toll has been enormous. The Great Leap Forward resulted in over 20 million excess deaths, although it is impossible to sort out the various causes such as malnutrition, disease, and accident (Aird 1982). The 1976 Tangshan earthquake is officially reported to have claimed 242,000 lives, and there are reports that fatalities were in fact up to three times higher (Ross 1984). The dimensions of some major events such as the Hubei floods and Hebei drought of 1979–80 only became known as a result of China's unprecedented petition for foreign aid (NYT, Mar. 18, 1981; Wu Zhonglun 1982). Other catastrophes have remained hidden behind the regime's veil of secrecy.

How can we reconcile contradictory impressions of a developing country sometimes outperforming its counterparts in disaster control, virtually exclusively through indigenous resources, with a country that still experiences catastrophes of almost unimaginable proportions? The answer lies in part in the choice of implementation strategy. For insights, I turn to a major comparative study of responses to disaster by researchers at the Battelle Human Affairs Research Center (Perry et al. 1981). They identified three separate approaches to natural hazards policy that correspond quite closely to the three implementation strategies found in China.

The first approach is to control the event threat, reducing the frequency or severity of the hazard. Although this opinion is not viable for earthquakes, it is feasible for floods or droughts through building reservoirs or levees or taking other measures that store or divert water to reduce the potential for damage. The second approach is to control human settlement patterns, reducing the danger from natural hazards by placing residential and economic centers in low-risk areas or by adopting hazard-resistant construction and other practices. This option can be expensive but becomes more attractive as the mapping of seismic activity areas, floodplains, and other event vectors improves, making it easier to predict where mitigation measures are needed. However, policymakers and ordinary citizens often prefer to live in low-lying coastal or other high-risk areas despite their vulnerability because of their economic and scenic attractiveness (Burton et al. 1978). Forecast and warning is the third approach. It seeks to reduce the damage from hazards by alerting the persons at risk to evacuate or otherwise modify their behavior through such measures as taking shelter. This approach is most common with regard to weather-related events such as floods, freezes, and cyclones. The Battelle researchers further subdivided this approach into four subcategories according to the timing and duration of evacuation, i.e., whether the evacuation and other navigation measures take place before or after the event (figure 1).

Chinese policy has rested primarily on a mixture of forecast and warning measures, particularly of a short-term nature, and on control of the event threat, with much less emphasis on control of human settlement patterns. Forecast and warning in China depends heavily on campaign-style mass mobilization to drill the populace in preparation for disaster and to carry out evacuations when forecasts of an imminent disaster are issued. Success in this regard benefits from the high levels of social organization and direct involvement by local leadership, which the party actively encourages. Such measures have low fixed costs and do not require permanent alterations in settlement patterns. That makes them attractive to a poor rural country. Advance warning also is essential, and China has achieved considerable renown for its attempts to predict earthquakes. Improvements have also been obtained in weather forecasting by the State Meteorological Bureau despite a lack of state-of-the-art technology.

Control of the event threat has been most pronounced with regard to floods and droughts. Most of the Ministry of Water Resources' budget has been directed to flood control rather than other functions. The flood control program has characteristically emphasized engineering or structural solutions to alter the forces of nature through dams, ditches, and reservoirs rather than less-expensive vegetative measures. Campaigns are involved in the actual construction process through farmland capital construction performed by commune members during slack seasons, but the overall approach is bureaucratic.

The system works quite well under some conditions. Accurate advance warnings facilitate emergency precautions and evacuation, and engineering measures can divert floods. The most notable success probably was the evacuation that preceded the Haicheng earthquake that struck Liaoning in 1975; many casualties were prevented (Ross 1984). Improved weather forecasts have greatly alleviated the human toll and property damage from floods, freezes, and the like.

The policy is also subject to severe limitations. Most obviously, the quality of forecasting and event control is still inadequate. Earthquake forecasting

		Duration of Evacuation	
		Short Term	Long Term
Timing of	Preimpact	Preventive	Protective
Evacuation	Postimpact	Rescue	Reconstruction

Figure 1. The forecast and warning approach to natural hazards policy as outlined by Perry et al. (1981).

in the late days of the Maoist era resembled a pattern of guesses made under political pressure on the basis of rather intuitive interpretations of the available evidence rather than more rigorous scientific criteria, despite widespread publicity to the contrary. Once scientific freedom increased in the post-Mao era, Chinese scientists conceded that they still lacked the ability to make accurate forecasts on the basis of tremors or other precursors. It is not surprising to learn that false alarms outnumbered accurate forecasts by a ratio of 10:1 (JPRS 79222 CST 131, Oct. 15, 1981: 43–44; Wilford 1983). The costs of overreliance on an unproven forecast technology can be severe. False alarms can result in unnecessary and costly disruption and possibly reduce the public's responsiveness to future warnings. Far more tragic, however, is the devastation that occurs when an event is not forecast in a situation where other mitigating measures have not been taken, as in Tangshan, where earthquake-resistant design and engineering was woefully inadequate.

There also is a political dimension to forecast and warning that may impair its capability. Local officials are critical actors in mobilization for natural hazards policy, with responsibility for annual flood-prevention campaigns and the like (ZRGGYG 1983 16: 723). Yet preventing disaster generally is of lower priority than increasing production or other responsibilities. That creates a tendency to slight preparations and, moreover, to delay actual mobilization until the last moment in order to minimize economic disruption. Such appears to have been the case in the Wuhan flood of 1983, when a sluice gate was left open too long in an effort to remove goods stored inside the ditches (Wren 1983). All these problems predated the post-Mao reforms but may have been aggravated since then by the decline in the regime's capacity to mobilize people for collective projects.

Local officials also may exaggerate their accomplishments and fail to report the full extent of damage lest their careers be affected. Such distortion of information in communications may lead the higher leadership to believe that large rescue or reconstruction efforts are unnecessary (RR, July 9, 1985). Relief efforts also suffer from inadequate financing. During the Sixth Five-Year Plan (1981–85), only 600 million yuan a year was budgeted for relief during a period when over 16.5 million hectares of farmland a year was suffering crop losses of 30 percent or more (ZNN 1985: 302; CD, Dec. 28, 1985). An extremely small amount of grain and other supplies is available for emergency relief, and victims are ordinarily required to repay all loans within a year (Lardy 1983: 174–75 and 209).

Event control is hampered by a lack of coordination, so the effectiveness of flood control reservoirs and other preventive measures often is offset by sedimentation and the draining of lakes and other natural drainage sites for the purpose of increasing cropland, dumping in rivers, and alteration of riverbeds by gravel mining. The great floods of 1981 that devastated the upper Yangtze and Yellow River valleys are widely believed to have been aggravated by the removal of forest cover on upstream catchment areas and the dumping of debris in downstream channels (Zeng Yibing 1983, Wang Mingzhong 1983). The floods that struck northeastern China in the late summer of 1985 were aggravated by similar problems, which scientists had previously analyzed to no avail (Li Zhixue 1985; CD, Feb. 11, 1986).

Forecast and warning relies heavily on campaignlike mass mobilization, while control of the event threat is heavily bureaucratic. The problem with regard to both forecast and warning and event control is that they do nothing to discourage development in vulnerable areas or to make structures less vulnerable to events. In fact, they may have a reverse effect and actually encourage movement into hazard-prone areas by encouraging a false sense of security.

Both have been favored in China over control of human settlement patterns. Construction standards and practices were frequently shoddy and were at best designed to resist disasters of relatively small magnitude. Structures in most areas of the country are designed only to withstand floods of a 10- to 20-year frequency, far less than the 50- to 100-year standard common in industrialized countries (Lampton 1983: 10). With regard to seismicity, the new construction code adopted in 1974 designated only a few facilities to withstand tremors one degree greater than the expected intensity, while most structures were assigned standards one degree below the expected intensity (Ross 1984). Meanwhile, population and industrial centers grew with little concern for minimizing the risks of disaster.

Control of settlement patterns typically involves a mixture of financial incentives and regulation to encourage relocation and to make structures less vulnerable to damage. Thus, it most closely resembles the market-exchange implementation strategy. Policy instruments feature insurance against floods, earthquakes, and other disasters, with the premium varying according to the risk involved. Thus, development is steered toward less vulnerable areas. Anyone who chooses not to purchase insurance implicitly assumes the entire risk himself. That discourages settlement in vulnerable areas while relieving the government of the political obligation to come to the rescue.

Insurance may not work by itself because disasters often seem so unlikely that an imbalance arises in the pool between subscribers and potential victims. Thus, a mixed market and regulatory approach may be preferred in which insurance is made compulsory. Insurance then can work in conjunction with zoning and construction regulations to reduce human vulnerability. The insurance provider works directly or indirectly with the government's police power to discourage vulnerable settlements in particularly risky areas in favor of low-intensity land uses such as farming and outdoor recreation. More extensive structural reinforcement and special building designs such as elevated structures may be required in floodplains and other high-risk areas in order to qualify for insurance. The purpose is to establish tighter links between individual land use and construction decisions and the costs they impose on society as a whole. The United States has achieved considerable success in this fashion with regard to flood control, although more work remains to be done with regard to this as well as other types of disasters, especially earthquakes (Dacy and Kunreuther 1969, Burton et al. 1978: 73–75).

Such measures were widely neglected in China for a long time. Indeed, the insurance industry virtually ceased to exist during the Cultural Revolution. Moreover, very little was done through zoning to discourage settlements in floodplains (Lampton 1983: 10–12). Construction standards for seismic resistance were weak or nonexistent, and in any event construction practices were extremely lax (Ross 1984).

The post-Mao era brought a big increase in emphasis on the control of human settlement patterns for several reasons. The leadership was sympathetic to market-exchange proposals, particularly those that promised to control the ballooning construction budget. Economists who favored market methods exerted more influence, and the society as a whole enjoyed more contact with foreign countries with greater experience in public policy. In addition, the damage caused by Tangshan and other major disasters in recent years was so great that the regime became anxious to reduce the human and budgetary impact of future events.

Even before the major floods of 1981, a national conference on water resources management held in the spring of that year proposed that the government establish regulations to acquire title to particularly vulnerable sites and conduct a study of flood insurance (JPRS 79630 CRA 177, Dec. 9, 1981: 4–11). The wisdom of this advice was confirmed during the floods later that year. Of the hundreds of thousands of people who lost their homes, only 210 were insured. Most commercial and industrial enterprises were not covered either (JPRS 82044 CAG 233, Oct. 21, 1982: 11–16; Ross 1983b).

Since the insurance industry resumed operation in 1980 there has been slow but nevertheless encouraging progress (Wai-Kown et al. 1984). The People's Insurance Company of China, a somewhat creaky monopoly, has begun to solicit business more aggressively, placing an emphasis on advising clients how to reduce their risks in the process of marketing its products (RR, Jan. 25, 1984). Riskier businesses, especially in the nonstate sector, were less likely to obtain coverage. By the end of 1985 property insurance of some kind was held by over 70 percent of state enterprises and over 15 million households (CD, Jan. 10, 1986; Zang Zhifeng 1983). During the Sixth Five-Year Plan (1981–85), over 290 million yuan was paid out to compensate policyholders for losses suffered in natural disasters, helping to restore production quickly (JR, Oct. 10, 1985). Growing appreciation of the role insurance can play in this regard led the State Council to order the Ministry of Civil Affairs to determine how it could subsidize insurance premiums to facilitate the extension of coverage to poverty-stricken areas as an alternative to continued reliance on relief measures.

The insurance company also provided some advice on damage-mitigation measures, although primary responsibility in this regard continued to rest with the ministries responsible (RR, Jan. 25, 1984). By the mid-1980s the Huai River Control Commission and other segments of the water conservancy community had conceded the impossibility of ever engineering absolute flood prevention over broad expanses. Therefore, they too endorsed expanded reliance on such nonengineering measures as flood diversions, detention basins, and especially flood insurance to steer development toward less risky sites (ZS 1985 3: 4–9). Allowing competition among insurance providers would also help to widen coverage and to lower rates, but that seems unlikely at present, although regulations do permit other insurance companies to be set up.

Similarly, more stringent architectural and construction standards for new facilities were adopted and a program for retrofitting some existing structures against earthquakes has begun. Under codes adopted in 1977–78 (TJ 23–77 and TJ 11–78, reprinted in *Jiegou Sheji yu Shigong Guifan* [Structural Design and Building Codes] 4: 1–121), more infrastructural elements are to be protected against earthquakes of greater than expected intensity, and most buildings in high hazard areas will be protected to withstand shocks of the predicted intensity. These measures are costly, but the State Seismological Bureau has successfully argued that the expense is justified (Ross 1984). Moreover, the Ministry of Urban and Rural Construction began to emphasize the systematization, strengthening, and enforcement of building codes in general.

The rise in attention given to human settlement measures, which best approximate market instruments, cannot be explained without recognition of the political changes that took place after Mao's death. During periods of leftist rule, natural disasters were frequently hidden under the rug while essentially campaign-based mitigation measures were favored despite a lack of adequate technology to make forecast and warning reliable. Concern for mitigation increased after Mao's death but sometimes focused on such low-cost measures as afforestation that have only a tangential relationship to flood control (Ross 1983b). Meanwhile, many bureaucracies, including water resources, if left to themselves would have continued to place excessive reliance on expensive and incomplete event-control measures. Only after the reforms gained momentum and scientific discourse became more open was it possible to take a more comprehensive approach, with balanced regard for all instruments including the control of human settlement patterns.

Conclusions

In this chapter I have argued that the market-exchange approach offers strong advantages in terms of both the economy and the environment. Market exchange encourages efficient use of scarce resources, reduces the need for ecologically disruptive construction projects, and reduces human vulnerability to natural disasters. These advantages have only begun to be realized in China, but based on findings in other countries there is little reason to doubt that market exchange will outperform the bureaucratic and campaign styles of implementation (Phelps et al. 1978, Gardner 1983). For example, an increase in irrigation efficiency of only 20 percent would supply North China farmers with at least as much water as promised by two of the three routes for the South-North transfer, and more than 100 times the volume to be supplied by that portion of the eastern route approved in 1983 and scheduled to begin construction during the Seventh Five-Year Plan (Liu and Ma 1983: 268–69). Although additional water supplies and engineering works will be needed to satisfy China's burgeoning demands, the magnitude will be greatly reduced by more efficient use of existing resources.

Some analysts have argued that market methods are inappropriate in less developed countries because the demand for water is not price elastic but instead responds solely to environmentally defined needs and the availability of water. Lee's study (1969) of municipal consumption in India is a case in point. It is true that pent-up demand is very high at currently low levels of consumption. However, Lee failed to consider variations in rate schedules. More importantly, he confined his study to residential water usage, which is relatively small and insignificant and generally less responsive to price incentives than industry or agriculture.

Others have maintained that campaigns are preferable to market methods and cost-benefit analysis because campaigns mobilize slack labor that otherwise would go for naught (Nickum 1978, Hinton 1983). Although that is true in part, many projects undertaken have been desirable on neither economic nor environmental grounds despite the best intentions of their proponents. Nor is it proven that a marketlike approach forecloses all options in terms of social cooperation. Although transaction costs involved in bargaining among multiple rights holders will be higher than under the coercive communes, a decentralized decision-making process that generates outcomes more in accord with the preferences of participants can actually enhance efficiency, even for public goods such as water resources. The history of the United States demonstrates, for example, that private mutual or stock companies are capable of building and operating water storage and distribution networks under a wide range of conditions (Gisser and Johnson 1983), while successful irrigation networks have been operated democratically in many parts of the world (Maass and Anderson 1978). In any event, decision making in China, even in authoritarian periods, has been plagued by incessant conflicts among collectives in bargaining over one another's labor obligations. Such conflicts involve the operationalization of such ideologically loaded terms as *mutual benefit* and *equal exchange* (Zhou Zishi 1983) without monetary values to guide the exchanges.

Of course, I am not unmindful of either the technical or the political impediments to market-exchange methods. They clearly are more appropriate for uses that involve water withdrawals than for instream uses such as navigation where it is hard to put a value on different uses. There are also bound to be enormous difficulties whenever any major change in implementation is attempted.

The primary considerations, however, are philosophical and political. Market exchange makes no pretense to cultivating sentiments of altruism and communitarianism, which have been considered two of the PRC's strongest features by many new and old China hands, as well as a fundamental basis for the power of party ideologues (GR, Dec. 11, 1983). Market exchange relies instead on appeals to the material self-interest of individuals and firms. It also rejects the need for all decisions to be made by remote bureaucracies.

Another way of understanding the differences among implementation instruments is in terms of equity. The bureaucratic and campaign approaches hold property rights largely in common and treat natural resources as cost free. In principle that allows the regime to limit inequalities within the country by increasing access for the poor as well as for future generations (Ingram et al. 1983). Although this limitation sometimes occurs, the major consequence is to redistribute resources to politically favored regions and sectors of the economy. By contrast, market exchange's conception of equity involves the assignment of costs to individuals according to their respective consumption of the commodity in question. That favors the efficient.

Moreover, campaigns or bureaucracies may not even be preferable on equity grounds. Maass and Anderson's comparative study (1978: 382–92) of irrigation systems showed that efficiency in fact is highly correlated with equity when one considers a community's capacity to cope with drought. That is to say, inefficient farmers are more vulnerable to drought than their efficient brethren. Thus, the market actually reduces income inequality in comparison to inefficient institutional forms of allocating water for irrigation because the latter encourage farmers to expand their operations beyond the point at which water is available under drought conditions, forcing them into insolvency.

Political factors are also associated with a transition to market-exchange approaches. The key item is the support shown by the post-Mao leadership, particularly by the reform elements but to some extent also by conservatives anxious to balance the budget. Top-level support is needed to overcome opposition from institutional interests, which are favored by the bureaucratic and campaign approaches. For example, the Ministry of Communications benefits from a monopoly of interprovincial inland shipping due to the planners' abhorrence of competition; it has also tended to free-ride on the Ministry of Water Resources' water projects. Unfortuntely, shippers suffer from indifferent service and a failure to develop the potential for navigation, since the Ministry of Water Resources naturally prefers to emphasize flood control, hydroelectric power, and navigation. The rivalry intensified during the planning of the Three Gorges project in the early 1980s. To overcome this problem, better coordination is required. The two ministries met in January 1985 and made solemn pledges in this regard, with the Ministry of Water Resources taking a particularly remorseful tack (Qian Zhengying 1985).

In general, however, more competition is needed to lower the monopolistic shipping rates that slow the development of inland shipping—a process that began in the mid-1980s, when approval was given to both centrally and provincially operated navigation companies to offer competing services on both main stems and tributaries and privately operated shipping companies were allowed to resume operations, albeit on a small scale (Ministry of Communications 1983; Ding Ming 1984; NYT, Jan. 28, 1985). Still, more progress is needed with regard to the allocation of project costs to each user in accordance with the benefits they expect to receive. In a related vein, the State Bureau of Environmental Protection and the Ministry of Water Resources are beginning to work with the provinces on more comprehensive pollution control projects covering entire river valleys, a major improvement over the central government's earlier focus on the main stems, which are generally less affected by pollution discharges than the tributaries (*Zhongguo Huanjing Bao*, Aug. 10, 1985).

Similarly, the Ministry of Water Resources and the various water management entities also will need to shift their mission from simply augmenting the supply of water to encouraging its more efficient use. It is no easy task to reorient long-entrenched bureaucracies to new patterns of operation. However, the pragmatist leaders' strong commitment to installing younger, better-educated, and more reform-oriented officials helps to make such changes possible. The bureaucracies' willingness to change can be further heightened if they stand to benefit from higher and more progressive rate schedules in terms of bigger budgets or stronger roles on other issues. The Soviet Union's history demonstrates, however, that there is great political resistance to price reform, which would decentralize power to individual enterprises and households, and thus water largely remains underpriced or even free (Gustafson 1981: 129, 137, and 141–42). No consumer is likely to favor higher prices for water. In China, any effort to further raise water fees will bring demands for consumer subsidies, which in turn will arouse the Ministry of Finance's hackles as guardian of the treasury. Moreover, conservation depends not only on more rational rate schedules but also on improved building codes and practices regarding plumbing and other design features, which still have a long way to go in China.

Any transition to a new implementation approach may also impair existing systems before the new approach is in place. As Orville Schell (1984: 74) and the Chinese media (JPRS 84257 CAG 270, Sept. 2, 1983: 33–41) reported, peasants in some areas have refused to pay higher water charges and have dismantled irrigation systems, removing the parts for their own use. Investment in water conservancy is said to have declined by as much as 70 percent (Walker 1984: 80). Since irrigation usually involves group efforts of some kind, such behavior clearly can become widespread under a more decentralized and private property rights regime.

It seems unfair, however, to discredit the post-Mao shift to market exchange on the basis of such incidents. Inefficiency was rampant under the previous system, and many areas were thirsting for water to irrigate their crops. Market methods and contracts are able to increase efficiency and make people more willing to cooperate if more democratic water distribution entities can be established in place of collective entities subordinate to state interests. A crucial requirement is legal reform if water resources are to be managed more efficiently. A water law is needed in which property rights regarding usage volume and priority are defined and enforced, both for surface water and for groundwater. For the latter, this would involve at a minimum a system of correlative rights to groundwater in which it is recognized that the right of any surface property owner to draw water is intertwined with the rights of his neighbors to draw water from the same aquifer. The history of the southwestern United States demonstrates that such regimes can reduce the mining of groundwater in arid regions. Similarly, the Chinese will need a codification of surface water rights specifying volumes and priorities, at least in arid regions.

Moreover, it ought to be recognized that China can go much further in the use of markets and prices. Markets for water rights can be developed that would encourage efficiency and investment because the investment can then be capitalized in property values (Anderson, 1983, Maass and Anderson 1978: 208–18). If these changes in property rights and exchange mechanisms are introduced, many of the social frictions associated with resource use observed in the early 1980s will diminish. China still has a long way to go in this regard, but the reformers' sympathy for market-exchange reforms of even a limited sort is an encouraging step forward. Further success may depend on how much influence they continue to wield in the political leadership.

IV.

POLLUTION CONTROL

We now turn to environmental pollution, focusing on the widespread belief that pollution worsens under market measures like those adopted in China since 1978. This prediction is based on three lines of reasoning. First, it is assumed that pollution is closely related to the level of economic activity. The more rapidly the economy grows, the worse pollution becomes. Since the Chinese economy has grown at a rapid rate during the reform period, pollution must have worsened. Second, pollution is considered to be a form of immoral or antisocial behavior. Such behavior is inhibited when the political economy highlights central plans and moral exhortation but becomes commonplace when self-interest is glorified. Self-interest has been given wider scope since Mao's death, albeit subject to the controversial bounds set by the conservative campaigns to "build a socialist spiritual civilization" and to check "bourgeois liberalism." Individuals have been encouraged to get rich to inspire other people to follow suit. Therefore, pollution must have been exacerbated. Third, pollution control is a form of regulatory policy in which the regime acts in behalf of the broader social interest. This is more likely where the governing ideology stresses service to the people than in a regime characterized by widening social stratification, in which case the government tends to be most responsive to the interests of industry and the dominant economic class. The post-Mao regime therefore would be expected to connive with industry, newly prosperous households, and foreign investors in environmentally ruinous acts in order to strengthen its base of support.

This chapter rejects the proposition that pollution necessarily worsens in a market system and assembles evidence to show that the situation in many ways has been getting better rather than worse since 1978. To begin with, pollution is not simply a function of the level of economic activity. Pollution consists of unwanted wastes or leftover materials that arise from the economic and social activities of mankind, i.e., the " 'nonproduct' materials or energy output, the value of which is less than the costs of collecting, processing, and transporting it for use" (Bower et al. 1977). Seen from this perspective, pollution amounts to the release of residuals in an untreated form without regard for the ultimate consequences of their deposition.

Although a primitive society obviously has fewer residuals to dispose of than a developing society, that really is beside the point since virtually all twentieth-century regimes are committed to rapid economic development. That was as true of China under Mao as it is of China under Deng, although the post-Mao regime is more successful at the task. The key question concerns economic efficiency, for the greater the efficiency the smaller the volume of residuals. Otherwise, the United States, Japan, and other advanced industrialized countries would necessarily be far more polluted than China. As I will show, however, pollution in China is proportionately much worse because of glaring inefficiency. A major purpose of the post-Mao reform has been to raise efficiency, which will in turn reduce pollution— in contrast to the Maoist era, when economic rationality was considered a dangerous manifestation of bourgeois counterrevolutionary thinking.

The second assumption, that maximizers of self-interest disregard broader social values, is well taken. Economists readily agree that pollution arises from market failure in which residuals are dumped on third parties or common property resources to minimize the costs of disposal. Nevertheless, it is erroneous to conclude on this basis alone that appeals to morality (Myers 1975, Ophuls 1977) or reliance on central planning (Kapp 1974, Hua Qingyuan 1971, McIntyre and Thornton 1978b) will produce superior outcomes. No body of evidence indicates that an official code of morality can ever completely suppress self-interest, in China or elsewhere. It is more likely that a cloak of self-effacement merely disguises self- or group interest, thus legitimizing pollution and other undesirable activities (Liu Wen 1980). For its part, central planning is gravely handicapped by lower-level officials who inevitably distort information to protect their own interests.

By contrast, a market-oriented approach exposes the conflicts between self-interest and broader social needs, turning the matter into a question of how well the two can be integrated. As I will show, the adoption of environmental statutes and regulatory standards have clarified the limits of permissible behavior while a major increase in treatment facilities and other measures is reducing the size of the pollution problem. Of particular interest is the institution of a system of effluent fees designed to force the polluter to directly assume the social costs of his behavior and thus to discourage pollution on the basis of self-interest.

The third assumption concerns the political predispositions of the regime. Although the placement of the prevailing ideology along a left-right spectrum affects policy, research by Crenson (1971) and Lundqvist (1980) indicates that political competition or openness is more important. Thus, although the post-Mao regime is further to the right politically than Mao and remains authoritarian and in some respects ruthless, on the whole its commitment to modernization leads it to be more responsive to external influences and to the social needs of the people. That is important for two reasons: the practice of pollution control is diffused outward from the advanced industrialized countries, and public opinion is a frequent impetus for regulation. By contrast, the Maoist regime tended to favor autarky while disregarding the material needs of ordinary citizens with regard not only to income, housing, and other necessities but also to environmental protection. Consequently, the post-Mao regime has tended to be more responsive to environmental considerations than its predecessors, although the specific influences on policy have varied according to whether reform—associated with Deng Xiaoping, Hu Yaobang, Zhao Ziyang, and their followers—or readjustment—associated with Chen Yun, Hu Qiaomu, Deng Liqun, and other more conservative officials—is dominant at any particular time.

It is by no means true that an environmental utopia has arrived. Long-standing problems can rarely be solved overnight, and new problems are emerging. Nevertheless, the changes made since Mao's death are likely to lead to a reduction in pollution while at the same time expediting economic development. I begin with a review of the pollution problem and then turn to policy changes. Along the way I will pay particular attention to the process of regulation.

Dimensions of the Pollution Problem

The severity of pollution in general depends on three factors: the volume of residuals, the composition or properties of the residuals, and the capacity of the environment to absorb or buffer the residuals. In China, the severity of the pollution problem is due first to a high level of residuals generated in the production process. Such performance is typical of less developed countries pursuing a resource-extensive development strategy. But the problem may be even more severe in China than elsewhere because energy production, the principal source of air pollutants such as suspended particulates and sulfur dioxide, is based on the use of fuels of low and uneven quality, including unwashed coal and household coal briquettes. Although this kind of air pollution is attributable in part to poverty and technological shortcomings, it is also a product of an economic system that fails to reward efficiency or technical innovation (Zhou Fuxiang 1980). For example, the average rate for fuel-conversion efficiency or energy utilization in China's factories and power plants (industrial kilns and furnaces) was reported to be only 28 percent in 1982, barely half that of the industrialized world (table 13), resulting in a correspondingly higher level of air pollution (Smil 1984: 115–17; JPRS 82241 WWEQ 377, Nov. 16, 1982: 1–16). Industry shows similar profligacy in its consumption of other raw materials.

Residuals are for the most part not properly treated before being released into the environment. Only thirty-seven small municipal sewage treatment plants were in operation by 1984, and over 90 percent of industrial and municipal wastewater is released untreated into the country's waterways (JR, Oct. 26, 1985; Liu Tianji 1980; JPRS 80462 CEA 217, Mar. 31, 1982: 14). On average, only about 20 percent of industrial residuals were recycled

Table 13

Energy Utilization Rates, 1982 (%)

	China	Advanced Industrial Countries
Thermal power plants	29	35-40
Industrial boilers	55-60	80
Industrial kilns and furnaces	20-30	50-60
Household stoves	15-20	50-60
Railroad locomotives	6-8 (steam)	25 (diesel or electric)

SOURCE: Lu Qi (1984).

before leaving the factory grounds (FBIS, Dec. 16, 1982: K6–7). Such high levels of untreated pollutants pose especially serious problems because of China's high population density and heavy reliance on effluent for irrigation and organic fertilizer. Water, soil, and other media thus are polluted at alarming rates, spreading the problem to the countryside (RR, Aug. 22, 1980; GR, Aug. 25, 1983; Cai Hanquan 1984).

The composition of residuals poses health risks (table 14). The estimated 42 million tons of residuals discharged into the atmosphere in 1981 included over 18 million tons of sulfur dioxide—more than four times greater than the volume in West Germany and near the 22.5 million tons of SO_2 discharged that same year in the United States, where economic activity is about six times greater (Li Jinchang 1984a, Kinzelbach 1983: 305). Sulfur dioxide is a mild irritant that can aggravate respiratory diseases and reduce lung function; it can also be converted to sulfates in the atmosphere and then be deposited on land in acid form.

Industrial effluent in China contains at least 130,000 tons of toxic substances, including over 4,000 tons of heavy metals, over 20,000 tons of phenols and cyanides, and over 80,000 tons of oily wastes (State Statistical Bureau 1985c: 240). Local concentrations can be alarming. Over 90 percent of urban groundwater and 25 percent of surface freshwater resources are considered contaminated, with 47 percent of stream bodies failing to meet surface water quality standards and 4.3 percent classified as biologically dead (Tian Chunsheng 1984, Smil 1984; 100–8, *People's University Industrial Economics Reprint Series* 1982 14: 101–4, Li Jinchang 1984a). Of seventy-eight major rivers surveyed, fifty-four were found to be polluted, including fourteen of particular severity. Included among the latter are portions of China's major rivers, the Yangtze, Yellow, Huai, Songjiang, Pearl, and Xiang. Kinzelbach (1981) cited internal sources in reporting that levels of organic mercury in the Songhua River downstream from Jilin ranged up to 20 micrograms per liter, which is up to five times higher than in Mina-

Table 14

Annual Discharges in China (Estimated)

		Wastewater	
Year	Volume $(10^9 m^3)$	Mass $(10^{10}$ tons)	Including Industrial
1977	--	--	--
1978	--	--	--
1979	--	--	--
1980	--	--	4.00
1981	--	3.03	2.42
1982	--	3.10	2.48
1983	--	3.09	2.39

Table 14

Annual Discharges in China (Estimated)
(Part 2)

	Gases			**Solid Wastes**	
Year	Volume $(10^9 m^3)$	Mass $(10^7$ tons)	Including SO2	Volume $(10^9 m^3)$	Mass $(10^8$ tons)
1977	8.0	--	--	--	3.6
1978	9.4	--	--	--	4.3
1979	9.9	--	--	--	4.5
1980	--	--	--	--	--
1981	--	4.2	1.8	--	--
1982	--	4.1	--	--	5.5
1983	--	--	--	--	--

SOURCES: Qu Geping (1983): 5; CD, Dec. 6, 1984; JPRS 80462 CEA 217, Mar. 31, 1982: 14; JPRS 80026 WWEQ 336, Feb. 4, 1982: 7; Fuyin Gongye Jingji (1982) 14: 104-4; Li Jinchang (1984a); Chongqing Huanjing Baohu (June 1985): 11.
NOTE: These data must be considered rough estimates until a more comprehensive and precise nationwide monitoring system is in place.

mata, Japan, during the epidemic of mercury poisoning in the 1960s. Less than 8 percent of Beijing's sewage received even primary treatment at the city's plant as late as 1978, and Beijing is better than most Chinese cities in this regard (JPRS 80026 WWEQ 336, Feb. 4, 1982: 43–50). Household and industrial sewage and saltwater intrusion have gravely affected Shanghai's water resources (Duan Shaobo 1984: 46).

The costs of pollution are high. Li Jinchang, a senior analyst working directly under the State Council, estimated that the annual bill for pollution was 9 percent of the gross value of industrial and agricultural output, or

75 billion yuan, in 1982 (CD, Dec. 6, 1984). Other estimates are lower but still amount to tens of billions of yuan (*Zhongguo Huanjing Bao*, Jan. 19, 1985). The economic costs include declines in fishing catches (GR, Sept. 12, 1983); the forced closure of urban wells and waterworks in major cities, including Chengdu and Shanghai, necessitating the construction of costly replacement facilities (Bangongting 1982; JPRS 82241 WWEQ 377, Nov. 16, 1982: 65); the pollution of almost 3 million hectares of farmland, including over 40,000 hectares contaminated with cadmium and mercury from which tens of thousands of tons of grain are harvested every year (Li Jinchang 1984a); the contamination of freshwater and sewage effluent previously suitable for irrigation (JPRS 82926 WWEQ 387, Feb. 25, 1983: 9); and the conversion of over 400 km^2 of land near cities into solid waste dumps (Qu Geping 1983).

The health costs of pollution are also high. Kinzelbach (1981, Editorial Committee 1979) suggested that the incidence of lung and some other cancers in Chinese cities is comparable to that of an industrialized nation in part because of pollution. In Shanghai, the incidence of lung cancer rose from 5.25 per 100,000 in 1960 to 35 per 100,000 in 1976, due in part to air pollution (Long Dehuai 1984). The incidence of respiratory disease is greatly aggravated by the use of inefficient coal-burning stoves at home and work (Lu Changmiao and Fu Lixun 1984). And there are many instances of human illness such as mercury poisoning attributable to pollution (ZHK, Jan. 1983: 8–11, February 1983: 49–52, and March 1985: 1–13; JPRS 80026 WWEQ 336, Feb. 4, 1982: 41–42).

Policy Development

For many years pollution was a nonissue in China. That was partly because of a worldwide lack of understanding of the problem but also because China placed first priority on economic development. Even the country's fabled public health programs only marginally involved pollution control. For example, the economic planning process concentrated on heavy industry, yet the 156 key projects built with Soviet assistance in the 1950s paid only slight attention to pollution control (Yu Guangyuan 1980: 16, Jiang Bikun and Guo Rui 1980). A few regulatory standards based on Soviet practice were promulgated in 1956 and revised in 1962 but were largely oriented to occupational health and were ineffective (Guo Li'ai 1985). The economic sector took little heed of pollution control because it was not included in enterprise norms and did not receive state investment funds (JPRS 83766 WWEQ 403, June 27, 1983: 40–54). Although concern about pollution increased dramatically elsewhere in the 1960s, China did not take part because of its isolation, which was aggravated by the anti-intellectual ferment of the Cultural Revolution and the lack of an institutional constituency to advocate environmental protection.

After the peak of the Cultural Revolution passed, it became possible for China to turn its attention back to practical problems of development, including pollution control. Environmental protection's advance on the policy agenda was hastened not only by an increase in the magnitude of pollution but also by China's reentry into the global community through rapprochement with the West and admission to the United Nations. The precipitating event was the United Nations Conference on the Human Environment, planning for which had begun in 1968 on the basis of a Swedish proposal. The conference, held in Stockholm in June 1972, forced China and other member states of the United Nations to address their environmental problems in a more formal and authoritative fashion than might have occurred otherwise. In this aspect the conference can be deemed successful (Caldwell 1984).

A leading group responsible for environmental protection was informally set up under the State Council in 1971 to supervise preparation of the Chinese delegation's position at the Stockholm conference. While many developing countries were wary of any trend that threatened to limit their options for economic development, China's position was the most ambiguous and confrontational. China acknowledged that pollution control was needed but placed primary responsibility for pollution on the large capitalist states, thus subordinating domestic causes of pollution in the Third World to international factors. Indeed, China defended the right of developing countries to exploit their own resources without interference from outside parties. Although suspicion of the environmental movement as a plot to suppress the development potential of Third World countries was widespread, China's role at the conference was the most disruptive. The Chinese delegation made unsuccessful efforts to include such tangential issues as the Vietnam War and nuclear testing in the conference declaration. The declaration was eventually approved without a recorded vote to convey an artificial sense of unanimity, but China pointedly announced that it had not taken part in the voting (PR, June 23, 1972: 8–11).

Nevertheless, the Stockholm conference provided impetus to China's own domestic environmental policy, as intended by the organizers. A conference on stack dust removal was held in Shanghai in April 1972 that would lead over the next several years to a pilot emission-control project in Shenyang, one of China's most polluted cities (*Huanjing Guanli*, January 1984: 3–12). The State Council simultaneously initiated a multiprovince project to improve water quality in Beijing's Guanting Reservoir, which had become increasingly fouled since its completion in 1954 (*BR*, Aug. 17, 1985).

In August 1973, the State Planning Commission convened a national conference on environmental protection work in Beijing. This conference led to State Council Directive No. 158, "Some Regulations on Protecting and Improving the Environment," which was provisionally approved in draft form. Both the conference and the directive placed primary emphasis on planning, which was hardly surprising given the nature of the regime and the sponsoring agency, while mass participation was also nominally encouraged. The major point was the need to incorporate environmental considerations into planning, while implying that this need not retard economic development. The spirit of environmental policy at this time was expressed in a thirty-two-character phrase that had first appeared a year earlier and conveyed a positive but very general message to different constituencies while papering over potential conflicts of interest: *Quanmian guihua, heli buju, zonghe liyong, hua huai wei li, yikao qunzhong, dajia dongshou, baohu huanjing, zaofu renmin* (Overall planning, rational distribution, comprehensive utilization, turning the harmful into the beneficial, relying on the masses, everybody lending a hand, protecting the environment, and benefiting the people) (Tang Ke 1972: 8; Jiang Bikun and Guo Rui 1980: 30; HB, Dec. 1983: 2).

Following the conference, the PRC began to establish a bureaucratic structure to deal with the problems that had been discussed by the assembled delegates. In 1974 an Environmental Protection Office with a small staff of twenty was set up under the State Council and its Leading Group for Environmental Protection, and similar units were formed at the provincial level in many parts of the country (National Environmental Protection Conference Secretariat 1973). As Boxer (1980: 465) noted, the national unit's designation as an office indicated an absence of vertical or line authority over subordinate levels of government in the fashion of a ministry or bureau. Instead, the office's duties were confined to coordination and planning, yet it lacked the prestige of a central commission. Since even central commissions must struggle to impose a common purpose on disparate operating agencies, environmental protection was in a tenuous position.

Several factors help to explain the absence of greater institutional support for environmental protection, in addition to the inevitable indecision and start-up pains associated with any new endeavor (Montjoy and O'Toole 1979). There is likely to have been some resistance from other agencies threatened by the establishment of a strong new agency. Industrial ministries may have feared infringement on their operating autonomy, while the Ministry of Public Health and other agencies that had historically been involved in environmental matters may have objected to the loss of peripheral functions.

The general political climate seems to have been the most important factor. China's initial efforts in pollution control coincided with the return of many pragmatists to political power. Following the elimination of Mao's erstwhile successor Lin Biao in 1971, the pragmatists were able to partially deflect China's attention from revolution to practical problems of development and rebuilding of the civilian government and party structures. Most notably, Deng Xiaoping was returned to office in April 1973. The pragmatists' ascendance did not go unchallenged by the left, however. By mid-1973, the Cultural Revolution leftists and the pragmatists were in an uneasy balance as signified by the personnel appointments and addresses made at the Tenth Party Congress held that August, just days after the conclusion of the environmental protection conference. Wang Hongwen became party vice-chairman, while the three other members of what later came to be labeled the Gang of Four retained their seats on the Politburo (Domes 1977).

By the beginning of 1974 the struggle to succeed Mao and fix China's future course was being waged in earnest. The pragmatists under the aegis of Zhou Enlai sought to neutralize the revolutionary symbolism of the left while gradually preparing a program to promote modernization. Although they enjoyed some success in this regard, the left actively sought to restore political redness to first place among credentials for office and to enforce the primacy of politics over all other considerations. Under the circumstances, official pronouncements and public discussion of environmental policy had to be conducted within the narrow confines of class analysis. For example, a major article by the pseudonymous Guo Huan ("National Environment") (1974a) attributed pollution to the nature of the social system and political line. Since it was dangerous to question the political line, China's achievements in pollution control of necessity were effusively praised in public, although the problem was actually worsening.

It was not until after the purge of the Gang of Four that progress on pollution control accelerated. The importance of environmental protection and pollution control was stressed at several national conferences convened in 1978 and in Central Directives 13 and 79 of that year. Environmental protection was raised in status to a state responsibility in the 1978 constitution. By later that year the Environmental Protection Office was issuing orders to key industrial facilities to halt pollution or risk being shut down.

In February 1978, the Leading Group on Environmental Protection under the State Council directed the environmental protection bureaus of seven provinces in industrialized northern and eastern China to draft a statute on environmental protection. This move toward the legal codification of policy took place as part of a broader commitment to restoring law and social order in the interest of stability and to preventing a recurrence of the ad hoc, rule-by-decree style of governance that had gotten out of hand during the Cultural Revolution. By April 1979 a draft statute had been prepared by these provincial officials along with specialists who referred to the experiences of foreign countries. The law was revised three times over the next several months to incorporate the views of other bodies such as the State Science and Technology Commission, with one change apparently involving the issue of flexible enforcement versus requiring the shutdown of factories found to be in violation of regulations (article 17). The statute was approved in draft form by the Standing Committee of the NPC on September 13, 1979 (Jiang Bikun and Guo Rui 1980: 32–38).

The law as presently constituted suffers from several problems. Like many other statutes, the law was issued in draft form or for trial use only (*shixing*). This trial-use format was intended to get laws into place quickly without making them permanent, for they were bound to be flawed. As Deng Xiaoping (1978: 157–58) explained at the decisive December 1978 Central Work Conference, where the Whatever faction of Maoist loyalists was defeated:*

> To ensure people's democracy, we must strengthen our legal system. Democracy has to be institutionalized and written into law, so as to make sure that institutions and laws do not change whenever the leadership changes, or whenever the leaders change their views or shift the focus of their attention. The trouble now is that our legal system is incomplete, with many laws yet to be enacted. Very often, what leaders say is taken as the law and anyone who disagrees is called a law-breaker. That kind of law changes whenever a leader's views change. So we must concentrate on enacting criminal and civil codes, procedural laws and other necessary laws concerning factories, people's communes, forests, grasslands and environmental protection, as well as labour laws and a law on investment by foreigners. These laws should be discussed and adopted through democratic procedures. Meanwhile, the procuratorial and judicial organs should be strengthened. All this will ensure that there are laws to go by, that they are observed and strictly enforced, and that violators are brought to book. The relations between one enterprise and another, between enterprises and the state, between enterprises and individuals, and so on should also be defined by law, and many of the contradictions between them should be resolved by law. There is a lot of legislative work to do, and we don't have enough trained people. Therefore, legal provisions will have to be less than perfect to start with, then be gradually improved upon. Some laws and statutes can be tried out in particular localities and later enacted nationally after the experience has been evaluated and improvements have been made. Individual legal provisions can be revised or supplemented one at a time, as necessary; there is no need to wait for a comprehensive revision of an entire body of law. In short, it is better to have some laws than none, and better to have them sooner than later.

Although well intended, this provision legitimized some evasion and noncompliance by polluters who insisted that the law had not yet taken effect. Meanwhile, enforcement was handicapped because the legal structure, including laws to govern specific categories of pollution and local legislation, was not yet in place.

Nevertheless, the environmental law did establish a statutory basis for future government action. Among its provisions were requirements that environmental assessments be prepared before new construction projects would be approved and that preventive or remedial measures be taken in the event of unavoidable impacts (articles 6 and 7); an organic charter for

*The Whatever faction, tied to Hua Guofeng, insisted that China must always adhere closely to Mao's policies regardless of changes in circumstances (Hu Jiwei 1979: U1).

an environmental bureaucracy (articles 26–28); sanctions and rewards (articles 32 and 33); and enforcement procedures, including possible suspension of operations (article 17) and a system of effluent charges and fines for excessive discharges (article 18) (Ross and Silk 1987). Administrative guidelines were subsequently issued governing the preparation of environmental impact assessments and other measures authorized by the statute (ZRGGYG 360, Aug. 30, 1981: 407–11). Legislation dealing with specific items, including water pollution control, marine environmental protection, and other subjects, were enacted in later years (Ross and Silk 1987).

Naturally, the effectiveness of any law depends on enforcement. In this instance, a great deal is lacking in terms of financing, personnel, and organization after decades in which the judicial system was relegated to the status of a formal appendage. Nevertheless, the higher leadership's support level has remained high. Recommendations to reduce the level of environmental protection until after industrialization has proceeded further (Mao Yushi 1982) have been rebuffed, most notably at the Second National Environmental Work Conference in December 1983 (*RR,* Jan. 8, 1984). Although primarily a result of greater support by the elite for environmental protection, the passage of additional and tougher laws and regulations may also reflect the segmented nature of policymaking under which each branch tends to make policy without extensive opportunity for other agencies, particularly those outside the branch's "general system," to influence its actions, although horizontal communication does take place on an informal basis (Oksenberg 1982: 180–81). Thus, a regulatory agency may at times be able to impose stronger formal requirements on regulated industries than would be possible under the extensive notice-and-comment rule-making procedure found in the United States (Heffron 1983). Conversely, the regulator may have greater difficulty implementing its policies in the absence of consensus on the scope of its authority.

The bureaucratic status of environmental protection was complicated in 1982 by its designation as a bureau of the Ministry of Urban and Rural Construction and Environmental Protection. Its power to compel other agencies to comply with its directives remained less than satisfactory, in part because the State Council simultaneously abolished its Leading Group on Environmental Protection along with the State Commission on Capital Construction, which had the authority to coordinate the various bureaucracies. Moreover, environmental protection resembled an appendage rather than an integral component of the new ministry, with most of its offices located in a separate compound.

In response, an Environmental Protection Commission was established in the spring of 1984, four years after it had been first proposed, to coordinate all agencies whose activities impact on the environment. Vice-Premier Li Peng was appointed chairman, with the Environmental Protection Bureau serving as the secretariat. Twenty agencies were represented by their heads (State Council 1984; RR, Sept. 5, 1980). Later in 1984, the bureau was further elevated to the status of a state bureau, making it largely independent of its parent ministry, although that is less true at the local level in some provinces (*Huanjing Fa* 1986 2: 53).

Interagency commissions fulfill an important coordinating and intra-governmental consciousness-raising function in China while relieving the State Council of the need to resolve technical issues and bureaucratic conflicts. The Environmental Protection Commission, set up to meet quarterly, convened for the first time in July 1984 to consider two items prepared for its consideration by the Environmental Protection Bureau: the control of smoke caused by the burning of coal, and the increasingly serious problem of pollution by small-scale rural industry. Both items were approved, with the second resulting in a State Council directive later in the year ("Directive on Applying Environmental Management to Rural and Neighborhood Enterprises," Sept. 27, 1984). Perhaps more important than these decisions themselves was the message delivered by Vice-Premier Li. Li reminded the assembled ministers that the polluter himself must assume responsibility for controlling pollution and that no construction would be approved without prior assurance regarding the alleviation of environmental impacts (HB, September 1984: 2–3; RR, July 11, 1984).

Commissions generally lack direct influence over agency budgets and operational procedures, however, so their power sometimes rests more on persuasion and consensus building than on the exercise of formal authority. The commission's weakness is typified by a directive issued at its second meeting in September 1984 on the protection of endangered flora. The document was prepared on the basis of a list of species that had first been prepared in 1980 by the Environmental Protection Bureau in conjunction with the Botany Research Institute of the Academy of Sciences; apparently little of direct import had been accomplished in the intervening years. Despite this lack of response, the commission's directive included measures no more forceful than propaganda and research in the "hope" (*xiwang*) of receiving cooperation from the relevant agencies (RR, Sept. 28, 1984).

Because the bureaucracies responsible for environmental protection are not fully able to secure compliance through their own devices, support by the central leadership is critical to policy success. Such support remained strong in the post-Mao era despite conflict over the general course of economic policy. The most dramatic evidence in this regard dates from early 1981, in the immediate aftermath of the decisive Central Work Conference that marked a shift in political emphasis from economic reform to a more conservative course of readjustment and consolidation. The State Council issued a directive calling for continued strict emphasis on environmental protection, including threats to close down or relocate violators. The cabinet's position was based partly on environmental factors, but it also was taken because environmental impact analysis could be used to slow down rampaging construction spending, which was contributing to alarming budget deficits and inflation (State Council 1981). Thus, environmental protection, which first blossomed in a period of liberalization, remained a priority item in 1981 in a more budget-conscious and politically conservative phase. Still, financial constraints on environmental protection remained tight.

At the end of 1983, with China on the verge of a more liberal phase that would follow the abortive Socialist Spiritual Civilization campaign, environmental protection received another boost at the Second National Environmental Protection Work Conference, called to mark the passage of China's first decade of modern environmental awareness. Speaking at the conference, senior Vice-Premier Wan Li and other leading officials in attendance all stressed the complementarity of protecting the environment and developing the economy. In their addresses, Vice-Premier Li Peng (RR, Jan. 8, 1984) and Ma Hong (1984), president of the Academy of Social Sciences, identified five goals to guide environmental protection work during the rest of the century: strive to basically control pollution; restore basically sound balance to the natural ecosystem; clean up, beautify, and restore order to the urban production and human environments; ensure that environmental quality basically remains in harmony with the rise in material and cultural well-being; and pursue the "three livelihoods" (economic, social, and environmental).* In terms of specific goals, Qu Geping, the head of the Environmental Protection Bureau, called for the removal of 96 percent of particulate matter from industrial emissions into the atmosphere as well as 42 percent of SO_2 emissions, recycling 80 percent of industrial effluent, treating 75 percent of all sewage, and recycling over 50 percent of industrial solid wastes by the year 2000. These overly ambitious targets actually represented a comedown by the bureau from its original position (JPRS CST-84-004, Feb. 14, 1984: 34–35).

Although economic development would obviously continue to receive far more funding, the principle was established that economic expansion would not be permitted to exceed the environment's absorptive capacity or the regulatory capability of the environmental protection apparatus. That represented a policy victory for environmentalists who insisted that economic development depended on environmental protection (JPRS 82926 WWEQ 387, Aug. 25, 1983: 4). By contrast, proponents of rapid development had argued that environmental protection was a luxury that should be pursued only after output had reached a much higher level (e.g., *Zhongguo Jianzhu* 1975: 105–19).

Funding for environmental protection has risen substantially in the reform era even though it remains primarily a local and enterprise, rather

---

*Economic and environmental development have clear meanings, but social livelihood is a vague concept implying both ethical behavior and support for socialism and the Communist party. In an earlier version of the "three livelihoods" designed to equate environmental protection with economic development, Li Chaobo (1980) referred to perfecting or reforming the economic structure as the third element.

than central government, responsibility (table 15). Funds for environmental protection must officially be included in construction and renovation plans, with a minimum of 7 percent of funds retained by enterprises for technological retrofitting earmarked for environmental protection (State Council 1984c). Shanghai claims to be devoting almost 6 percent of funding for new construction on environmental protection. That is less than the 20 percent demanded by the environmental protection agency but nevertheless represents a big increase over past years (JPRS 82241 WWEQ 377, Nov. 16, 1982: 106–7; Li Yangming 1982). Beijing spent over 6 percent of its technological renovation funds in 1984 on environmental protection and pollution control, more than twice as much as in 1983 (*Beijing Economic and Statistics Yearbook* 1985: 232 and 1983: 63).

Nationwide, 1.5 percent of technological renovation funds were devoted in 1984 to environmental protection and pollution control per se (table 16). That does not include energy and raw materials conservation, which accounts for nearly 5 percent and has a direct payback in terms of improved environmental quality (ZTN 1985: 453). The percentages are much higher in major cities—a harbinger of future trends.

As table 15 shows, overall funding has increased substantially, from 0.28 percent of the gross value of industrial and agricultural output (GVIAO), about 2.3 billion yuan, in 1982 to 0.5 percent of GVIAO and about 5.4 billion yuan in 1984. By 1990 the figure is expected to rise to 1 percent of GVIAO, and then to 1.5 percent by the end of the century (Li Jinchang 1983 and 1984a; JPRS CST-84-004, Feb. 14, 1984: 34–35; *Zhongguo Huanjing Guanli*, January 1986: 6–7). Staffing levels have also risen substantially (table 17).

The rise in priority of environmental protection generally, and of pollution control in particular, is due to several factors. Most important is

Table 15

China's Environmental Protection
Expenditures, 1980-1984

Year	Amount $(10^9$ yuan)	% of GVIAO[a]
1980	1.8	0.25
1981	--	--
1982	2.3	0.28
1983	3.7	0.40
1984	5.4	0.50

SOURCES: Li Jinchang (1983 and 1984a); CD, Dec. 6, 1984; JPRS CST-84-004 (Feb. 14, 1984): 34–35; ZTN (1985): 24.
[a]Gross value of industrial and agricultural output.

Table 16

Investments in Technological
Renovation in China, 1981–1984

Year	Industrial Waste Treatment (10^6 yuan)	(%)	Environmental Protection (10^6 yuan)	(%)	Total (10^6 yuan)	(%)
1981	337	1.5	135	0.6	22,460	100
1982	412	1.4	225	0.8	28,978	100
1983	475	1.3	177	0.5	35,783	100
1984	652	1.5	300	0.7	44,203	100

SOURCES: Chinese Statistical Yearbook 1984, 336, and 1985, 453.

Table 17

Employment in China's Environmental
Protection System, 1981–1983

Year	Scientific and Technical	Overall
1981	10,442	22,467
1982	13,419	26,771
1983	15,336	28,278

SOURCE: State Statistical Bureau (1985c).

active support, or at least tolerance, by the higher leadership, which encouraged proponents to express their positions. Scientists and other intellectuals made use of the more open research and publishing climate made possible by the liberalization of science policy to press their concern over environmental degradation. Although the Four Modernizations that served as the rallying cry for Premier Zhou Enlai and the moderates was primarily an economic policy, the party Central Committee at its decisive Third Plenum in December 1978 approved the Environmental Protection Leading Group's report declaring that pollution control and environmental protection were indispensable aspects of modernization and economic construction (Qu Geping 1984: 54). Thus, the Four Modernizations did not prove to be a license to ignore environmental factors, although some officials may have interpreted it that way. Instead, environmentalists used the new respect accorded science to argue that modernization was impossible without environmental protection. Although the proponents of the Four Modernizations originally may have been concerned only with economic growth, the relative permissiveness of their policy allowed other concerns to be expressed.

As emphasis shifted to balanced development, it became easier for environmentalists to communicate their positions through journals, conferences, and professional societies. Particularly notable was the Second National Environmental Protection Work Conference convened in 1983, ten years after its predecessor marked the beginning of environmental policy. As Li Peng explained, population control and environmental protection were critical national needs to be attained by 2000 in the fashion of the Four Modernizations. Although Li agreed that considerable progress had been achieved with regard to population control, he warned that environmental protection remained a glaring deficiency (RR, Jan. 8, 1984). Environmental protection was consequently assigned a prominent place in the Project 2000 systems dynamics forecasting models to be built in the fashion of similar work performed in the West.

Funding levels provide another glimpse of how environmentalists were able to advance their views. In classic bureaucratic fashion, they presented a set of alternative funding levels to the leadership. In terms of GVIAO, it was said that 0.5 percent would lead to continued deterioration, 1 percent would halt further degradation but would not allow for improvements, 1.5 percent would permit modest improvements, and 2.5 percent would allow major improvements to be made but at considerable cost to the economy (*Zhongguo Huanjing Guanli*, January 1986: 6–7). Clearly, 1.5 percent was the only sensible choice, even though the spending intervals were set widely apart and the projects to be funded were not specified. Of even greater interest is the fact that the 1.5 percent figure was already being exceeded if capital construction, technological renovation, and effluent fees were included in the calculations. In other words, environmental officials and scholars defined their revenues narrowly to justify additional appropriations, while they conversely claimed a broad mandate to intervene in all activities that could be construed as affecting the environment.

Popular protest was also a factor. Factory pollution was a major source of local discontent. Information is scanty, but in 1979 alone, Shanghai reported 339 incidents involving confrontations between factories and the public over pollution, resulting in forty-nine full or partial shutdowns. The loss of production totaled over 30 million yuan. The number of incidents fell in later years, but the four-year toll still amounted to almost 50 million yuan in the period 1979–82 in China's largest city (Deng Jianxu 1983; JPRS 81609 WWEQ 365, Aug. 23, 1982: 13–15). Letters to the editor and other more conventional forms of expression were naturally more common and also increased in number.

Given the high risks faced by anyone engaging in irregular political conduct, the fact that many hundreds of demonstrations were taking place each year is significant. It indicates that the regime was more tolerant of protest on issues of daily life that did not directly challenge the Four Cardinal Principles of governance (socialism, proletarian dictatorship, party rule, and Marxism–Leninism–Mao Zedong Thought) proclaimed by Deng Xiaoping in 1979. Rather than ignore or simply repress the protests, the leadership even occasionally supported them as a means to gain leverage over recalcitrant local officials and bureaucrats.

A prominent example of intervention by the central party leadership involved coal transportation. The Changjiang (Yangtze River) Shipping Administrative Bureau's port facilities in Wuhan were old and poorly maintained. Whenever coal was loaded or unloaded, large clouds of black dust spread into the neighboring residential area, and:

> The residents repeatedly sent their views to the Wuhan Port Office and the Changjiang Shipping Administrative Bureau demanding that the pollution problems be resolved but were never able to arouse the attention of the leaders of the two bureaus and thus became very dissatisfied. On 3 days, 5–7 July [1982], some angry masses broke into Pier 41 three times when it was in operation. They forced a halt to the unloading of coal, smashed some equipment and caused direct losses amounting to more than 11,000 yuan. After the incident, leading comrades of the CCP Central Committee severely criticized the leaders of the Changjiang Shipping Administrative Bureau for neglecting the people's interests and for their bureaucratic work style.

Vice-Premier Wan Li read an internal press account of the incident and forced an investigation that led to criticism of the port administration. Substantial progress was reported over the next six months. Dust hoods were installed over the unloading facilities to capture fugitive dust emissions. Raw coal piles were hosed down regularly to reduce dust and incidentally remove some impurities. It was reported that steps also were taken to reduce the runoff of polluted water back into the river (JPRS-CST-84-017, June 11 1984: 142–44; Ross and Silk 1987).

This case is important because of what it tells about the political process. When the polluter declined to take remedial action on its own, the environmental protection authorities and the parent Ministry of Communications were unable or unwilling to compel compliance with the Environmental Protection Law. Therefore, direct intervention by the Central Committee was required to compel action in order to placate the populace and assure continuity of production. Intervention by the central authorities obviously cannot be anticipated in the normal course of events, but the fact that it occurred on several occasions in the 1980s served as a powerful reminder to local officials of the dangers they ran when ignoring environmental considerations. Although positive response to protest on such issues may seem trivial in comparison with the arbitrary arrest and jailing of genuine dissidents, it represents a sharp contrast to the leftist politics of the previous decade. At that time individuals who spoke out against pollution from nearby factories were liable to arrest as counterrevolutionaries (Ross and Silk 1985, Sun Xiangming 1984).

Moreover, the post-Mao regime placed greater emphasis on raising the standard of living to induce workers to work harder. While this move depended primarily on increases in procurement prices for agricultural products and improved wages and bonuses for workers, it also incorporated improvements in welfare benefits, including a major expansion and upgrading of the housing base in city and countryside alike.* Meanwhile, Beijing, Hangzhou, Suzhou, and Guilin, as well as other areas of scenic and cultural importance, were instructed to improve their environment even at the expense of relocating or shutting down older industrial facilities (State Council 1981). Environmental protection proved more compatible with this broad emphasis on raising social welfare than it had been with leftist asceticism.

Nor was sustained concern for the environment possible during the height of the succession crisis in the mid-1970s when the lack of consensus at the peak of the political system kept the country in turmoil. Although pilot projects and individual cleanups began, it was impossible to carry out major changes because leadership backing was fleeting. In the absence of clear signals from above, the lower echelons remained immovable.

In this respect, my analysis of China tends to confirm the findings by Lundqvist (1980) for Sweden and the United States. Lundqvist found that the more open the system, the broader and more immediate are its responses to policy problems. In the absence of consensus, however, it becomes impossible for such open systems to carry through a new policy. Therefore, a closed and consensus-oriented system may start slower but can eventually catch up with a faster-starting, open, conflict-oriented system.

Lundqvist's analysis can be broadened by creating a two-by-two matrix, which yields twice as many categories as his original analysis (figure 2). Both Sweden and post-Mao China then belong in the lower left (open-consen-

		Openness	
		Open	Closed
	Conflictual	United States (hare)	Cultural Revolution China
Consensus			
	Consensual	Sweden post-Mao China (tortoise)	Soviet Union

Figure 2. A two-by-two matrix showing relations between the political systems and policy change.

*In the five-year period 1979 through 1983, the state financed the construction of 395 million m² of housing, which is equivalent to three-quarters of total state construction over the previous thirty years. In addition, private individuals and collectives were encouraged to build housing on their own that amounted to 97 million m² (Zhu Qinfang 1984: 30, ZTN 1985: 448 and 456). New rural housing during the same period totaled 2.8 billion m² (JR, Oct. 10, 1985).

sual) cell rather than the lower right (closed-consensual) cell. My analysis of the evolution of policy in China indicates that only if a country is open to external political influence from the broader society and beyond its borders will it respond to new problems. Conversely, the leaders of a closed-consensual system such as China's under leftist rule have no incentive to consider new ideas. Clearly, some liberty has been taken by placing post-Mao China in the consensual category in light of its factional conflicts, but the absence of political competition makes this placement essential. In addition, post-Mao China is less open than Sweden, but it is far more open than earlier Chinese regimes. Although I hesitate to compare countries in the upper left (open-conflictual) and lower left (open-consensual) cells in terms of performance, I would predict that both would respond more quickly to new problems than would regimes on the right side of the matrix, with the upper right (closed-conflictual) cell the most resistant to change.

Implementation Strategies

Having traced the evolution of policy, I now must take a look at its effectiveness. For this, I turn to an analysis of implementation, examining the three alternative strategies employed in previous chapters.

Campaign-Exhortation Implementation

Governments influenced by Confucianism are predisposed to rule by publicizing models for popular emulation. In China, that includes governments on both the right and the left of the political spectrum. Nevertheless, the left has tended to emphasize campaigns to a far greater extent because of its preference for ideological indoctrination. This preference applies to pollution control as well as other policy sectors.

The campaign response to the discovery of pollution as a serious problem was to stress political indoctrination in order to alter behavior in the desired direction. Enterprises were exhorted to collect and recycle the "three wastes" (liquids, gases, and solids, or slag). These otherwise useless wastes would then be dialectically transformed into useful by-products (Gao Fengxiang 1973, Zheng Xiaojing 1973). In keeping with the campaign bias toward normative incentives, enterprises were urged to engage in pollution control without regard for profit or other material compensation (JPRS 81737 WWEQ 367, Sept. 10, 1982: 29). Enterprises that did well in this regard were then praised as models for others to emulate. For example, a paper mill in Jilin was widely praised for recycling on a self-reliant basis (Gao Fengxiang 1973). Similarly, a forest products plant after undergoing arduous line struggle was reportedly able to double its materials utilization rate by converting residues into artificial board (Yu Hong 1970). Models like these were of particular relevance to a country struggling to overcome persistent shortages of materials.

The fact that some enterprises subordinated their immediate interests to the interests of the larger community was presented as proof of the superiority of socialism as manifested in struggle with capitalism. At the height of Cultural Revolution anti-intellectualism, it was even argued that line struggle was conducive to recycling and that the masses could solve their pollution problems without expert advice or outside funds (Guo Huan 1974a).*

The campaign strategy thus amounted to a politically inspired effort to promote altruism among those responsible for enterprise administration, with *altruism* defined as "a willingness to act in consideration of the interests of other persons, without the need of ulterior motives" (Nagel 1970: 79). In practice, the campaign strategy proved woefully inadequate. Although there must have been exceptions, state enterprises were generally unwilling to subordinate their direct interests in fulfilling production plans to the vague need to reduce pollution.

The clearest evidence in this regard lies in the country's very low recycling rates. As noted in chapters 2 and 3, industrial recycling rates for wastewater and forest products residues are distressingly low. Yet they appear to be typical rather than exceptional. For the economy as a whole, the recycling rate was only 20 percent in 1980 despite official expressions of dismay (Li Jinchang 1984b: 4). The discussion by Kinzelbach (1981: 6–7) on this point deserves quotation in full because of his personal experience working on environmental management in China.

> There is a general belief that China offers a good example as far as the recycling of wastes is concerned. This may be true for human and animal feces. It is certainly not true for most industrial wastes. One example of an industrial bulk waste is coal ash. About 15 million tons of ash are annually discharged into rivers. Only 15 percent of the total amount created by industry and power plants is made use of. In West Germany the percentage is almost 5 times higher.
>
> Without disqualifying the recycling and reuse of feces, waste paper, orange peels, or bones I daresay that they originate from necessity due to the general shortages rather than from environmental consciousness and whether they will prevail once those shortages vanish is hard to say.
>
> As the technical ability for recycling of industrial wastes will increase, the desirability of the recycling of human wastes will decrease. One reason is

---

Line struggle nominally refers to a conflict between ideologically based and internally consistent policy doctrines that can split society from top to bottom, as in struggle between the "capitalist road" and the "socialist road." As Dittmer (1977) argued, line struggle actually consists of policy differences that widen in the course of a struggle for power and only acquire the label of line struggle when one of the leadership contestants seeks to enhance his position by dramatizing the issue to a wider audience, so that it becomes intelligible to lower-level officials and, if necessary, the mass public.

the growing application of persistent pesticides which will be recycled to-gether with the feces. Another is the mixing of industrial waste waters with human waste waters. The sludge from one of Shanghai's municipal waste water treatment plants which used to be taken away as manure formerly is no longer in demand as the growing admixture of industrial wastewater increases the poisonous residues in the sludge. The composition of house-hold garbage in Peking is changing too. Formerly it contained practically only ashes and organic waste from food preparation (cabbage leaves, etc.). Now the paper component is growing and the garbage is no longer of large interest as soil conditioner to the farmers of the south.

The neglect of recycling was not a function of the chaos in industrial administration that arose during the Cultural Revolution but rather is due primarily to the subordination of environmental considerations to output and other norms established within the planning process. No amount of exhortation could be expected to prevail in the face of a planning process instituted with little regard for factors extrinsic to production itself, es-pecially because campaigns are cyclical. Thus, recycling suffers a loss of emphasis whenever competing campaigns to fulfill production norms, con-serve energy, or police the grounds are under way (GR, June 7, 1980). Thus, voluntary recycling in China as in the United States (Baumol and Oates 1979: 284–87 and 306), is unlikely to exert more than a modest impact on a massive and growing problem.

Recycling could acquire a continuing stimulus by raising prices for scrap products to complement the strongly normative and ascetic thrust of cam-paigns. But recycling has actually been impeded by low prices, the absence of a competitive scrap market, and a lack of investment in recycling tech-nology (Weisskopf 1983), with the result that large volumes of reusable materials have simply been discarded, while new materials and machinery are also poorly cared for.

The campaign strategy was also subject to another fundamental defi-ciency. By placing virtually exclusive reliance on recycling, it ignored the prospects for reducing the volume and toxicity of residuals through changes in technology. Conversion to purer or alternative raw materials and redesign of the production process can usually raise efficiency and reduce the volume of residuals more effectively than recycling. Meanwhile, the remaining residuals may well be more amenable to reuse (Zhao Zongliu 1981). This is particularly serious since up to half the volume of residuals has been attributed to resource and energy waste (Qu Geping 1983). How-ever, campaigns are blunt instruments that tend to focus on simple, uniform targets such as the volume of trash collected rather than on complex, diffuse tasks such as technological innovation (RR, July 26, 1979). Therefore cam-paigns are ill suited for the more demanding work of pollution control.

That does not mean that campaigns have no role to play. They are in-expensive instruments that rely to a large degree on unpaid, low-skilled labor. They are particularly appropriate for controlling litter, traffic noise, and similar forms of pollution that originate among millions upon millions of individuals who are too numerous for society to monitor yet not very susceptible to material incentives. Social pressure and community pride can and should be enhanced to encourage private and public cleanups.

Even campaigns of this sort, however, are often merely vehicles for broader political purposes that can deflect attention from the substantive goals involved. For example, beautification and environmental protection were among the "five stresses and four points of beautification" included in a campaign that began in 1980. This campaign was part of a broader effort by conservative elites to halt or at least slow down the reform process, which was a threat to their power. Acting in the name of building a Socialist Spiritual Civilization, the conservatives led by Deng Liqun and Hu Qiaomu tried but largely failed to win the full backing of Deng Xiaoping and, as a result, the reforms continued despite several interruptions (Gold 1984, Dirlik 1982). This campaign exemplified problems that arise whenever environmental protection or any other ongoing policy is swept up in the maelstrom of a political or ideological campaign. Technical considerations are shunted aside in the quest for immediate results, apathy and cynicism develop among the populace at large when they see public affairs being manipulated for partisan purposes, and paralysis can set in if the leadership splits over the campaign's goals and intensity.

Bureaucratic-Authoritative Implementation

Operating within a planned economy yet suddenly aware of the severity of pollution, many policymakers stressed improving the planning process as the key to improving the environment. They recognized that pollution is due in large part to the perverse emphasis within the planning process on increasing physical output to the virtual exclusion of all other considerations. They argued that the real superiority of socialism would manifest itself only after the planning process had been broadened to incorporate environmental protection as a goal. In this respect, the command and control features of centralized planning were considered both readily adaptable and essential to pollution control, since the problem was defined in terms of individual decision makers following inappropriate cues and overproducing residuals or waste products. More comprehensive instructions were needed to guide enterprise managers and other decision makers on a course of economic expansion without sacrificing environmental quality.

The case for central planning was cogently presented by McIntyre and Thornton (1978a). They argued that pollution control requires the maximization of information flows to the decision-making center so that environmental and economic factors can be considered simultaneously. Only central planning has this feature. They also stressed that the hierarchical administrative system found in such countries as the Soviet Union is conducive to the effective enforcement of what are likely to be more comprehensive policies.

McIntyre and Thornton err, however, in assuming that information itself is not subject to distortion and withholding. Because officials manipulate information to enhance their own interests, the quality of information tends to be worse rather than better under central planning in comparison with a more pluralistic system (Ziegler 1980). McIntyre and Thornton similarly exaggerate the capacity of decision makers to consider a broad range of alternatives before acting (Braybrooke and Lindblom 1963, Etzioni 1967). Although centralized supply of services may be environmentally as well as economically superior in the case of public utilities, for example, this superiority is a function of the goods in question rather than the general properties of the system (Williamson 1975).

Because Chinese policymakers were ideologically predisposed to welcome planning, they naturally favored planning or bureaucratic instruments in the environmental protection sector as well. This political bias was reinforced by the worldwide predominance of a direct controls approach to environmental regulation at the time even in market systems, not solely because of its merit but also because of the prevailing logic that problems arising from market failure require nonmarket solutions. In the United States, regulation tended to stress the imposition of mandatory emission controls and often the installation of particular technologies to lower pollution levels, e.g., New Source Performance and Best Available Technology standards, which regulators enforced through their power to approve construction projects or to impose shutdowns and fines. Meanwhile, the government stepped up the treatment of remaining pollutants by increasing the capacity of publicly operated or licensed facilities such as sewage treatment plants and landfills.

Direct controls are often more politically popular because they offer the appearance of strict enforcement. They also gain bureaucratic support by enlarging the budgets of regulatory agencies involved in implementation. Substantively, technological controls may be easier to administer because the regulators only have to observe design, procurement, and installation rather than the performance of industrial facilities. Although public opinion exerts only marginal influence in Chinese politics, bureaucratic backing is an important consideration, as is the central government's recurrent struggle to keep the lid on capital construction. Direct controls offer advantages in all these respects.

China's first set of environmental standards, "Provisional Public Health Standards for the Design of Industrial Enterprises (101–56)," copied Soviet industrial hygiene standards of the 1950s. They were refined and formally issued in 1962 (GBJ 1–62) by the Ministry of Public Health during a period of bureaucratic regularization as part of a package of health-related measures. A remarkably large number of substances were included, ranging from criteria pollutants such as sulfur dioxide and carbon monoxide to emissions of man-made chemicals such as benzene and turpentine. The standards for air quality, however, affected only the work places and residences and not the broader environment as would befit an industrial health measure. Nevertheless, the water quality standards governed sewage effluent and also to some extent ambient surface water quality (JPRS 49725, *Translations on Communist China* 88, Jan. 30, 1970: 13–24). However, officials later reported that these standards were widely ignored with impunity.

A second set of standards (GBJ 4–73, "Provisional Regulations Governing the Discharge of the Three Wastes By Industry," reprinted in Guo Li'ai 1985: 117–28) was issued in 1973 shortly after the First National Environmental Protection Work Conference. These regulations defined multiple sets of emissions ceilings for each industry without clearly indicating which one would apply. They failed to prescribe sanctions and were frequently disregarded, although that was due in part to the post–Cultural Revolution disorder, which still paralyzed the central government.

Regulation in most respects did not commence until the late 1970s, after Mao's death, when there was broader appreciation of the fact that the lack of laws and regulations had implicitly legitimized pollution. The first major move in this regard was based in technology. In late 1978, 167 leading industrial enterprises were ordered by the State Planning Commission, the State Economic Commission, and the Environmental Protection Leading Group to take pollution control measures by 1982 or risk shutdown (ZBN 1980: 564; PR, Nov. 24, 1978: 31). This measure subsequently was extended to all construction projects built under state or local plans (FBIS, Nov. 6, 1980: L2). Environmental impact statements or reports—but not true assessments—were subsequently required before construction was permitted to proceed (ZRGGYG 360, Aug. 30, 1981: 407–11.)

In practice, the precise nature of the measures deemed acceptable was not clearly defined and there seems to have been no genuine prospect of closing or relocating such major enterprises as the Baotou Iron and Steel Company in Inner Mongolia, the Shenyang Smelter, the Capital Iron and Steel Company in Beijing, or the Daqing General Petrochemical Works because of noncompliance. These major polluters were instead targeted for pollution cleanups. Initial progress was said to be halting (Yu Guang-yuan 1980), in part because of a lack of funds, but compliance improved once the state provided subsidies to finance technological retrofitting. By 1983 over 80 percent of large and medium-sized enterprises were said to be in compliance, including all twenty-eight targeted enterprises in the petroleum industry and three-quarters of those in the metallurgical industry, particularly the giant Anshan complex in Liaoning (BR, Oct. 4, 1982: 7–8; HB, Dec. 1983: 2; FBIS, Sept. 15, 1980: L14–15; Zhao Zongliu 1981; JPRS 84521 CST 209, Oct. 12, 1983: 267–68). Small polluters, by contrast, were relocated away from major downtown areas in large numbers.

It is important to note that the first targets of regulation were major industries, suggesting that their economic importance did not exempt them from external influence. That was true in Shenyang, Hunan, and elsewhere (JPRS 84521 CST 209, Oct. 12, 1983: 274–75), although many small polluters such as electroplating workshops also were targets of crackdowns (JPRS 83010 WWEQ 388, Mar. 4, 1983: 168). Larger enterprises may be easier to regulate despite their greater economic importance because political supervision and the planning process are more effective with regard to a few concentrated industries than to many small firms.

In addition, although the directive did not explicitly distinguish between new and existing sources of pollution, an accompanying directive issued jointly with the State Capital Construction Commission focused on new construction or renovation projects. This latter directive publicized what became known as the "three simultaneous points," i.e., no project would be approved unless an environmental study had been conducted and the prescribed measures taken in each of three stages: design, construction, and operation (PR, Nov. 24, 1978: 31). A similar requirement had been incorporated into the 1973 standards (article 4) but had been widely disregarded. This provision was subsequently formalized in the State Planning Commission's "Circular on the Strict Implementation of the Three Simultaneous Points in Capital Construction and Technological Renovation Projects" of 1981. It required the preparation and approval of an environmental assessment and inclusion of funding for environmental protection in all reports and preliminary designs (Ross and Silk 1987).

The focus on new construction rather than older facilities represented an effort to concentrate pollution control on facilities where improvements could be installed more easily and uniformly. It was soon extended to expansion and renovation projects at existing factories by the State Council in "Some Regulations on Integrating Technological Renovation with the Prevention and Control of Industrial Pollution" (Central Directive 20, 1983; Ministry of Urban and Rural Construction 1983). It also amounted to recognition that the government's leverage, though far from absolute, was greatest over new construction, through control over land acquisition permits, construction permits, and especially capital funding. At a minimum, these regulations made it illegal to contemplate the acquisition of new technology on a stripped-down basis by omitting pollution controls.

The Environmental Protection Law issued in 1979 (for trial implementation) provided the authority for the two directives noted above and also authorized the issuance of pollution control standards. Shortly thereafter, the Environmental Protection Bureau and the Ministry of Public Health issued a host of ambient air and water standards that had been waiting on the shelf until the law was approved. The 1979 standards (TJ 36–79, "Public Health Standards for the Design of Industrial Enterprises," in Guo Li'ai

1985: 72–105) were still classified as public health measures but were considerably more comprehensive and stringent than their predecessors. These standards specified the maximum allowable concentrations of specific hazardous substances on both a single-event and 24-hour daily average basis. For example, the maximum allowable concentrations for carbon monoxide in the atmosphere in residential areas are three milligrams per cubic meter in any thirty-minute period and one milligram per cubic meter on a twenty-four-hour average. The comparable levels for sulfur dioxide are 0.50 milligrams and 0.15 milligrams per cubic meter, respectively. In other cases only one standard was issued, e.g., only a thirty-minute maximum was set for oxides of nitrogen. Similar standards were published for surface water. These standards generally were similar to their counterparts in industrialized countries.

The 1979 standards were superseded by a host of more elaborate standards beginning in 1982. The newer standards were first issued under the exclusive imprimatur of the State Council Environmental Protection Leading Group and later, after its formation, by the Ministry of Urban and Rural Construction and Environmental Protection. These standards exhibited a more professional and environmentally oriented cast than the older public-health-based standards, although in many instances the values themselves remained unchanged.

The standards are regional and not uniform for the entire country. In terms of air quality, the most stringent standards apply to class I areas, which are nature preserves and similar areas of relatively pristine quality. Class II areas include most of the country, while class III areas are heavily polluted urban and industrial areas (table 18). Although these standards appear to condemn the most polluted industrial areas to higher levels of pollution than the rest of the country, in practice they approximate the three-class system found elsewhere, with values falling between those of the Soviet Union and the United States. In fact, class I is stronger than in the United States, although class III is far weaker (table 19). These standards take account of the highly uneven economic burden of meeting air quality goals, so that only the most pristine and economically least important areas should be expected to meet the highest ambient standards.* They may even expedite air pollution control by facilitating the construction of newer and cleaner plants that will allow older facilities to be closed down

---

*The standards are expressed in terms of units of mass per unit volume air or water. Because air and water density vary by altitude, more stringent standards may be needed in high-altitude areas. That suggests a need for vertical as well as horizontal differences in standards, which may most easily be accomplished by reformulating standards according to parts per million, a purely volumetric measure. A similar regulatory scheme for water pollution control based on each stream's self-assimilative capacity will also be introduced to minimize the need for costly water treatment plants (Wang Baozhen 1984; GR, Jan. 25, 1986). Water pollution discharge standards are still inadequate, however, in part because they continue to emphasize the concentration or density of discharges to the exclusion of their mass.

Table 18

China's Ambient Air Quality Standards (mg/m^3)

Pollutant	Averaging Time	Class I	Class II	Class III
Total suspended particulates	24 hours	0.15	0.30	0.50
	Single event	0.30	1.00	1.50
Fly ash	24 hours	0.05	0.15	0.25
	Single event	0.15	0.50	0.70
SO2	Annual (arithmetic mean)	0.02	0.06	0.10
	24 hours	0.05	0.15	0.25
	Single event	0.15	0.50	0.70
NO_x	24 hours	0.05	0.10	0.15
	Single event	0.10	0.15	0.30
CO	24 hours	4.00	4.00	6.00
	Single event	10.00	10.00	10.00
Photochemical oxidants (O_3)	1 hour	0.12	0.16	0.20

SOURCE: <u>Ambient Air Quality Standards</u> GB 3095-82.

Table 19

U.S. Ambient Standards and Allowable PSD Increments ($\mu g/m^3$)

		Controlling NAAQS	Allowable PSD Increments		
			Class I	Class II	Class III
SO2	Annual	80	2	20	40
	24-hour	365	5	91	182
	3-hour	1,300	25	512	700
TSP	Annual	75	5	19	37
	24-hour	150	10	37	75

NOTE: 24-hour and 3-hour standards are not to be exceeded more than once a year. NAAQS = National Ambient Air Quality Standards (maximum allowable pollution concentrations). PSD = Prevention of Significant Deterioration increments that are designed to give extra protection to airsheds already in compliance with NAAQS.

faster than would be possible if plants in all parts of the country were held to the same very high standards.*

Several aspects of the standard-setting process are worth noting. Most obvious is the speed with which the standards were adopted. A process that would have taken years in the United States, where extensive opportunity is provided for public comment, took hardly any time at all in China. That was due largely to the lack of opportunity for political participation but also can be explained in terms of a phenomenon that appears to operate with regard to regulation as well as economic development: a late developing country can close the gap in regulation by emulating standards already set in advanced countries. That not only eases the standard-setting burden for developing countries but also legitimizes the regulatory agencies' mission. Usually small and lacking in political influence, regulatory agencies often find themselves hard pressed to win an audience for their concerns. The availability of internationally recognized standards helps them to persuade their country's leadership that environmental protection, or any other form of regulation, is simply a part of modern nationhood. China's adoption of international standards in this regard became official upon the promulgation of the "Procedures for the Management of Environmental Protection Standards" on October 11, 1983, over the objections of some industries (Li Zhangong 1984).

For the time being, there is no explicit link in China between emissions by individual polluters and the attainment of the designated ambient standards. The first ambient air or water quality models are only now being developed to analyze the effects of individual sources and to predict the effects of changes in emission levels. More importantly, for quite some time there was no real permit process for the Environmental Protection Bureau to regulate discharges and then penalize violators by suspending their operating permits when discharge limits were exceeded. Until the Marine Environmental Protection Law and the Water Pollution Prevention and Control Law were passed in 1983 and 1984, respectively, there was no way to keep track of all pollution sources. Consequently, only the largest or most visible polluters were subject to ongoing regulation (Shen Xin 1984). When we also consider that enforcement mechanisms were geared to emission levels rather than to changes in ambient quality, it becomes apparent that the ambient standards had little significance beyond serving as a benchmark to evaluate environmental quality and justify tighter emissions controls in most cities.

Ambient standards will remain a peripheral factor at least until networks of monitoring stations are in place around the country and analytical ca-

---

*Older facilities, however, are still closed down less frequently than they deserve to be no matter how outmoded they are because of low depreciation schedules and a complex web of employment and social obligations that restricts the freedom of regulators as well as enterprises.

pabilities are enhanced. Impressive progress is reported, with some 10,000 monitoring stations in place and 100,000 personnel involved in all phases of pollution control work, but the system remains far from complete (JPRS 82926 WWEQ 387, Feb. 25, 1983: 4, and 84521 CST 209, Oct. 21, 1983: 36–37). In the interim reliance must be placed on emission standards alone. They are simpler to administer but bear no direct relationship to ambient quality, particularly when economic growth results in an increase in the number of polluters. Emission standards also create new complexities and inequities of their own as separate standards must be calculated for each industry and even individual plants (GB 3544-3553-83, 4274-4283-84, and 4286-4287-84, "Emission Standards for Pollutants From Industry").

Nevertheless, stringently enforced emissions guidelines can be expected to produce demonstrable improvements. In this respect the Chinese authorities have continued to reiterate the "three simultaneous points," as in the State Council's "Decision on Strengthening Environmental Protection Work in the Period of National Readjustment" (JPRS 84521 CST 209, Oct. 21, 1983: 36–37; State Council 1981). Moreover, new source performance standards contain some welcome flexibility. For example, power plants burning low-sulfur coal are not required to satisfy the same sulfur dioxide removal criteria as plants that burn high-sulfur coal, although formal standards have yet to be issued in this case (Zheng and Salib 1982: 122). By contrast, their American counterparts are expected to satisfy more uniform sulfur removal criteria as part of a congressional compromise to win over both environmentalists and states with high-sulfur coal mining (Crandall 1983). This difference may reflect the fact that regional interests are less capable of affecting national policy in China, where there is also less economic mobility.

The enforcement of emission or performance standards has not gone smoothly. The primary problem was that standards as well as all other criteria for environmental protection remained outside the state plan. Industrial polluters, when faced with a conflict between their production norms and external regulations, emphasized the former. Although environmental protection departments in principle had the authority of the law behind them, in practice their mandate was highly ambiguous, especially while the new laws and regulations remained in the vague state of "for trial use," which was sometimes interpreted to mean that compliance was a matter of convenience rather than a legal obligation (Chen Ren 1984).

Coupled with the weakness of the procuratorial and judicial institutions, that left the environmental protection bureaus without independent recourse in the event of noncompliance. Instead, if they elected to pursue violations, they were forced to appeal for support from the local political leadership or, failing that, to seek favorable press coverage. For example, Wu Songmei, an environmental engineer and National People's Congress deputy, went public in a *People's Daily* interview to complain about a lack of support from local officials and other bureaucracies (RR, May 31, 1984).

In other cases even hundreds of letters to the press (which serves a quasi-ombudsman function) failed to bring relief (JPRS 84521 CST 209, Oct. 12, 1983: 145–46).

Because of the chancy prospects for outside support, the environmental protection sector argued in favor of making specific provisions for environmental protection in the state plan. Li Chaobo, head of the Leading Group on Environmental Protection, endorsed this point at a 1979 conference on environmental protection work, and he and others repeated this call on many occasions thereafter (Li Chaobo 1979, Zhou Fuyang 1982, Gao Yusheng 1981). Environmental protection was included in development plans for the first time in 1979 when the city of Shenyang prepared a municipal environmental protection plan for 1980–85. Shenyang is a center for heavy industry and had been serving as a test case, or experimental point, for the entire country with regard to pollution control since 1972 (*Huanjing Guanli*, January 1984: 3–12).

Following the introduction of urban planning in 1979, environmental protection began to be included in municipal development plans, beginning with eighteen key-point cities. Beijing, the national capital, was newly designated a cultural city. Rather than continue to concentrate on heavy industry, the city was now called on to enhance its quality of life to serve as a national cultural showplace (Tao Zhenni 1982). The Beijing cleanup really took shape in 1984 with the approval of twelve major projects, including factory relocation (*Summary of World Broadcasts* W1280/A/5, Mar. 28, 1984). Hangzhou, Suzhou, and Guilin were similarly ordered to emphasize their cultural and tourist appeal (FBIS, Sept. 14, 1983: O6). That resulted in the compulsory pollution abatement, shutdown, or relocation of many industrial establishments, particularly small shops involved in dirty technologies such as electroplating that release heavy metals and acids into waterways. Even major cities with less famous cultural heritages are following suit through zoning and other administrative controls. This focus on improving the quality of life in urban areas represents a direct reversal of the long-standing Maoist bias against the nonproductive, "parasitic" cultural and service character of cities (Special Commentator 1984, Mao Zedong 1949: 365).

Far more critical is the incorporation of environmental protection, including pollution control, as a specific chapter in the state plan. As the minister of urban and rural construction and environmental protection explained at the Second National Environmental Protection Work Conference (Li Yangming 1984, Special Commentator 1984), inclusion in the plan largely assures that specified assets will be allocated to environmental protection and increases the pressure on economic ministries and enterprises to comply with regulations that function as production constraints. Such inclusion occurred for the first time in the Sixth Five-Year Plan 1981–85, which was not finalized until the end of 1982. The fact that environmental protection was listed only as chapter 35 in a 36-chapter document is an indicator of its continued subordination to agriculture, industry, and the rest of the economy (BR, May 30, 1983: XVI). Nonetheless, environmental protection's place clearly is higher in the Sixth Plan than it was in its predecessors and the short-lived Ten-Year Plan (1976–85) that was drafted in 1975 and released in 1978 in the initial modernizing fervor at the end of the Maoist era (Yu Guangyuan 1980; ZRGGYG, October 1982: 467–68). These earlier plans gave virtually no attention to pollution control in their haste to expand the country's economy, primarily through heavy industry.

Although pollution control still faces an uphill battle, further gains are promised in the Seventh Plan, the first five-year plan to formally include social development alongside economic development. The plan's goals include a 30 percent reduction in urban airborne dust levels and a rise of nearly 150 percent in the number of houses served by central heating (JR, July 4, 1986; CD, May 27, 1986).

An essential accompaniment to the enhanced status of environmental regulation in the state plan is the construction of new pollution treatment facilities and other infrastructural elements. For many years treatment capacity was terribly neglected, with the result that less than 10 percent of industrial effluent received even primary treatment before discharge and most urban households are not yet connected to overloaded central collection and treatment facilities (FBIS, Dec. 16, 1982: K6–7).

More aggressive support for pollution control is turning the situation around, although there still is a long way to go. By 1983 industrial wastewater treatment was able to handle 17 percent of the effluent volume, well short of the 1985 target of 25 percent but a marked improvement nevertheless. Every year an additional 27.5 million tons of wastewater treatment capacity is being added (ibid.; HB, December 1983: 2). Xi'an, Guangzhou, and other major cities recently have added substantial new treatment facilities and more are planned.

Seen in this light, it is apparent that regulation, planning, and bureaucratic supply are vital policy instruments. In many instances, including centralized wastewater treatment facilities, they are indispensable. Although planning undertaken without regard for environmental quality gravely aggravated pollution control, improved planning and centralized directives can exert a strongly beneficial impact by setting more comprehensive goals and committing the resources needed to achieve them.

Nevertheless, there are several reasons why the bureaucratic-authoritative approach produces suboptimal solutions. Although technology or engineering standards often are the most attractive choice from an administrative perspective, they tend to be the most expensive in terms of investment—a serious problem in a capital-poor economy. Therefore, Qu Geping, head of the Environmental Protection Bureau, has said that other approaches in general must be favored over technology standards during the readjustment period (Qu Geping 1982). Moreover, technology standards are extremely demanding in terms of design and prescription because they require separate provisions for each industry and sometimes each plant. Such knowledge can only be acquired at great expense. The consequence of reliance on prescriptive technologies is likely to be long delays in the issuance of standards that are often outmoded by the time they are issued.

Technological requirements also suffer from other drawbacks. The imposition of uniform technologies despite substantial variation in ambient conditions, e.g., upstream vs. downstream or deepwater vs. shallow water polluters, imposes higher costs on the economy. Reliance on technology standards also displaces the locus of regulation from the emissions themselves to emission control devices, virtually legalizing pollution in the event of breakdowns or faulty operation of the control equipment. Even in a highly industrialized country there is a high incidence of downtime because of breakdowns, cold starts, and faulty operation during which the level of emissions rises (Crandall and Portney 1984). The problem is more severe in China, where preventive maintenance is a novel concept and complaints are frequently voiced that expensive pollution control equipment is left unused while factories remain in operation (Liu Wen 1980: 72–75). One survey of 6,000 factory wastewater treatment facilities installed since the 1970s found that they averaged only a 60 percent operating rate and 50 percent effectiveness (Chen Youxiang and Xu Gangxi 1986).

Emission standards are somewhat more flexible because they focus on discharges per se rather than on the design of specific technologies. They tend, however, to be applied most stringently to new facilities. Although this bias may be preferable from an engineering perspective, it raises the cost of new plants. That can delay the introduction of newer, often more efficient production processes, with the paradoxical effect of extending the life of older, less productive, and more polluting factories (Lave and Omenn 1981).

Although a well-constructed regulatory approach can work effectively, emission standards also suffer from other serious limitations. They tend to be applied uniformly to all polluters without regard for differences in their cost structures. Meanwhile, polluters have no incentive to reduce their emissions below the maximum allowable ceiling. The result is that low-cost polluters tend to pollute up to the maximum emissions limit while high-cost polluters face severe economic difficulty satisfying the standards. Thus, even if the socially desired level of pollution is attained, the cost of attainment is likely to be unnecessarily high.

A regulatory approach also tends to generate politically related enforcement problems. In the United States, industries that are most affected by the standards use political pressure and judicial maneuvers to delay or avoid regulation (Anderson et al. 1977). The absence of electoral competition and procedural due process might at first appear to rule out such strategems in China, and indeed regulations when reinforced by strong political backing from higher levels can result in prompt compliance by polluters. For example, numerous factories and workshops were ordered closed in 1982 by Guilin, a noted tourist attraction (FBIS, Sept. 15, 1980: L21). Nanjing claimed major improvements in 1975–82 thanks to pollution control investments totaling 150 million yuan, much of which was recovered through stepped-up recycling. Nanjing attributed its accomplishments to greatly increased political support and stiff enforcement, with over 7,000 polluters ordered to pay fines or suffer other penalties in 1982 alone, although the problem remained severe (H, Feb. 1984: 20–21). But even senior Vice-Premier Wan Li has acknowledged that for the most part enterprises respond only to shutdown threats, which local governments and economic decision makers are reluctant to make (Wan Li 1983).

Moreover, the political morality of regulation is somewhat ambiguous because regulatees claim that they too are acting in the national interest by increasing production. That in turn legitimizes evasion and delay (BR, Jan. 4, 1982: 26). Most enterprises are not yet governed by environmental protection norms; nor do they assemble data on their performance in this regard. That makes it difficult to operationalize state plans down to the local and enterprise levels (HB 1984: 2–4; FBIS, Dec. 17, 1981: K12–13). Even where enterprise plans include pollution control, the criteria to evaluate pollution are less clear and more uncertain in their effects than the physical production indicators used to evaluate the economic side of enterprise performance. In any event, pollution control standards tend to be subordinated to output norms by the parent ministries and enterprises alike, as is the case in Eastern Europe, where only output or profit performance results in tangible rewards (NYT, Sept. 12, 1982).

To the extent that economic output is measured in monetary rather than physical terms, pollution control is hampered by the fact that the standard economic yardstick, the gross value of output, not only fails to incorporate environmental protection but also tolerates waste, which is incorporated in product value (JPRS 84374 CEA 384, Sept. 21, 1983: 99–109). Moreover, the planning process tends to focus on a limited number of indicators, resulting in such economic distortions as making producer and consumer goods in only a narrow range of varieties to ease the burden of the producer regardless of consumer demand. It is also a problem for pollution control because it may be possible to meet particular standards by transforming residuals into different but no less dangerous forms or at the cost of increasing other pollutants.

Chinese analysts recognize that their failure to develop clear norms for pollution control provides enterprises and lower-level officials with the opportunity to conduct business as usual. Therefore, several efforts are under way to improve planning targets and to develop indicators of environmental quality (GR, July 21, 1984). For example, Li Jinchang (1984b), of the Technical Economics Research Center under the State Council, proposed that a set of quality-of-life or social indicators be constructed. This work is supported by Ma Hong, a leading party theoretician. Under the "three live-lihoods" *(san sheng)* principle, environmental protection and social welfare would receive official consideration alongside economic production for the first time, although the latter still would enjoy greater proportional weight: 0.4 for production, 0.3 for social welfare, and 0.3 for ecology.

The difficulty involved in meshing regulation with a planning regimen is apparent even in Li Jinchang's admirable exercise (table 20). His environmental quality indicators seem to be chosen not because of their intrinsic nature but because they are measurable and satisfy important political constituencies. Forest cover presumably ranks highest because of its accustomed status as an environmental value even though it is only tangentially related to human health, unjustifiably elevates one form of land use above all others, including grasslands and erosion-resistant farming, and is at best only a crude measure of the state of forest resources. Recycling similarly is an indicator of questionable value; it lumps together toxic and nontoxic waste products, and thus a high score can be attained even if small volumes of extremely dangerous residuals are discharged or if the recycled products themselves are contaminated by toxics. Both the recycling and industrial wastewater treatment rates continue the unwise emphasis on treatment of residuals after the production process has been completed, a practice that fails to provide any incentive to minimize the volume of discharges. Mean-

Table 20

Proposed Environmental Indicators

Indicator	Weight (%)	1980 (%)	1981 (%)	1982 (%)	2000 (%)
Forest cover	0.30	12.7	12.7	12.5	20
Cities in attainment of ambient sulfur dioxide atmospheric standard	0.15	75.0	78.0	80.0	100
Cities in attainment of ambient suspended particulates standard	0.15	15.0	17.0	13.0	80
Industrial wastewater treatment rate	0.20	14.0	15.0	17.0	76
Comprehensive utilization of residuals	20.00	20.0	22.0	24.0	60
Index Value	1.00	1.00	1.06	1.07	3.16

SOURCE: Li Jinchang 1984b.

while, only two criteria pollutants, sulfur dioxide and suspended particulates, are included in the ambient air quality measure, while none at all are specified for ambient water quality. Other indices of environmental quality in addition to Li's are being urgently developed, but they too are prone to inconsistencies and operational shortcomings.

Yet another problem concerns enforcement. Violation of regulatory standards can result in fines or orders to curtail operations, relocate, or even close down. However, these sanctions are blunt instruments that are not easily calibrated to the offense. Fines can be treated as simply an expense of doing business, although they are in principle not to be included in an enterprise's costs of production. Although more severe fines and sanctions can be imposed (FBIS, Aug. 19, 1980: L11–12), politically favored polluters can ignore them (Liu Wen 1980). To cite one example, a shutdown order issued to a fireproofing products plant in Jiaojiang City went unenforced because of the municipal government's opposition, resulting in an angry letter to the editor by an environmental engineer who was concurrently a deputy to the provincial people's congress (RR, May 31, 1984). Conscious of their political vulnerability, environmental protection officials often simply ignore persistent violations rather than run the political gauntlet that springs up when regulatory actions are threatened (RR, May 31, 1984).

Market-Exchange Implementation

To what extent do market methods provide a suitable alternative to bureaucratic controls? The market approach also involves the regulation of pollution, but the process is indirect. It is a decentralized form of implementation that makes an explicit appeal to self-interest while reducing the day-to-day involvement of politicians.

There are two basic types of market or economic instruments for pollution control policy: effluent charges and pollution markets. Like the bureaucratic approach, they require the setting of ambient environmental quality goals and the monitoring of emissions. Both are predicated on the assumption that the polluter is behaving rationally by releasing untreated effluent into the air and water when such action costs less than reducing or treating his discharges. As one Chinese resource economist explained, industry will continue to discharge its effluent untreated so long as water amounts to no more than 1 or 2 percent of its production costs despite widespread freshwater shortages, making it cheaper to use more water than to recycle the effluent. Meanwhile, low or even zero sewage treatment charges contribute to the further overload of already inadequate municipal treatment facilities. Thus, it is not surprising that over 30,000 reservoirs are considered seriously polluted (Chen Huaizhi 1982).

Charges or emission fees discourage such behavior by introducing taxes or fees that are based on how much of the environment's assimilative capacity a polluter consumes, i.e., the polluter pays for the damage he causes.

The purpose is to alter management incentives in the direction of behavior that takes into account the environment or the public without sacrificing the efficiency of the market. Thus, a polluter's charges decline when he reduces his pollution and conversely rise when pollution increases.

Government must establish and enforce these charges as agent for the commons because no natural markets for pollution exist. The monitoring requirements are substantial but do not exceed those required by the bureaucratic approach. In general, the level of charges is set in order to achieve a desired ambient quality. Polluters then know in advance what their charges will be. To the extent that the charges equalize the polluter's marginal costs of reducing his discharges and the marginal social costs of pollution, an efficient solution will emerge. In practice, as Rose-Ackerman (1977) and Russell (1979) argue, a uniform set of charges cannot be expected to achieve a socially optimal solution when polluters have different cost structures. Although it is theoretically possible to adjust charges for each polluter, in practice this is neither technically nor politically possible.

Nevertheless, any well-designed charge system promotes innovation among polluters. It converts regulatory standards into readily comprehensible monetary costs, thus encouraging polluters to lower their costs by reducing their discharges. It differentiates among polluters so that industries with higher treatment costs make smaller cuts in pollution than those with lower costs; pollution thus can be reduced at a lower overall cost to society than under uniform regulatory standards. Moreover, the revenues obtained can be earmarked for pollution control or other environmental protection programs, putting into practice the "polluter pays" principle of economic equity and diminishing the need for general fiscal obligations by government.

Since effluent charges have encountered indifference and outright opposition from businesses afraid of higher costs as well as skeptical environmentalists and legislators even in a market economy such as the United States (Kelman 1981), China's reception might be expected to be completely hostile. Indeed, a few Chinese economists have publicly expressed unease that the de-emphasis on planning inherent in modern environmental economics leads to a perverse encouragement of selfishness, although they have not been able to present a theoretically consistent Marxist alternative (Li Kaiwang 1984).

In actuality, the loosening of ideological shackles since 1978 has led to surprising support for effluent charges. Many economists and environmental specialists conversant with the Western literature used the post-Mao liberalization to explain and promote the application of charges in China. Their case was based not only on the promised environmental benefits but also on the prospects for greater economic efficiency (Wang Weimin 1980), which is highly valued by reformers and to some extent even by the more conservative readjusters in the leadership.

The first major event in this regard was a conference on environmental management, economics, and jurisprudence held in Taiyuan in February 1980. Yu Guangyuan, a party theoretician sympathetic to the reforms presided. He stressed not only that economics and environmental quality were intimately related but also that it would no longer do to simply wait for socialism to automatically demonstrate its superiority over capitalism in either sector. Indeed, Yu pointedly noted that Japan and some other capitalist countries actually had lower levels of pollution than China despite much higher levels of economic development. Although Yu agreed that pollution control and environmental protection should be included in state plans and declined to endorse some of the more extreme views presented by others, his emphasis was quite clearly on the need to employ market methods (Yu Guangyuan 1980).

Numerous economists have sought to apply market approaches to pollution control issues. For example, Ye Yuhui (1984) suggested ways to calculate resource productivity. Although his formulae are not based on price, he explicitly suggested that resource users should be charged or taxed on the basis of their consumption to encourage greater efficiency.* A related argument had been made several years earlier by Liu Wen (1980), who stressed the interrelationship of irrationally low resource prices, waste, and pollution. Liu explained how rational individuals seeking to further public goals like economic growth in fact caused pollution, so reforms were needed to better differentiate between what was good and bad for society.

Another positive factor was the attitude of the most involved government agency, the State Bureau of Environmental Protection. This bureau is a new agency, with most of its personnel having been transferred from other agencies. It lacks an established niche in the policy process and is striving to increase its share of budgetary appropriations. Yet the bureau's pollution control and resource protection mission will ultimately cost many billions of dollars and involve it in nasty confrontations with more powerful ministries. Thus, the bureau is more open to novel policy proposals than its more hidebound counterparts and, like all Chinese bureaucracies, is highly receptive to any option that promises new or discretionary funds. Without a product to sell, effluent charges seemed an especially attractive option (Li Yangming 1982). Moreover, charges provided regulators with welcome flexibility when responding to recalcitrant polluters. Politically difficult fines and shutdown orders could be held in abeyance while legally enforceable

---

*Ye Yuhui's formulae included three equations:

1. Resource production rate $= \dfrac{\text{useful product (1)}}{\text{investment in natural resources (2)}}$

2. Renewable resource rate $= \dfrac{\text{resource regeneration volume (3)}}{\text{resource consumption volume (4)}}$

3. Resource productivity rate $= \dfrac{(1) \times (3)}{(4)^2}$

charges automatically accumulated until paid by the polluter, reducing the regulators' dependence on local political leaders anxious to keep factories operating. This consideration was a factor in the preparation of the Water Pollution Prevention and Control Law of 1984 (RR, May 13, 1984). In fact, charges are multiplied by a factor of one or more in the event of noncompliance to spur cleanups by recalcitrant polluters (JPRS 84521 CST 209, Oct. 12, 1983: 265–66 and 269–71; FBIS, Apr. 23, 1981: R1; GR, July 19, 1980).

For these reasons, charges have not been merely an academic exercise. Instead, they have been introduced on a widespread basis since 1979, primarily with regard to water pollution (FBIS, Apr. 23, 1981: R1). They were authorized in 1979 by the Environmental Protection Law (article 18) and endorsed at a national forum in Wuxi the following year. Charges soon were introduced in some of the most heavily polluted cities and streams, including Guangzhou, the Heilongjiang River in the Northeast, and the Yangtze River valley. All funds derived from charges officially are earmarked for environmental protection work. At first, all such funds could only be used to meet program expenses as opposed to administrative expenses or staff welfare, but this limitation subsequently was lifted. Nevertheless, most revenues retained by the environmental agencies are still devoted to such program needs as pollution control and developing the monitoring network (RR, Sept. 20, 1980).

Although the charges approach began in the economic reform period, it continued even after the conservative readjusters gained greater political influence in December 1980. The decision by the State Council (1981) on environmental protection in the readjustment phase gave prominent attention to charges. After a period of trial implementation, the State Council issued the "Provisional Methods for the Assessment of Effluent Fees" in May 1982 (ZRGGYG 1982: 4). Reliance on the charges concept was modified by stressing that payment of charges did not constitute relief from the polluter's obligation to clean up pollution or compensate victims, i.e., the polluter must control his own pollution. Nevertheless, the basic approach remained one of imposing charges in a progressive or stepwise relationship according to the volume and severity of discharges (JPRS 81737 WWEQ 367, Sept. 10, 1982: 25–28; for the text governing the Beijing municipal charges system, see HB, July 1982: 2–6).

The pollution control rebate is a particularly interesting feature of effluent fees. Usually, 70–80 percent of the revenue derived from charges is reserved for subsidizing treatment measures taken by polluters. All polluters are eligible for a rebate of their assessed charges if they show a good-faith cleanup effort. They can submit a proposal for pollution control which, upon approval by the Environmental Protection Bureau, makes them eligible for a rebate (Cao Fenglin 1982; JPRS 84521 CST 209, Oct. 12, 1983: 265–66). This provision results in the formation of a quasi-coalition between the regulator and the polluter, with the latter requesting additional funds from its parent ministry for effluent fees, which are in turn partially rebated to the polluter for control measures. This can be an effective inducement since the polluter can reduce his liability by taking remedial measures that are financed in part by outside funds. The polluter must demonstrate good faith because there is competition for such funds and not all expenditures are eligible for reimbursement. On average, only about half the control expenditures are financed through rebates.

A related measure involves subsidies. A three- to five-year tax holiday and exemption from the requirement to remit profits for the sale of goods made from recycled materials, for example, was authorized by the State Council in its 1979 directive "Some Measures on Accelerating the Development of the Building Materials Industry" (FBIS, Feb. 6, 1980: L5) and then reiterated in the 1981 "Circular on Reaffirming the Tax Exemption for Recycled Industrial Wastes" (*Compendium of Policies and Decrees on Chinese Economic Development* I: 291). As Baumol and Oates (1979: 246–50) argued, however, subsidies have their drawbacks. They are difficult to design in terms of performance benchmarks; they focus on specific technologies rather than on the desired behavior; and they tend to result in expensive giveaways that are hard to terminate. Ziegler (1982) argued that in the Soviet Union such subsidies are typically diverted to purposes unrelated to pollution control because the output norm remains the dominant target. Nevertheless, subsidies are often politically more attractive than negative sanctions. More importantly, the post-Mao reforms have substantially transformed China's political economy, making it more responsive to economic instruments. Thus, it is not surprising to find that environmental officials regard charges as a useful supplement to administrative controls, and some regard them as their most effective tool.

In 1982 alone, 500 million yuan in charges was collected. That amounted to almost one-quarter of state spending on environmental protection. Some 45 percent of the total receipts were rebated to enterprises to assist them in pollution control (HB, December 1983: 3). For example, several cities in Jiangsu, including Suzhou, a terribly polluted city of canals known historically for its beauty and aesthetic sophistication, began to introduce charges in 1979. Officials reported a decline in pollution once public waterways were no longer treated as free and inexhaustible disposal media.

Guangzhou began to assess charges in August 1980, soon extending the system to nearly a thousand of the city's largest polluters. The head of the municipal environmental protection office reported that charges energized previously lackadaisical factory management to take action. The Guangzhou Silk Filament Bleaching and Dyeing Factory, for example, purchased water pollution control equipment through a special grant for technological upgrading. But the factory refused to employ the equipment for over two years because operating expenses had to be financed out of its own working capital. The prospect of effluent charges led it and many other factories to take quick remedial action. The city found that the charges provided substantial additional funds for environmental protection work that could be used to upgrade monitoring and enforcement (Cao Fenglin 1982; for Hubei, see Wu Furen 1983; for Wuhan, see Ren Guofu 1985; for Changchun, see Shi Hongwen 1985; for Sichuan, see JPRS CST-84–004, Feb. 14, 1984: 120).

Effluent fees are rising in importance. In 1983, 630 million yuan in charges was collected from polluters, with one of every four large and medium-sized enterprises already subject to assessment. By 1985 the total had risen to over 900 million yuan, Some large units such as Wuhan Steel face annual bills in the eight-figure range, and in some cases charges can exert a very significant impact on enterprise costs and profits (Wu Furen 1983; Lei Kai 1985; *Zhongguo Huanjing Bao*, Jan. 5 and Aug. 3, 1985).

Many drawbacks still remain to be overcome for charges to function effectively. On the technical side, monitoring is at best inexact and takes place at irregular intervals, often no more than once a quarter rather than on a continuous basis, and the variation in charges for different pollutants is still crude. Most fundamentally, price controls and uneven profit rates across industries complicate a charge-setting process that is difficult even in the best of circumstances. The target for revenues generated from charges seems to be about 1 percent of profits, 0.5 percent of local revenues, and 0.1 percent of gross output value, although in problem cases the percentages may be much higher (Cao Fenglin 1982). The relationship among these three norms is likely to have uneven effects when applied to any particular industry. Charges generally may be too low to affect production decisions, or they may be unrealistically high. Charges have been set below the marginal costs of control for political and economic reasons, which is self-defeating, although they are being increased in many areas despite the qualms of the Ministry of Finance and the industrial ministries. For example, Shanghai used its local discretion to raise charges 17 to 64 percent higher than the national rate schedule set in the 1982 "Methods for the Assessment of Effluent Fees" (Chen Ziqun 1985; cf. Butterfield 1980 and Zhou Fuyang 1982).

Industries also operate under differential pricing systems and tax rates and thus are unevenly affected by emission charges. Whereas the relatively low-polluting petroleum industry enjoys a low tax rate, the high-polluting coal industry suffers from both low prices for its products and a relatively high tax rate (ZTN 1985: 378–79; Solinger 1982: 1245; Lockett and Littler 1984: 63). The resulting inequity greatly reduces the funds available to the low-price, high-tax industries (coal, forest products) for pollution control while permitting their more favorably treated high-price, low-tax counterparts (petroleum) to handle effluent charges as merely a cost of doing business without appreciable effect on their operations (figure 3). That may explain why the petroleum and metallurgical industries have earned considerable praise for their pollution control efforts. Unequal treatment of this sort might be justifiable if the favored industries happened to be the

Product Prices

		High	Low
Taxes and Compulsory Profit Remissions	Low	Petroleum	?
	High	Textiles	Coal Forest products

Figure 3.   The political economy of pollution control.

worst polluters, but the cause is actually bias in planners' prices. Unequal treatment leads inevitably to foot-dragging and bureaucratic opposition by the less favored ministries.

Political opposition also can be a severe impediment as revealed by the difficulties encountered by some local environmental protection agencies when collecting charges. In Huzhou, Jiangsu, over twenty factories refused to pay their charges on the grounds that their plans made no provision for such expenditures, and because neither the Ministry of Finance nor local government was willing to authorize such payments (RR, May 31, 1984). In such cases, strong backing by higher-level officials and the judicial system is necessary to ensure that fees are paid (Jin Ruilin and Cheng Zhengkang 1983). Similarly, the Ministry of Finance and the banks must facilitate the assessment process and enforce the requirement that rebates be spent for the intended purpose (JPRS CST-84-034, Oct. 29, 1984: 39–42). In Gansu, for example, the Finance Administration's own smelter was cited for exceeding emission standards but resisted paying its fines until the courts intervened. Such judicial action is clearly the exception. Therefore, the extent to which charges stimulate innovation and obtain pollution control at lower cost is dependent on price reform and economic decentralization so that enterprises can be held genuinely accountable for their actions.* Otherwise, enterprises will continue to emphasize satisfaction of their production norms while ignoring charges (*Huanjing Fa* 1986 2: 53–54, Yang Xinzheng 1980, Wan Li 1983). For this reason, some sophisticated policymakers initially favored sanctions based on wages and bonuses rather than charges because the former are more readily adaptable to a command-based planning system (Epstein 1984), but such sanctions have their own problems.

Because charges encounter enormous problems even in market economies, many analysts have urged the establishment of markets in pollution rights instead. Dales (1968), Rose-Ackerman (1977), and others argued that a system of tradable pollution rights would greatly simplify the govern-

*Of course, enterprises have lots of slack resources in an economy as inefficient as China's, but there would appear to be no incentive for them to become more efficient under a system governed by plans and commands.

ment's burden of determining the costs of pollution by creating markets in which prices would automatically be set in transactions between buyer and seller. The government's obligation would be reduced to one of determining in advance the desired ambient carrying capacity for pollutants, which it has to do in any event under a system of charges or of emission standards. An initial assignment of property rights would then be made through lottery or auction or simply through assigning rights to current polluters. Future assignments of rights then would be made through trades among individuals free to buy, sell, or save their permits. Such trades would be subject to overarching requirements that aggregate emission not exceed ambient environmental quality goals, with polluters not exceeding their allowable discharges.

Markets provide other advantages beyond simplifying administration, which may itself be a considerable plus, especially in a developing country where trained talent is scarce and routines are makeshift. Polluters acquire an incentive to devise innovative control strategies because any surplus pollution rights can be sold or reserved for future expansion. A market system can also accommodate growth and the entry of new polluters by simply allowing newcomers to express their demands through higher prices for pollution rights. By contrast, effluent charges require periodic recalibration to account for economic expansion. Pollution rights can even incorporate usage priorities. For example, holders of second-class rights can be permitted to discharge wastes into rivers only in the high-water season, while holders of first-class rights would be allowed to discharge year round. Should society or the government prefer a level of pollution below the maximum allowable in the interest of preservation, all that is required is public purchase and withdrawal of some pollution rights to ensure that pollution remains below the ecosystem's carrying capacity. Meanwhile, the revenue obtained by government from the sale of rights or through the levying of taxes on private sales can be earmarked for pollution control.

So far there is no sign that China is considering pollution rights, which must seem to be an extreme departure from past practices. However, should price reform resume, there is a possibility of progress in this regard. At a minimum, more rational prices would increase efficiency, which by itself would reduce the waste that accounts for so much pollution (Qu Geping 1983).

Conclusions

Since the early 1970s China has addressed her pollution problems in an increasingly serious way. As leadership concern grew, directives were issued, statutes were enacted, funding was increased, and a bureaucracy was created. Measurable progress has been reported in major cities and river valleys as district heating networks are extended, while elsewhere households convert from coal briquettes to bottled gas for cooking (CD, Nov. 15, 1984), older factories are renovated, and newer facilities satisfy more stringent standards (e.g., FBIS, Sept. 13, 1983: R5 for Shijiazhuang; RR, Nov. 24, 1983, for the Songhua River).

As I have argued, the severity of the problem can be attributed in substantial part to deficiencies in the political economy. The planning system, with its wastefulness and rigorous emphasis on heavy industry, magnified pollution while the closed nature of the polity, especially during leftist periods, restricted the raising of concern about pollution. Progress has been much greater in the post-Mao era. The shift to an intensive or efficiency-conscious development strategy has reduced the volume of waste products being generated by industry and led to increased emphasis on resource recovery. Meanwhile, the political system's greater openness to outside influence and popular concerns has helped pollution control rise higher on the political agenda.

I have also shown that good intentions are not enough—there also must be a sound implementation strategy. The past emphasis on moral exhortation through campaigns was an inexpensive but woefully inadequate strategy. People could not be persuaded to consistently subordinate their personal interests in behalf of a vaguely defined social interest. That does not mean that exhortation has no role to play. It is appropriate when there are large numbers of polluters, the problem can be clearly defined, the costs of supervision are high, and the property is public and thus not susceptible to the carving out of private property rights. Examples are litter control and recreation management. Exhortation also may be effective when the benefits to the individual are clear and compelling, as in campaigns to quit smoking. In the latter case, campaigns are as much educational as exhortational. Nonetheless, campaigns were overdone in China, particularly in periods of leftist rule, and they merely diverted attention from more effective implementation strategies while discrediting the government.

Regulation is much more common and effective worldwide and should be easier in China because the economy is largely government owned and operated, reducing the scope for conflicts between the private and public sectors. Regulation alone, however, cannot generate efficient outcomes and tends moreover to be a very blunt instrument—prescribing particular technologies or ordering factory shutdowns. It therefore arouses political opposition and delay and sometimes results in inappropriate solutions.

Consequently, economists have urged greater respect for market principles in pollution control. Effluent fees and pollution rights can be used to transpose the efficiency and entrepreneurship of a market economy into an arena defined by externalities and publicly owned property. Paradoxical though it may seem, it is possible to use market measures to address problems like pollution that derive from market failures. As we have seen, China in the post-Mao era has welcomed effluent fees with surprising eagerness to spur efficiency, circumvent the opposition of entrenched bureaucracies, and increase funding for pollution control. Fees may generate only a fraction of the billions of dollars needed for pollution control, but their policy effects exceed the amount of money involved because of their differential impact on particular enterprises (Wu Furen 1983).

Market methods have also been applied to recycling. Reorganization of the low-profit scrap industry, along with limited competition from private dealers, has facilitated the movement of waste products from where they are generated to where they are needed, a substantial improvement compared with the long-standing neglect that central planning had visited upon this industry (Zhu Hanxue and Zhang Zhao 1983; CD, Oct. 30, 1984, and Dec. 17, 1985; Weisskopf 1983). The use of market methods even applies to consumer goods such as beer, which continues to be in scarce supply despite rapidly rising output. Part of the problem lies in the distribution system, which makes it hard to buy beer but even harder to return the empty bottles. The refusal of many stores to accept empty bottles and cases slows up the already creaky distribution system for want of containers. Enterprising individuals began to fill the slack in the mid-1980s, offering consumers half-rebates and then returning the empties directly to the breweries (*Beijing Wanbao*, Oct. 5 and Nov. 1, 1985).

Unfortunately, the regime's support for market methods is qualified by a persistent tendency to regulate the terms of trade by which wastes are bought and sold out of fear that the planned sector of the economy will be unable to compete and that excessive profits will be made, as revealed in the State Economic Commission's "Provisional Regulations on Some Problems in Developing the Comprehensive Utilization of Materials" (JR, Oct. 14, 1985). Price ceilings and barriers to market entry can only obstruct the development of the industry, with unfortunate consequences for the environment.

Market methods are not the complete answer, of course. Regulation is a more appropriate policy instrument in emergencies, when highly toxic substances are involved or when there are large numbers of polluters, each of whose emissions are too small to be tradable. That would appear to be the case with regard to rural and neighborhood small-scale industry, one of the most widely praised features of the Maoist economic development strategy (Sigurdson 1977a). Few took notice of the fact that these factories tended to be proportionately worse polluters than modern, large-scale enterprises. That has changed since 1980, with rising concern expressed about the danger they pose to both human health and agriculture. Several conferences were held (RR, Aug. 22, 1980, and July 25, 1983; GR, Aug. 25, 1983; HB, Aug. 1983: 7–9; Cheng Yaping 1983) and then, in the fall of 1984, the State Council issued the "Directive on Applying Environmental Management to Rural and Neighborhood Enterprises" (ZRGGYG 447, Nov. 10, 1984: 917–18). Vice-Premier Li Peng called this a critical need at the second meeting of the Environmental Protection Commission (RR, Nov.

20, 1984). Noise is another example of a pollutant where campaigns, zoning, and technological standards are more appropriate than market measures (GB 3096-82; JPRS 84521 CST 209, Oct. 12, 1983: 21–25; *Faxue Yanjiu,* June 1982: 43–47).

In many instances mixed approaches are likely to emerge. For example, regulations can be complemented by effluent charges. Should the polluter fail to pay, shutdowns might be imposed. Hangzhou claims that a mixed approach of this sort has helped reduce pollution (JPRS PSM 4, Jan. 11, 1984: 34; FBIS, Feb. 10, 1984: O3). Similarly, exhortation is a useful complementary measure in most cases. Nevertheless, if the political leadership directs the legal system to further define and enforce property rights and if price reform provides better information on the scarcity value of all goods, including natural resources, economic methods may play a surprisingly large role in a country once virulently opposed to anything resembling capitalism.

V.

COLLECTIVE ACTION

Not many years ago it would have seemed preposterous to write a book on China based on the impact of individual preferences and property rights on policy outcomes. Well into the 1970s, China was widely regarded as a model of economic development based on revolutionary ascetism. Collective or group action appeared to be ubiquitous as a people once said to have been riven by selfishness and disregard for the common good (a "sheet of loose sand," according to Sun Yat-sen) was transformed into a throbbing mass of humanity working together for shared purposes. Yet, as we have seen, it was not merely economic development that was found lacking. Even public goods such as environmental quality and resource conservation (not to speak of human rights) were widely neglected during the first decades of the People's Republic.

Heavy pollution loads in socialist countries contradict the general expectation that public ownership of resources, coupled with appeals to social values, will increase the supply of public goods. Part of the explanation lies in the strong bias within Marxism toward industrial development at the expense of other values, the refusal to countenance the expression of countervailing interests by environmentalists and other groups, and the economic system's failure to apply scarcity pricing to natural resources—factors that were analyzed in preceding chapters.

Environmental problems are also indicative of broader aspects of collective action in socialist countries. In particular, from the perspectives of game theory and social choice theory, it appears that the collective goods appeals and political campaigns so prevalent in the Maoist period actually weakened the foundations for collective action. Coercion came to be the regime's only alternative, and coercion proved incapable of generating sincere effort on the part of the populace. By contrast, I suggest that the post-Mao market-oriented reforms actually can enhance collective action by creating a sense of trust and a social learning process among the populace, provided there is policy stability. I begin by examining the Chinese case in terms of competing theoretical explanations of collective action.

Game Theory

Collective action can be analyzed in terms of a noncooperative game in which the players act independently instead of attempting to coordinate their strategic decisions. In other words, individuals are assumed to be selfish or indifferent to the desires of other players. Because individuals are motivated only by the short-term pursuit of their own personal interests, the resulting outcomes are socially inferior. In the classical prisoner's dilemma game:

> Two prisoners who are suspected of having committed a crime are interrogated separately by the police. If both maintain silence, at most they can be booked on a minor charge. Each is encouraged to incriminate the other with a promise of leniency if he is not himself incriminated. If they double-cross each other, they are both in trouble (Shubik 1982: 217 and 254).

As shown in figure 4, although both players collectively stand to benefit by cooperating in a posture of silence (1, 1), when each player acts rationally the natural outcome is defection (-1, -1) because Confess dominates Do Not Confess.

During Chinese political campaigns, the regime shrewdly manipulated this defection impulse to induce persons who were subjects of political criticism to confess their complicity in trumped-up crimes. Confession was regarded as a sign of contrition, particularly when it was accompanied by denunciation of one's friends or neighbors for similar offenses. The regime was gradually thwarted, however, by quiet agreements among close friends to confess only to relatively innocuous charges and by the growing popular realization that any confession exposed the individual to danger in the next campaign, when old charges could be dredged up and exaggerated to grotesque proportions (Whyte 1974, Chan et al. 1984: 207–10).

The prisoner's dilemma game also is directly applicable to environmental policy. Consider forestry as an example. Although everyone gains from an increase in forest resources in terms of environmental amelioration, soil conservation, and the like, each individual will personally come out further

		Prisoner 2	
		Do Not Confess	Confess
	Do Not Confess	1,1	-2,2
Prisoner 1	Confess	2,-2	-1,-1

Figure 4. The prisoner's dilemma.

ahead by cutting trees down and selling or using the timber, while hoping that everyone else continues to plant and manage the woodlots. But because all individuals share the same calculus of decision, the result is deforestation and neglect of forest management (figure 5).

If that is the problem China faces with regard to environmental policy and other public goods, how can socially superior outcomes be obtained? Several alternatives may be considered. First and most obvious is the transformation of people's preferences. If people can be persuaded to prefer social benefits to individual benefits in the manner of a "new socialist" or "new communist" man, the dilemma would disappear. Rational individuals would get more pleasure from conservation than from the private benefits of deforestation. Following this logic, Carens (1981) analyzed the potential for altruistic behavior in a world of perfect socialization or "new socialist men." But such exercises are speculative to the extreme. Despite all of the Communist party's efforts in propaganda and social control, there is no real indication that the populace holds self-abnegating preferences, so the problem resurfaces whenever coercion is relaxed. Campaigns such as Obligatory Tree Planting initiated in 1981 to spur afforestation for the public good often have proved to be sideshows to factional politics, with little positive impact on the problem at hand. Indeed these campaigns often create a tragedy of the commons effect by stressing public ownership that aggravates the problem of deforestation, thereby ultimately dampening collective values (Ross 1987, Lan Xiuliang 1984). That is not to deny that popular preferences change over time. Rather, it is to stress that the pattern of change is far more complex and uneven than ideologues imagine; values are either resistant to officially endorsed changes, or they change in directions that the regime does not necessarily welcome. Most notably, the post-Mao reforms revealed a deep-seated sense of household loyalty and a yearning for material things—just what the leftists had sought to suppress.

Reciprocity and Conditional Assurance

Far more interesting is the notion that self-interested individuals may be persuaded to set aside their real preferences and behave according to a social-regarding calculus. Writing amid the hoopla surrounding the Cul-

		Woodsman 1	
		Conserve	Deforest
	Conserve	6,6	0,8
Woodsman 2			
	Deforest	8,0	2,2

Figure 5.   The woodsman's dilemma.

tural Revolution, Sen (1973: 98) argued that "even if the people involved continued to have the same Prisoners' Dilemma type preferences, but behaved . . . *as if* they had the 'socially conscious' preferences . . . they could be better off *even in terms of their true preferences.*"

The issue addressed by Sen was the socialist conundrum of how to get people to work hard once extra or even ordinary effort is no longer entitled to greater reward. Arguing against the inevitability of shirking, Sen concluded that people could be induced to behave as if social benefit was worth more to them than individual effort. Specifically, he began by assuming that individuals' preference structures reveal an inclination to free-ride. When an individual's alternatives are to work hard (I_1) or not to work hard (I_0), and the other members of society R have the same choices (R_1 and R_0), the individual ranks alternative outcomes beginning with the most preferred in the order $I_0R_1, I_1R_1, I_0R_0, I_1R_0$. Converted into matrix form, this means that I's preference ordering is c,a,d,b and R's preference ordering is b,a,d,c (figure 6).

If each player follows an individually rational strategy, choosing I_0 and R_0 respectively, the socially inferior outcome d results. Sen argues that the universally preferred outcome a will emerge instead if all players choose according to the principle of "reciprocity," i.e., I works hard (I_1) if R works hard (R_1) as well, but I slacks off (I_0) if R slacks off (R_0). The new ordering $I_1R_1, I_0R_1, I_0R_0, I_1R_0$ reverses the ranking of the first two choices for both parties so that I's alternatives are ranked a,c,d,b and R's choices are ranked a,b,d,c. I goes first and chooses a, which is reciprocated by R with the consequence that both I and R enjoy a higher degree of satisfaction than if they simply pursued their individual interests.

Unfortunately, Sen fails to explain satisfactorily why the Chinese should be expected to follow the reciprocity principle and thus transform the prisoner's dilemma into a game of conditional assurance. His explanation is predicated upon the notion of "cultural orientation," by which he refers not to national character but rather to the ethic of selfless service promoted during the Cultural Revolution. Although Sen (1973: 100) clearly considered the Cultural Revolution a pathbreaking development in terms of bridging the gap between Marxian social values and social optimality, in reality only a small segment of the populace responded with alacrity to its goals. More importantly, shared allegiance to Maoist ideology soon dis-

	R_1	R_0
I_1	a	b
I_0	c	d

Figure 6. Conditional assurance.

solved into bitter fighting between competing factional alignments over their respective revolutionary bona fides. Most enthusiasts were urban youths, and within a few short years they became bitterly disillusioned and many were exiled to the countryside (Chan et al. 1984).

Sen's proposition that China is culturally exempt from the prisoner's dilemma cannot be sustantiated on empirical grounds. Indeed, research on factory work life (Walder 1984) and agriculture (Lardy 1983) as well as environmental policy reveals that individual or household interests are important determinants of behavior in China. Indeed, the family is generally regarded as the enduring nucleus of Chinese society. In practice, the reciprocity principle is most effectively applied only when the Communist party is prepared to make concentrated use of both coercion and persuasion, as in the campaign for single-child families.

Group Size and Altruism

Another way of approaching cooperation is to consider group size and values as variables influencing collective action. Following Olson (1965), small groups are considered "privileged" in terms of organization and maintenance when wealthy benefactors or political entrepeneurs can provide a larger share of the needed resources themselves, when the group can offer greater solidary incentives such as friendship that are an important source of gratification, and when the members can observe one another to guard against defection. By contrast, large groups are handicapped because each individual's contribution is smaller and prevention of defection is more difficult.

Approaching this issue from an organizational perspective, Ouchi (1980) argued that the issue is a matter of goal congruence as well as size. The lower the level of congruence in an organization, the higher the internal transaction costs and the lower the efficiency. Conversely, the higher the goal congruence, the lower the internal transaction costs and the more efficient the organization. The high-congruence organization or "clan" tolerates greater ambiguity in terms of organizational communication and thus is advantaged in comparison with such low-congruence organizations as markets and bureaucracies.

Hardin (1982: 38–49) generalized the concept of the size principle in terms of the k factor, where k is equal in size to the smallest subgroup that stands to benefit from providing a collective good even without participation by other members of society. Although k equals one in a purely atomized society, larger k values may be found elsewhere. In China, many observers have noted the strength of subgroup identities at the production-team, factory-workshop, and similar grass-roots levels. Group formation is facilitated by the regime through exhortation and subsidies, overcoming some of the start-up costs that otherwise impede organization (Hansen

1985: 94). Small units then are pyramided in behalf of national goals by the Communist party and its auxiliaries, resulting in a higher degree of cooperation (Popkin 1981: 57–58, Ishikawa 1984: 18).

The increase in group formation and cohesion at the basic level does not, however, necessarily lead to higher levels of collective action. That is partly because groups are subject to great stresses during ideological campaigns, forcing their members into uncomfortable roles as accusatory witnesses. These incidents create rifts that often prove difficult to bridge later on, while unintentionally encouraging the development of group conventions to reduce the intensity of mutual accusations. Because of political turbulence and other factors, small groups have often been unable to transform their members' values in the transcendent direction desired by the regime (Whyte 1974).

Moreover, small-group cohesion often grows at the expense of cooperation in behalf of societal goals because each unit (*danwei*) has considerable discretion to define collective goods in its own interest. For example, as rural production teams acquired corporate identities, barriers developed between neighboring teams that inhibited horizontal cooperation on irrigation, flood control, and other projects whose dimensions overlapped unit boundaries (Parish and Whyte 1978: 303–4 and 313–14). Similarly, urban development is plagued by conflicts between utilities and developers over the allocation of building space, with the former sometimes obstructing project completion until they receive a share of the apartments or offices (Butterfield 1982: 111–12).

The conflict between small-group and large-group interests also qualifies the thesis that cooperation is a function of altruistic values. Margolis (1983) argued that social choice can be understood in terms of distinct dual preference orderings; S for private goods or self-interests and G for group or social goods, rather than a single integrated utility schedule. Since the individual benefits from the consumption of both S and G goods, the key determinant of altruism or G-oriented behavior when the two conflict is the marginal rate of return. Individuals will devote themselves to societal or G goods whenever their rate of return exceeds that for S goods.

This is an important contribution to the study of altruism. In practice, however, Margolis's approach is valid only to the extent that G goods are defined uniformly across all members of the group. If, by contrast, the members of the group or society define social goods in terms of their own conflicting interests, cooperation will not emerge (RR, Dec. 5, 1984). That is the nature of bureaucratic politics where each organization regards its own mission as the key guarantor of the national interest.

Such bureaucratic conflict occurs universally but appears particularly widespread in countries such as China where state ownership of property and central planning are prominent institutions, yet traditional solidaristic organizations have been weakened. A major example in environmental policy is the interagency disagreement between the forestry and water conservancy bureaucracies over flood control measures; forestry favors vegetative controls while water conservancy favors engineering, and neglect of the former leads to accelerated sedimentation of reservoirs and streambeds (Ross 1983b). Another example is the conflict between the central government, which is responsible for the main stems of rivers, and the provinces, which are responsible for the tributaries, resulting in costly offloading and neglect of shipping channels in tributaries. Still another example is the rivalry over pesticide efficacy and efficiency between the user-oriented Ministry of Agriculture and the producer-oriented Ministry of Chemical Industries. There are also conflicts between the Environmental Protection Bureau and regulated industries; the regulator insists that pollution control is a public good that everyone must contribute toward, but the industries behave as if their own vertically assigned production plans were the primary public good (Liu Wen 1980). Although in principle these conflicts can be adjusted by the State Planning Commission, in practice each agency responds primarily to the directives assigned by its parent ministry or system (*xitong*), which reflect more parochial concerns. That in turn necessitates the creation of additional coordinating commissions, such as the State Commission on Environmental Protection and the Central Greenification Commission.

Iteration

The approaches examined so far are all based on single-play games that exaggerate the tendency for the players to maximize their own self-interest. In reality, life consists of ongoing interactions in which the participants acquire a fuller understanding of the benefit structure and the needs of other actors. Reality requires multiple iterations of the same prisoner's dilemma game to be played in order to determine the likelihood of social cooperation. As Axelrod (1981: 307) noted, the iteration must be of an infinite nature, for otherwise all players will treat the last play of the game as a single play and then, through a process of backward unfolding, treat each and every play as a single play. By contrast, there is a potential for social learning when the game continues indefinitely.

Following Shubik (1982: 290–92), multiple iteration is modeled in three rounds where the player's next choice is dependent only on his opponent's play in the just-concluded round (figure 7). A two-by-two matrix then unfolds into an eight-by-eight matrix where each cell depicts the average payoff. All eight strategies are displayed along the margins (figure 8).

Returning to the earlier model of forest conservation, CCC means that player 1 begins by conserving C, continues to conserve C if the other player conserves C, and conserves C once again if the other player conserves. By contrast, CCD means that player 1 begins by conserving C, continues to conserve C if the other player conserves C, but deforests D if the other player deforests D.

	C	D
C	6,6	0,8
D	8,0	2,2

Figure 7. Iteration a:
two-by-two matrix.

	CCC	CCD	CDC	CDD	DCC	DCD	DDC	DDD
CCC	6,6	6,6	0,8	0,8	6,6	6,6	0,8	0,8
CCD	6,6	6,6	4,4	2,2	6,6	4,4	4,4	2,2
CDC	8,0	4,4	4,4	0,8	8,0	4,4	0,8	0,8
CDD	8,0	2,2	8,0	2,2	8,0	2,2	8,0	2,2
DCC	6,6	6,6	0,8	0,8	6,6	6,6	0,8	0,8
DCD	6,6	4,4	4,4	2,2	6,6	2,2	4,4	2,2
DDC	8,0	4,4	8,0	0,8	8,0	4,4	4,4	0,8
DDD	8,0	2,2	8,0	2,2	8,0	2,2	8,0	2,2

Figure 8. Iteration b:
eight-by-eight matrix.

	CCC	CCD	CDD	DCC	DDC	DDD
CCC	6,6	6,6	0,8	6,6	0,8	0,8
CCD	6,6	6,6	2,2	6,6	4,4	2,2
CDD	8,0	2,2	2,2	8,0	8,0	2,2
DCC	6,6	6,6	0,8	6,6	0,8	0,8
DDC	8,0	4,4	0,8	8,0	4,4	0,8
DDD	8,0	2,2	2,2	8,0	8,0	2,2

Figure 9. Iteration c:
six-by-six matrix.

Because CCD dominates DCD (all payoffs under CCD are equal to or
better than payoffs under DCD) and DDC dominates CDC, the inferior
strategies are eliminated, reducing the game to a six-by-six matrix (figure
9). CCD dominates both CCC and DCC, reducing the game to a four-by-
four matrix (figure 10). CCD dominates DDC, resulting in a final three-
by-three matrix (figure 11).

CCD is the weakly dominant strategy. Each player begins by conserving
C, continues to conserve C if the other player conserves C, but deforests
D if the other player deforests D. That of course is the tit-for-tat strategy
in which cooperation is rewarded by further cooperation but defection is
punished by defection. As Axelrod (1981) discovered in a fascinating simu-
lation involving prominent scientists, tit-for-tat consistently produced
higher payoffs than all other strategies.

	CCD	CDD	DCC	DDD
CCD	6,6	2,2	4,4	2,2
CDD	2,2	2,2	8,0	2,2
DDC	4,4	0,8	4,4	0,8
DDD	2,2	2,2	8,0	2,2

Figure 10. Iteration d: four-by-four matrix.

	CCD	CDD	DDD
CCD	6,6	2,2	2,2
CDD	2,2	2,2	2,2
DDD	2,2	2,2	2,2

Figure 11. Iteration e: three-by-three matrix.

Applications to China

The dominance of the tit-for-tat strategy depends on policy stability and strong, positive links between individual choice and benefits. Without stability, iteration dissolves into a series of single-play games, foreclosing the possibility that social learning will lead to higher levels of cooperation. In a related vein, the socially superior outcome is obtained only if individuals can perceive differences in payoffs. When payoffs are vaguely defined, individuals will be more hesitant to act or will exercise inconsistent choices.

Of critical importance to China is the modern historical legacy of policy instability or cycling in which the pendulum swings rapidly from left to right and back again. That creates great apprehension among the people, who fear that falling out of step with the higher leadership will expose them to denunciation, particularly in leftist periods. Even after the post-Mao shift in economic policies toward market methods, many Chinese continued to fear a policy reversal. It is not change per se that is the issue but rather a "communist wind" restoring collective ownership at the expense of individual incentives. The "communist wind" can be interpreted as defection on the part of the regime vis-à-vis the populace and is bound to induce defection on the latter's part as well. The problem is serious in all sectors of the economy, but it is critical in long lead-time production processes such as forestry, where capital is immobile for years and years. Fear of a policy shift discourages investment in forestry, exacerbating soil erosion and the shortage of wood products. Therefore, officials in favor of the post-Mao reforms stress the need for the regime to honor its promise that the cultivator will enjoy the profits and to avoid any sharp dislocations. Property rights instead must be further clarified and strengthened (Zhu Zanping 1984).

The significance of policy stability has much wider import, however. Throughout society, lower-level officials have tended to qualify their commitment to regime policies out of concern for future policy reversals. They have learned that no policy course is permanent and that newly dominant factions target the most prominent proponents of discredited policies for punishment. Officials therefore learn to be cautious in order to minimize the risks they face. Unfortunately, the resulting tepidity hampers implementation. Performance tends to be slow and half-hearted. With regard to pollution control, regulated industries are emboldened to delay compliance with regulations, while the regulators themselves are reluctant to publicize the dangers posed by pollution lest powerful enemies be aroused.

The role of policy stability in facilitating social cooperation also helps to explain variation in the performance of policy instruments. Campaigns are intermittent organizations in which brief episodes of intense activity interrupt longer periods of routine activity. Campaigns are the key elements in the policy oscillations or cycles that have characterized PRC history: policy surges out of a state of normalcy into mobilization and then high-tide phases, followed by deterioration, retrenchment, demobilization, and then a new cycle of normalcy and mobilization (Skinner and Winckler 1969).

Policy cycles are important elements in Chinese political history, and some scholars have argued that they function as social learning devices. Petrick (1981) contended that oscillations enable a regime to scan the universe of policy alternatives faster than does a more deliberate policy process, and thus help the regime to quickly determine which policies are best. This argument appears to explain the change in views of Deng Xiaoping, a loyal Maoist through the 1950s whose political shift toward the right was accelerated by the debacles of the Great Leap Forward and the Cultural Revolution. It fails, however, to take full account of factional conflict. Each faction jealously defends its own campaigns and other policies, and that actually reduces the potential for social learning. After all, it took nearly ten years for the Cultural Revolution to wind down, during which time the radical leftists continually tried to reignite the flames of Maoist ideology.

Indeed, the early post-Mao leadership under Hua Guofeng remained faithful to many of Mao's precepts under the guise of the "two whatevers": "We shall resolutely defend whatever policies Chairman Mao devised and shall unflinchingly carry out whatever instructions he gave" (RR, Feb. 7, 1977). Had it not been for the purge of both the Gang of Four and the Whateverists after Mao's death, it is not at all clear that any reforms would have been introduced. To Deng Xiaoping's credit, though, he and his colleagues were reluctant to unleash campaigns lest they get out of hand, and they retreated quickly on such occasions as the "Combat Spiritual Pollution campaign of 1983–84, when popular fears of a policy reversal were revived. Countercurrents of conservatism are always just beneath the surface, however, and they reemerged with a fury in the winter of 1986–87.

In terms of game theory, each movement of the policy cycle is tantamount to defection by the regime vis-à-vis the populace. Such moves soon break down the trust that is essential if social cooperation is to develop and instead produce irrational behavior among the people. During leftist upsurges, surviving elements of the private economy are destroyed to cut off "tails of capitalism" while the decline in investment efficiency of the overall economy accelerates. Whenever a window of opportunity for the advancement of private interests opens, as in the early post-Mao period, embezzlement and other crimes become commonplace and capital shifts toward consumption to maximize short-term gains before the window closes again.

By contrast, although market methods originate in self-interest, the process of exchange by which they operate tends to create mutual cooperation (Lan Xiuliang 1984). No exchange in principle takes place unless it is to the advantage of both parties. Although each party has an incentive to cheat in a single-play game, over time the parties themselves establish conventions and contracts to place their transactions on a more trustworthy basis while excluding cheaters. Otherwise, it is understood that transaction costs will rise as each party seeks to reduce the other's opportunity to defect, ultimately resulting in a decline in the number of transactions—to everyone's disadvantage. In this respect, markets function as tit-for-tat games that produce higher levels of cooperation than campaigns or other forms of altruistically motivated implementation instruments.

This counterintuitive result indicates that regimes anxious to increase the supply of goods ought to concentrate on enhancing markets rather than suppressing them. With regard to environmental policy, that includes the establishment of free markets in natural resources and artificial markets in pollution rights. For example, more efficient patterns of water usage can in many cases be attributed to the introduction of more realistic utility schedules based on replacement value. That frees water for downstream consumers as well as for ecological needs that were historically slighted in water-short areas (JR, Aug. 27, 1985).

Naturally, markets also have their limitations. When transaction costs are prohibitive, internalization through agencies such as water resource management districts is in order, although such bodies best operate as quasi-market institutions with regard to the purchase and sale of commodities. To the extent that consumer information is inadequate or that monopolies create unfair advantages for one party to a transaction, some regulation may be required, but caution is in order because regulation frequently creates more monopolies than it relieves (Bates 1984). This latter pattern emerges under central planning, which creates enormous inefficiencies and assigns monopolistic power to every state bureaucracy.

The other major problem concerns third-party transactions or externalities such as pollution. Even here, however, the most reasonable approach is not the superficially easy route of planning or regulation involving the arbitrary designation of appropriate technologies or maximum emission levels for each polluter, but rather the maximal use of markets to allocate pollution rights and to tax emissions.

The scope of bureaucratic implementation therefore is best left to those commodities or issues for which markets are not feasible, such as nature preserves. Meanwhile, the regime can maximize social cooperation by facilitating the operation of markets. Particularly needed in this regard are the clarification and the enforcement of property rights through stable and fair jurisprudence, as well as assistance in capital formation, market development, and other functions already performed by government in most countries on the western Pacific rim.

The post-Mao regime has made extraordinary progress in this regard, but let caution be our concluding thought. The task of transition from planning and campaigns to a market orientation is enormously difficult and continues to arouse political reactions. Although there appears to be a substantial groundswell of support for the reforms, there is no guarantee against a reversal during or after Deng Xiaoping's tenure. China's most essential need is for further progress in the transition from the traditional pattern of rule by individual leaders setting personal examples—a pattern still prominent during Mao's rule and one highly vulnerable to idiosyncracies and factionalism—to a pattern combining the rule of law with government by representatives responsive to their constituents. Only in this fashion can citizens be expected to cooperate in behalf of societal interests as well as their own.

VI.

AGENDA SETTING AND THE POLICY PROCESS IN CHINA

In the course of analyzing environmental policy, I have discussed the merits of market methods and their newly won prominence. In so doing, I have begged critical questions about how new issues come to the fore and why policy instruments rise and fall in favor. After all, the prospects for increased attention to issues such as pollution control and habitat preservation and greater reliance on market methods were not entirely propitious in the 1970s. Like other developing countries, China in its recent history had shown little regard for environmental pollution. The economic system and powerful production-oriented bureaucracies stood in the way of proposals to divert resources to conservation and social programs. There was little opportunity for direct popular participation or for scientists to question the existing state of affairs. Yet without minimizing present-day pollution problems, we have seen that both environmental concern and reliance on market methods increased substantially, although not as much as many concerned parties would have wished. How did these changes occur? For answers, I will examine the process of agenda setting as revealed in environmental policy and the secondary literature.

There are two types of agendas: informal, or societal, and formal, or institutional. Informal agendas consist of values held by some or all of the populace regarding those issues which they feel are important. On rare occasions, the entire populace shows unanimity, but these occasions tend to be short-lived episodes focusing on issues of an emergency nature, such as winning a war or fighting a natural disaster. Even then, unanimity is obtained only when the issue is framed in general terms.

Most of the time, people's issue awareness is low and, to the extent that they perceive an issue's importance, they differ on its priority and solutions. In other words, public opinion tends to be inchoate until it is given shape by politicians, the mass media, organized interest groups, or other intermediaries. Organized interest groups, politicians, and others mobilize the general public only when additional support is needed. Otherwise, they are content to advance their social agenda through their own resources (Kingdon 1984).

Social agenda status is sufficient for a decision to be made on private matters, but when it comes to public policy, proponents must first move their issue onto the agenda or calendar of one or more formal institutions through an "outside initiative" strategy (Cobb et al. 1976). Social agendas are much less important under an authoritarian or communist regime than in a democracy because the private sector is much smaller and the public has been denied the freedom to organize in order to advance its interests. That, however, does not completely nullify the importance of social agendas. At a minimum, individuals determine the enthusiasm with which they comply with public policy. A dissatisfied public responds lethargically and is prone to evade onerous policies. The more the regime depends on energetic, efficient, and creative responses, the more likely it is to tailor its policies to the felt needs of the public regarding compensation, justice, and other values. The post-Mao regime demonstrated a major improvement in this regard. Similarly, the more the regime concentrates its attention on particular issues as opposed to a quest for total control, the more influential the private sector becomes with regard to social aspirations and related values outside the scope of official concern.

The number of formal agendas reflects the number of institutions. In an absolute monarchy or one-man dictatorship, there can be only one agenda, with one vote tantamount to decision. The number of agendas rises in accordance with structural differentiation and the diffusion of power. In a complex democracy such as the United States, where the constitution ordains checks and balances, the number of institutions and the built-in conflicts among them are high. This setup greatly expands agenda access but also increases the prospects for stalemate to the advantage of defenders of the status quo.

To cite a dramatic example, the Reagan administration entered office in 1981 with a substantial electoral mandate and promptly went to work on a far-reaching set of agenda changes. The administration was extraordinarily successful on some issues such as tax reduction and defense spending and helped create a new public mood on issues such as labor-management relations and a reduction in the role of government. But the administration was much less successful with regard to environmental policy, where its proposals centered on regulatory reform through mandatory cost-benefit analysis, increasing the role of markets in the allocation of resources, and defederalization of resource management. Some successes were achieved with regard to cutting spending and reorienting the regulatory agencies—decisions that lie in whole or in part within the scope of the president's executive authority—but for the most part the administration was unsuccessful and actually aroused a major political backlash.

The administration's problems in this instance were due in part to the appointment of unusually abrasive individuals, including James Watt and Anne Gorsuch. But problems arose primarily because the proposals represented a drastic departure from the political status quo in the face of overwhelming congressional and public opposition. Rather than focus on reform per se via greater reliance on economic or market instruments that would have promised greater efficiency and might have won public approval, the administration adopted a negative and apparently antiregulatory posture. Yet without control of the House of Representatives or key committees in the Senate, the administration had trouble even formulating a legislative agenda. The result was perpetuation of the legislative status quo: sunset legislation such as the Clean Air and Clean Water Acts were simply renewed on an annual basis rather than allowed to expire. This move cheered environmentalists, who generally were satisfied with the legislation of the 1970s with a few exceptions such as the lack of stringent controls on acid rain and toxic pollutants in the atmosphere. Not until its second term did the Reagan administration actively pursue efficiency-oriented environmental regulatory items such as pollution banks, a course that promised to win broader support from other actors in the environmental policy sector in the fashion of previous coalitions, which had secured passage of the Coastal Barrier Resources Act in 1982 and the conservation easements provisions (Title XII) of the Food Security Act of 1985.

By contrast, China has a smaller number of formal agendas and the content of these agendas is closely monitored from above by the Communist party, where power is based in central leadership organs: the Politburo, especially its Standing Committee; the Secretariat; and, for military affairs, the Central Military Commission. These institutions mostly operate as collegial bodies with decisions not taken until after a consensus emerges. That puts a premium on elite coalition building, an "inside access" strategy in which leaders carefully build support for their positions. As Lieberthal (1978) argued, this process involves the painstaking gathering of data and preparation of reports to win approval of central documents, the policy memoranda by which central decisions are communicated to lower echelons. When circumstances permit, however, leaders try to purge their rivals and replace them with their own supporters in an unending game of factional politics (Pye 1981). The process can take a long time; actually, it never ends because new factional alignments are always in the process of being formed. But once an alignment's opponents have been co-opted, bypassed, or replaced, changes can be rapidly instituted because the Communist party is the only source of legitimacy.

The policy process may also involve officials at lower levels who are "mobilized" by senior leaders as part of the coalition-building process. The latter have considerable flexibility in this regard; they can convene a variety of meetings, conferences, and forums under various rubrics to promote their positions. In exceptional circumstances, an extremely powerful leader may even disavow formal decisions made by the central party organs when he enjoys broad support among provincial officials or the populace at large, as Mao Zedong did in the collectivization drive of 1955 and the Cultural

Revolution. In most instances, however, mobilization is used in tandem ✓
with elite coalition building.

The process of mobilization also provides lower echelons with the opportunity to promote their own interests among higher-level officials.
Bureaucracies and localities seek endorsement of their own positions, especially with regard to funding and on issues that supersede organizational
boundaries and thus require interagency coordination. Pollution control
and water resource projects are issues that fall into both categories. Conversely, these bureaucracies will also try to defend their sense of organizational mission or key interests by persuading senior officials to modify
policies they oppose. Failing that, they may delay or modify implementation
in the hope of minimizing a policy's impact on their interests. Thus, the
problem for the central leadership is one of how to build support for policy
proposals without relinquishing their power to implement them later on.
Indeed, once an issue acquires agenda status, different constituencies will
acquire a vested interest in maintaining its priority, making difficult the
leadership's attempts to reshape it or lower its priority.

Although the process is dominated by artful, goal-oriented behavior,
outcomes do not necessarily reflect intentions. Policymaking instead sometimes resembles the garbage-can model of organizational choice in which ⟩
problems, solutions, and careers chase each other in a random fashion ⟩
(Cohen et al. 1972). Officials may disguise their true ambitions to prevent
opposition from forming, or they may try to piggyback one issue onto
another to increase their prospects for success. Newly discovered problems
become magnets for solutions no matter how tangential their relationship.
For example, after the Hundred Flowers period (1956–57), Mao tended
to respond to any criticism of his policies as if it were an instance of class
conflict, thus justifying harsh repression of his critics regardless of their
past service.

In the following pages, I will discuss the agenda-setting process in terms
of a sequence of gates or ports through which issues and solutions must
pass before they can be considered. Each gate or port represents an opportunity for agenda access whose dimensions vary with the political climate
and the nature of the issue.

Factional Politics

The Communist party in the Leninist tradition seeks to perpetuate its
own monopoly of political power by exercising close control over state
organs and transmission-belt-style, mobilizational interest groups. Subject
to the rare and extremely short-lived exceptions of the Hundred Flowers
period and the Beijing Spring (1978–79), all fundamental challenges to
party rule are illegitimate. These ground rules for political discourse were

reaffirmed by Deng Xiaoping in 1979 in the Four Cardinal Principles (upholding socialism, proletarian dictatorship, party leadership, and Marxism-Leninism-Mao Zedong Thought). They were enforced during the student demonstrations of December 1986–January 1987.

Despite official denials (FBIS, Mar. 29, 1985: W12–13), the party itself inevitably falls far short of the Leninist ideal of internal unity and selfless discipline. Like any "total organization" in which rewards are distributed in response to loyalty rather than more impersonal norms, it is marked by internal cleavages along functional, regional, generational, and hierarchical lines. The most serious involve factional struggle over both power and ideology, with each faction striving to eliminate or neutralize its rivals (Tsou 1976). Although interpersonal relationships *(guanxi)* form the cement that binds factions together, factions ultimately tend to split ideologically.

The most serious split in recent years focused on development strategy and the role of the party. The Gang of Four defended an increasingly doctrinaire view regarding the validity of Maoist revolutionary ideals in a postrevolutionary society but was purged within weeks of Mao's death by a coalition of senior party officials. The latter also soon divided. The Whatever faction led by Hua Guofeng most closely adhered to Maoist doctrine but was largely squeezed out of power by the end of 1978. Afterward, the competition for power centered on the pragmatists, or reformers, who tended to favor major changes in the political economy in a market direction, and conservatives, or readjusters, who were only prepared to support alterations in the proportional balances and other features of central planning on a foundation of heightened discipline (Schram 1984).

Each faction assembles a stable of advisers and publicists to refine its preferences and advance its cause through the media, although inevitably the advisers themselves acquire a measure of influence as well. In Mao's case, Chen Boda, a party theoretician, was a strong influence from the left for over thirty years (Wylie 1980). For the most part, however, Mao's advisers in later years are better described as propagandists or courtiers dependent solely on the favor of their patron for their positions in the policy process (Dittmer 1978). As for intellectual advisers, Mao himself had a pronounced anti-intellectual streak that led him on many occasions to disparage academic norms and orchestrate campaigns against scholars in the fashion of the Yellow Emperor, to whom he was often compared.

√   By contrast, the reformers have tended to prefer men of ideas within the party who are comfortable with the sciences and academia in general. Deng formulated a proposal to reform science policy in the mid-1970s with input from supportive officials in the Academy of Sciences (Lieberthal 1978). Such intellectuals as Yu Guangyuan, vice-chairman of the State Science and Technology Commission and vice-president of the Academy of Social Sciences, and Xu Dixin took the lead on environmental policy. In various articles and conference proceedings, Yu (1980) helped to define the interdependence of economic development, environmental quality, and regime policy by encouraging many reforms while rejecting the more far-reaching views put forth by others (e.g., Liu Wen 1980). The role of advisers has become increasingly institutionalized in such bodies as the Research Center on Rural Development, which is affiliated with the party Secretariat's Rural Policy Research Institute; both the center and the institute are headed by Du Runsheng. The proliferating professional and scholarly societies such as the Chinese Society of Environmental Economics also serve an advisory function ("Historical Review," 1984, 8–9). Permanent organizations of this sort, although generally subordinate to governmental agencies that serve as their patrons, increase the ability of factional advisers to broker ideas and mediate relations between the regime and the intellectual community, screening out heterodox proposals while attempting to shape their patron's views (Schram 1984, Xu Xing 1983).

Because the party enjoys a monopoly of power, the identity of the dominant faction and the extent of its power at any point in time are critical aspects of the agenda-setting process. Unlike a democracy, the Chinese system is one in which no alternatives can be publicly presented by other political parties, interest groups, or the media without the approval of the dominant faction. The only exceptions come during periods of factional interregna such as Mao Zedong's last years, when the absence of a single dominant faction encouraged the factions to engage in more public competition, and periods when the dominant faction's ideology encourages more openness in policy discourse. The latter include the post-Mao reform period (1980–82 and 1983–86), but even then, as Rudolph (1984) and Halpern (1985) argued, the mass media and specialized journals alike slant their coverage and editorial content to suit the preconceptions of the dominant faction. As General Secretary Hu Yaobang explained, journalism cannot be allowed the freedom to express differences because all elements of the official press must assume a unified stance under the leadership of the party (FBIS, Apr. 15, 1985: K1–15).

The party's agenda-setting role can be visualized in the abstract in terms of a gatekeeper (figure 12). If all issues or alternatives range from a to z, the party's historical tendency has been to consider only leftward issues a through j. At the height of Maoist intolerance during the Cultural Revolution, only a narrow range of issues b through d were considered. By contrast, the reformers have shifted the location of the gates rightward and opened them wider, so that g through s may pass through.

The importance of factional struggle is confirmed in the cases examined in preceding chapters. The major changes in forestry policy toward pri-

```
                        Pragmatists
                       ‾‾‾‾‾‾‾‾‾‾‾‾
Left    a b c d e f g h i j k l m n o p q r s t u v w x y z    Right

        Ultra-left                        Conservatives
```

Figure 12. Factions and gates in the Chinese Communist party.

vatization and decentralization could not have occurred while the left was in power, for this faction bitterly resisted the reforms that Deng Xiaoping sought to introduce with regard to science and agriculture as a whole (Lieberthal 1978). Similarly, the left's proclivity for ideological self-justification lessened the prospects for a meaningful pollution control policy.

These items changed after the downfall of the left. The process of change was uneven and sometimes abrupt. The first two years under Hua Guofeng featured the grandiose Ten-Year Development Program (1976–85) (Hua Guofeng 1978), whose scale made it reminiscent of the Great Leap Forward, which had resulted in enormous environmental damage. As the power of the Whateverists was curbed in late 1978, many overly ambitious projects such as massive land reclamation in the Sanjiang region of Heilongjiang— which would have legitimized deforestation and reduced wildlife habitat— were trimmed back (Woodward 1982: 244; CD, Dec. 31, 1985).

Some projects were even used as political ammunition to attack the Whateverists. The Baoshan steel complex outside Shanghai became the subject of heated discussion, not only within the party but also at the Third Session of the National People's Congress in September 1980. Most of the controversy centered on the need for a six-million-ton annual capacity plant at a cost of five billion dollars in foreign exchange to acquire dated Japanese technology. Some of the most dramatic charges concerned site selection, including the filling of wetlands and the danger to Shanghai from air pollution and solid wastes. Baoshan's proponents were put on the defensive, and the project's target completion date was set back several years while many modifications were introduced. Ironically, even in its original design the plant included more advanced pollution control technology than any other steel mill in China (Weil 1982: 382–84).

The rise to power of the reformers in December 1978 opened the way for a host of changes involving greater emphasis on the definition of individual rights and obligations as well as material incentives. These changes included the passage of various statutes, including the Forestry Law (for trial implementation) in February and the Environmental Protection Law (for trial implementation) in September 1979. These statutes began the process of establishing a legal foundation for defining and enforcing property rights and distinguishing between legal and illegal behavior. Prior to this period, property rights and behavioral norms had been only loosely defined and were often subject to arbitrary political redefinition (Ross and Silk 1987).

Privatization of forestry and agriculture and market-exchange methods for allocating resources also were greatly extended beginning in late 1978. Although these changes necessarily amounted to a reduction in government control of land and other resources, they were justified on other grounds. It was argued that the contract guarantee system of management and other reforms were needed to alleviate the defects associated with overly centralized and restrictive planning. The poorest and most remote areas would be permitted the greatest latitude in production and market autonomy regarding agriculture and, by extension, forestry management. That meant that the issue of privatization was not framed strictly in teleological terms but rather as an economic-development and equity-enhancing measure.

The reformers' command of the political structure nonetheless remained insecure. Beginning in late 1980, there occurred a series of alternations between reform and readjustment impulses as each side seized opportunities to build support within the leadership. The reform side stressed the need for economic and cultural modernization to close the gap between China and the developed countries. The more conservative readjusters pointed to worsening budgetary imbalances and rising inflation in late 1980 to compel a slowdown in spending and construction, to a decay in morals in 1983 to criticize cultural imports from abroad, and to an epidemic of corruption in 1985 to justify the reimposition of tighter state controls on the economy (JPRS 84262 CEA 379, Sept. 7, 1983: 106–7; FBIS, Dec. 7, 1984: K3–4).

The intense competition compels each faction to gild the lily and speed up policy implementation when it is in charge in order to solidify its position. Unfortunately, this process impairs policy coordination and heightens the danger of system overload. In chapter 3 we saw the effects of such a process on water resources: under the left, when construction campaigns led to enormous waste and disregard for technical criteria, and under the right, when management decentralization preceded the clarification of property rights and financial arrangements. Rival factions exaggerate the problems associated with a policy to blacken their rivals' reputation and win the favor of the top leader when the latter is uncommitted.

Of particular importance in this regard are pilot programs and investigations that are used to build momentum for a new direction in policy or to assail an old one. Pilot programs have a long pedigree in CCP history as expressed in such concepts as proceeding from "point to plane" (to refine a program at one or more sites before diffusing it widely) and the "mass line," in which programs undergo iterative modifications on the basis of experience. The process of site selection and project evaluation is not randomized and independently audited, however. Rather, ranking officials cultivate units and communities to serve as test sites for their policy initiatives. Candidates for such status tend to be put forward by officials with personal ties to leaders who themselves may have served there earlier in their careers. Pilot programs thus have little analytical value in predicting a program's success in general application (Travers 1982; FBIS, June 14, 1982: R3–5). They can be used, however, to build a groundswell of support for a policy initiative or to gather ammunition to attack a rival proposal, as well as to train personnel to carry out the program.

For example, former party general secretary Hu Yaobang's ties to the Taihang Mountains dated back to the Anti-Japanese War. Hu apparently cultivated these relationships for many years. In the late 1970s and early

1980s, when Hu was anxious to promote privatization and diversification as the keys to economic development, particularly in hardscrabble mountainous regions, he returned to the Taihangs on several occasions, during which he cited the accomplishments of Yixian County, Hebei. Yixian became an important element in Hu's effort to extend economic reforms, despite opposition from more conservative elements in the party and from the state bureaucracies, including the Ministries of Forestry and Water Conservancy (*Important Documents in Forestry Work* 5: 9; FBIS, July 8, 1982: R2; Yang Zhong 1986). Yixian's role in the post-Mao era is similar to the one it played in the promotion of material incentives and the decentralization of the communes in the early 1960s during the recovery from the Great Leap Forward, although privatization and market exchange have gone further in the more recent period (ZL, February 1961: 12–13).

Naturally, policy advocates also try to attract leadership support by creating pilot projects of their own. One example involves ecological agriculture in which farmers are encouraged to practice diversified, energy-conserving, closed-loop agriculture. The wastes from each activity, e.g., poultry raising, are used as fertilizer or feed for another activity such as fish farming. One model brigade was sponsored by the Beijing Environmental Protection Research Institute and the State Bureau of Environmental Protection. To garner increased publicity, Yu Guangyuan was invited to visit and lend his approval, which was published as the lead story in China's foremost economic journal (Yu Guangyuan 1984). Similar units have been established in Guangdong, Sichuan, and other places where influential local patrons have been cultivated.

The most striking instance of the role of pilot projects in the policy process is the model Dazhai Brigade, which was widely praised beginning in the mid-1960s for its miraculous accomplishments in agriculture in the face of a harsh, forbidding environment. Dazhai was praised not so much for its economic achievements as for the political style in which the brigade was said to be run, featuring self-reliance and political motivation as opposed to state assistance and normative incentives. Within three years of Mao's death, however, the Dazhai facade crumbled under withering charges of inflated production statistics, widespread state subsidies, and political corruption. The most prominent allegations regarding environmental quality included pork-barrel politics involved in the construction of a wasteful water-diversion project to irrigate Dazhai's fields and the fact that fewer than one in five of the 300 heralded clonelike Dazhai-style counties had made the progress in greenification required for certification (FBIS, Feb. 11, 1981: L9; Zhao Mingguang 1984). In other words, the Dazhai experience in mobilizing human labor to reshape the countryside had been based on false premises and failed to produce the intended results, sometimes damaging the environment and reducing producer enthusiasm in the process.

The decimation of Dazhai as a model was a part of the purge that claimed

Politburo members Hua Guofeng and Chen Yonggui, two of the most faithful adherents of Mao's line. Both were closely associated with Dazhai, Chen being the brigade's former leader (Tsou et al. 1982; FBIS, Apr. 26, 1985: W3–5). Only after Dazhai had been discredited was the ascendance of the contract guarantee responsibility system assured, with heavy reliance on the household as opposed to the collective. Had Dazhai not been refuted, it is hard to imagine the reformers' being able to elevate their own models, such as the individual household entrepreneur Li Jinyao in forestry, or the regime's being able to credibly promote dryland farming over irrigation in the arid Northwest.

Somewhat similar to pilot programs are investigations of selected locali- ties and units that leaders initiate to acquire a grass-roots grasp of policy performance and the popular mood. The information so obtained can then be used to justify a need for policy change or to confirm the merit of current policy. Mao Zedong was so convinced of the value of investigations, based on personal experience he had gained in the countryside in the 1920s, that he insisted that no one had a right to speak unless he had first conducted an investigation of his own. Mao, however, was still wont to dismiss data (and their sponsors) when they conflicted with his own preconceptions.

The areas selected tend to be ones that the leader is personally familiar with. For example, Politburo member Chen Yun maintained ties with his home county, Qingpu Xian, west of Shanghai, and returned there in the summer of 1961 to familiarize himself with the consequences of the Great Leap Forward. Chen's stay in Qingpu confirmed his expectations that smaller collectives were superior to communes and that households were more efficient in some activities such as pig farming (Chen Yun 1961).

Although investigations produce local data that might otherwise be hard to obtain, they are subject to biased reporting and conflicting interpretations. Mao's investigation of rural society in Hunan produced findings that have been described as a "fantasy" by a leading scholar specializing in that era (Hofheinz 1977: 35). Because the findings of investigations can affect the fate of policies and careers, the sponsor of an investigation runs serious risks if it challenges a sacred cow. Peng Dehuai, for example, visited Mao's native village in 1959 to discover whether reports of extraordinary leaps in production were credible. He found exaggeration and a myriad of problems (Peng Dehuai 1959: 1). Yet when he presented his findings at the party's Lushan conference that summer, Mao rejected Peng's findings and demanded his removal from office.

Even when investigations are not conducted in areas selected for their dramatic effect or to confirm the leader's own predispositions, they may be hamstrung by local officials who doctor their books or otherwise seek to present an artificial image. Therefore, officials may resort to covert methods to conduct investigations. Mao himself relied in part on the capital guard to report domestic developments back to him. Wang Guangmei, wife of then president Liu Shaoqi, spent months in Peach Garden Brigade,

Funing Xian, Hebei, in the winter of 1963–64 gathering data incognito on cadre behavior and corruption in the countryside in the Socialist Education Movement. Wang subsequently was attacked by the left for driving a wedge between local officials and the masses in order to divert the focus of the movement from alleged "capitalist roaders," including her husband (Ahn 1976: 105–9).

Although the Maoist criticism of Wang was a factional maneuver, it points to the methodological dilemmas associated with investigations. These dilemmas include the selection of units, how much time and effort leaders should spend away from their posts, how to acquire data without revealing the full purpose of the investigation to local officials, and how to assess the validity of findings from a single point in time and space. Leaders have to decide who to sponsor and when to reveal the results of investigations, knowing full well that premature disclosure risks disgrace.

To improve the quality of information needed to run the country, the post-Mao regime has devoted great effort to rebuilding the statistical services and encouraging more open media coverage. Although investigations of model units will continue, they will be subordinated to sample surveys and other statistical procedures (He Huanyan and Chu Xuejin 1984: 105–6). With regard to environmental policy, this new focus involves a major investment in pollution monitoring and reporting services (Nantong Municipal 1982). In terms of natural disasters and accidents, the mass media are now much quicker both to report their occurrence and to analyze likely causes (CD, Mar. 26 and Apr. 8, 1986). As Bordevich (1983) explained, the media were specifically ordered to do more accurate reporting on such events as a deadly landslide in Gansu, in contrast to the situation only a few years earlier when news about droughts, floods, and other major natural disasters was suppressed.

Media coverage can also precipitate an official response. *Zhongguo Huanjing Bao,* the nationwide environmental newspaper that began publication in 1984, ran a series of articles on the danger Tianjin faced from industrial pollution of the Luanhe River, and it claimed that the articles led to remedial action by polluters and local officials (FBIS, Jan. 3, 1985: 81–84, and Feb. 5, 1985: 93–94). The Bureau of Environmental Protection actually encouraged the press to report instances when local officials willfully overrode the regulations in order to provide the bureau with greater regulatory leverage. Such an incident occurred in the summer of 1985 when the authorities in Wenzhou sought to locate a factory in an area off limits to polluters (*Zhongguo Huanjing Bao,* June 22, 1985; RR, July 7, 1985).

Without exaggerating the extent to which information has become more widely available, especially following the purge of Liu Binyan, China's most prominent investigative reporter, in January 1987, it should be clear that the dominant faction faces a risk in this regard. Attacks by the press on its rivals can create enemies, while any revelation of bad news can be used as ammunition by its rivals to snipe at the press. The reformers were badly damaged when budget imbalances, inflation, crime, and credit overruns became known, first within the party and then in society at large (Naughton 1983, Lardy and Lieberthal 1982: xxxvii–xxxviii). It would have been more prudent to discourage the assembly of data on such problems and to censor their publication, in the time-honored tradition of dictatorships in Eastern Europe and elsewhere (Curry 1984: 218–27). Doing so, however, would have deprived the dominant faction, too, of needed data, and would have foreclosed the possibility of enlivening the economy, stimulating science, and unearthing hidden problems. The reformers therefore elected to loosen the channels of information, subject of course to the limits enunciated in Hu Yaobang's condemnation of press freedom in the spring of 1985 (FBIS, Apr. 15, 1985: K15). Hu nevertheless was purged in January 1987, in part because of his tolerance of a more active press and greater intellectual freedom, limited as it was.

Bureaucracies and Public Opinion

It would be short-sighted to regard agenda setting as the province of factional politics alone. Even though China is not a democracy, groups and individuals have particular interests which they seek to further. The most important actors are the institutional interests—the bureaucracies and geographical units of government, especially the provinces. They are legitimate entities with reasonably secure manpower and financial resources and are remarkably resistant to external influences, even when these influences emanate from the higher leadership. That is because of their permanence and their control of information and expertise within their own spheres of jurisdiction, a control that, when taken to the extreme, leads them to be called "independent kingdoms." As Harding (1981) argued, they tend to retain their shape regardless of changes in policy goals.

To control the bureaucracies, the higher leadership can employ a variety of formal and informal measures. The most fundamental are the state plan and party discipline. As we have seen, environmental protection officials were very determined to include pollution control and related matters in the state plan in order to increase their leverage over regulated ministries (Gao Yusheng 1981), while forest management officials similarly favored broadening the timber production planning process under the unified *yi ben zhang* (single-ledger) principle to control excessive logging. Personnel changes involving the replacement of recalcitrant officials with more responsive substitutes and creation of interministerial coordinating bodies such as the State Environmental Protection Commission are also critical measures. On the whole, however, the center's formal organizational power is limited; personnel appointments are not completely determined by a central roster, and bureaucracies and provinces enjoy off-budget funding. As Harding (1981) argued, the Maoists were most prone to devising extra-bureaucratic political campaigns to raise the status of their pet issues, while conservatives tended to favor administrative rationalization. By contrast, the reformers, or pragmatists, have shunned campaigns, which they regard as destabilizing and inefficient. Campaigns sponsored by the reformers have been relatively mild, as they prefer to rely on a mixture of internal and external pressures. These pressures include laws to define agency rights and responsibilities, selective debureaucratization of some administrative functions such as woodlot management, and positive incentives to raise efficiency by converting many bureaucracies into quasi enterprises. The reformers' problem is partly one of ensuring that the bureaucracies do not simply use their newly acquired freedom to continue past behavioral patterns or to purloin state assets without improving their performance. For example, the bureaucracies-cum-enterprises engaged in a binge of raising bonuses and employee perquisites in late 1984–85 (FBIS, Apr. 2, 1985: W1–2). Although the regime cracked down on the excesses, it had to tread cautiously lest it smother the foundation for the reforms (FBIS, Feb. 28, 1985: W1–3).

To the extent that discretion allows, bureaucracies seek to mold policy in their own interests, often demonstrating considerable alacrity in this regard. The Ministry of Forestry, which is traditionally committed to asserting tight control over the production and marketing of forest products, was unsympathetic to reform proposals in 1978–79 to decentralize forest management down to the household level. It regarded this change as tantamount to legitimizing deforestation with its attendant ecological consequences (Ross 1983b: 213–15). Its efforts were to no avail at the time, but revelations about deforestation received close attention in December 1980 when the readjusters had gained dominance and were about to impose economic retrenchment. As a result, the ministry was given extraordinary power to control the production and marketing of forest products (RR, Dec. 6, 1980). That in turn aroused reaction against overly rigid controls. After a few years, the reformers regained the top spot and were able to greatly advance privatization in forestry, helped along by the appointment of Yang Zhong as forestry minister in 1982. The strength of the ministry's traditional views was still visible in 1984, however, when some forestry officials publicly blamed deforestation on the economics and profit-making orientation then in vogue, in contrast to State Economic Commission personnel who believed that price distortions were the major problem (JR, Apr. 26, 1984).

In other instances, the outcomes have been less predictable because issues, solutions, and interests interact in random patterns. The severe 1981 floods in the Yangtze and Yellow River valleys helped the ministry make a prima facie case that deforestation was the ultimate cause of flooding. The ministry also benefited from the fact that vegetative measures cost less than engineering projects, making the former more attractive in a period of economic retrenchment. The principal outcomes, however, were hardly what the ministry would have ordered. General Secretary Hu Yaobang accepted the concept of revegetation but proposed that it be conducted in a decentralized fashion by households rather than by collective or state units (Ross 1983b). Afforestation also was incorporated into the Support Socialist Civilization campaign, a half-hearted and largely symbolic effort to minimize the disruptions occasioned by market-oriented modernization and thus deflect criticism from the political left. The result was the Obligatory Tree Planting campaign, an underfinanced and poorly organized urban greenification program of little direct relevance to flood control or soil conservation (Ross 1987).

Ordinary citizens and economic enterprises also influence the policy process, although the extent of their participation is limited by the ideology of the dominant faction and the overall structure of the system. For the most part, public participation has been employed selectively to validate particular policies. Mao mobilized grass-roots cadres and peasants in the 1950s to advance collectivization and communization faster than many of his colleagues would have preferred. Because the people responded to the promise of immediate material benefits, the policy changes were swiftly implemented, although in deforestation, for example, the price was long-term ecological disruption. Mao's ability to mobilize these groups greatly diminished in the 1960s after the disaster of the Great Leap Forward (Baum 1975).

Deng Xiaoping and the reformers, operating from a different ideological perspective, counted on popular support for their policies to deter opposition from other factions. Deng said on several occasions during the negotiations over the retrocession of Hong Kong that his policies of opening China to the outside world and invigorating the domestic economy would never be reversed because most of the people supported them. "If the road is correct," he said, "no one can change it because any change would be unpopular. People like the changes that have taken place in the past few years, so they will be continued" (BR, Apr. 30, 1984: 10, and July 23, 1984: 16; FBIS, Jan. 2, 1985: K1–2).

Deng's prognosis was partly correct in the sense that the populace had responded favorably to the opportunity to become wealthy, resulting in an impressive economic boom. The prognosis also implied acceptance of a greater role for public opinion in defining the context of public policy and acting as a restraint on unpopular policies. Popular influence increased not only in response to the reformers' preferences but also because central policy directives tended to be imprecise and to lag behind events, with the result that policies were defined in critical respects by popular responses (O'Leary and Watson 1982). With regard to forestry policy, the initial declarations in favor of the production responsibility system failed to alleviate producers' anxieties about a policy reversal and confiscation of their holdings. That resulted in a wave of deforestation. To relieve these worries, the regime was impelled to spell out and liberalize policy on the terms of responsibility management contracts, rights of inheritance, and the size of households. In this fashion, the entire rural sector, including forestry, moved much faster in the direction of privatization and household management than the reformers had originally intended.

A similar example involves the urban rustification movement (*shang shan xia xiang*), which was intended to slow urbanization and promote rural development by relocating many big-city youths to the countryside, including frontier areas. Unpopular from the outset, the campaign aroused bitter opposition among the youths selected during the Cultural Revolution, when the program was greatly expanded and used as a tool to quell urban disorder (Bernstein 1977, Whyte and Parish 1984: 259). Widespread discontent forced the regime to virtually halt the program after Mao's death and to allow many of the unhappy migrants to return to the cities. Nevertheless, the regime refused to allow all participants to return to their former homes. It also refused to totally renounce the policy of relocating urbanites to rural areas because of the burdens that would have placed on the government and because most future urban graduates might refuse postings to the countryside. The consequences would have been especially severe in teaching, forestry, geology, water conservancy, and similar professions. Therefore, the concept of the program was kept alive but the terms were greatly modified. The regime assured rural assignees that they could retain their urban residence permits and return to the cities after several years (CQ, September 1985: 559; RR, Jan. 31, 1986).

This sequence of events indicates that popular influence is reactive and indirect: the populace responds to official policy, the leadership factions monitor mass behavior, and then policy adjustments are made to assure a closer fit between the leadership's goals and popular predispositions. The public's role expands during factional struggles as one or another faction seeks to mobilize popular support. The leadership's response is colored by ideology in the sense that the reformers have been uniquely tolerant of the popular quest for a rising standard of living, a yearning which the Maoists failed to appreciate and which contributed to their downfall (Dittmer 1977).

In other instances, popular participation is more direct and voluntary. The National People's Congress, historically a moribund rubber stamp, and other "democratic" organs have acquired somewhat greater opportunity to question official policy and voice dissent (Burns 1985, Solinger 1982). The right of individual citizens to supervise or influence the policy process on issues affecting their livelihood has been given greater legal standing in some legislation, including article 8 of the Environmental Protection Law (for trial implementation), which affirms the right of citizens to act as pollution monitors.

Two examples in the post-Mao era are local protests against pollution and the organization of more democratic utility-management institutions in the countryside. In each case, there has apparently been a substantial increase in participation because of a reduction in the political risks associated with expressing one's views on such matters and because the separation of political and economic institutions in the countryside as a result of the breakup of the communes decreased the power of local officials. The Pier 41 incident involving pollution in Wuhan is an outstanding example of how popular protest generated a positive response in Beijing to a serious problem that had gone unattended by local officials, but it is just one instance of a phenomenon that saw substantial increases in the number of popular protests and letters to the authorities concerning pollution (Rose and Silk 1985).

On the whole, however, because of the prohibition against horizontal links among community groups and the establishment of broader, more permanent organizations (FBIS, Dec. 12, 1984: K1–2), popular participation is likely to remain indirect and focused on the most visible problems. More subtle and remote issues cannot be so easily influenced by the public. Nevertheless, the public's role will expand if the regime continues to relax its control over social behavior, allowing individuals a larger sphere of personal freedom. Consumer demand rather than the plan will exercise greater influence over economic decision making and popular culture; these factors in turn will affect politics.

Although these developments generally conform with the reformers' preferences, rapid rises in economic and social expectations and protests against corruption and inflation or for more freedom such as those that flared up in 1985 and late 1986, put unwelcome pressures on the regime. In these cases, the regime moved rather quickly to co-opt the protesters and ban public demonstrations; nevertheless, it did respond to public opinion by slowing the reforms and cracking down on perceived excesses. In this way, public opinion bolstered the conservative factions in the elite by revealing popular dissatisfaction with the untoward effects of the reforms or by showing how a relaxation of authoritarian controls could quickly lead to challenges to the authority of the Communist party and the dictatorship of the proletariat.

International Linkages

International linkages have become much more important in the policy process in the post-Mao era. Imperial China frequently resisted foreign experience and culture as well as military aggression. Under Communist rule China has exhibited a pronounced tendency toward autarky to prevent foreign culture from threatening its revolutionary virtue. The principal exception was the decade of Sino-Soviet friendship during the 1950s, when China assumed the role of dutiful younger brother to its elder brother from the north. Many Chinese, especially Mao, chafed under Soviet tutelage and demanded a more equal relationship. When the Soviets proved unable to accommodate them, China turned on the Soviet Union in a rapid reversal that changed their alliance into a virtual cold war. Hostility to the Soviet Union and opposition to the West combined to shift China into a pronounced xenophobia in relation to the entire outside world during the Cultural Revolution. Feelings of inferiority and national pride were joined in a closed-door policy more rigid than at any time since the turn of the century.

This xenophobia had serious repercussions on the policy process, extending even beyond national defense and foreign trade. Autarky meant that Chinese leaders, unlike their counterparts in many developing countries, rarely traveled abroad and did not have to respond to foreign constituencies. Indeed, China at times took a deliberately disruptive attitude toward the world community as reflected in its dismissal of nuclear nonproliferation as a superpower plot. Never having traveled abroad, leaders were more secure in their prejudices, including the notion that pollution was more severe in capitalist countries than in China.

Autarky also meant that intellectuals, dissidents, and national minorities were less able to challenge official policies because they lacked support from abroad. Furthermore, autarky isolated the Chinese policy process from new information from outside, a particularly serious problem in a country where only a minuscule percentage of the population was university educated. During the late 1960s and into the 1970s foreign publications were almost entirely unavailable and personal contact with foreigners was forbidden. With regard to environmental policy, that meant that the Soviet model, which underpriced natural resources or treated them as free goods, remained intact even though the Soviets themselves were making some modifications (Yu Guangyuan 1980).

Deng Xiaoping and the pragmatists greatly expanded China's ties with the outside world, especially the advanced industrialized democracies. Their major motives were strategic—to expand ties with the United States to deter a Soviet attack and otherwise help China to pursue its interests regarding the recovery of Taiwan and Hong Kong—and economic, in the broad sense of expediting the Four Modernizations through the acquisition of modern technology and capital.

In the course of opening China's doors (the closing of which had been due in part to the American-orchestrated containment policy in the postwar era), the policy process was substantially affected even with regard to tangential sectors such as the environment. National leaders acquired international responsibilities and a foreign constituency, which they felt bound to honor to some degree. As early as 1972, China had to prepare a statement on environmental policy for the United Nations Conference on the Human Environment in Stockholm following her admission into the world organization. Although the document consisted of little more than a set of self-serving platitudes about the superiority of the Maoist approach, it led to the establishment of a staff office on environmental protection under the State Council that was elevated to ministerial status a decade later. Thus a small bureaucratic locus for environmental issues was established and began to act as a counterweight to the production-oriented ministries.

At the individual level, officials began to travel and read more widely and acquired a comparative basis for judging the deplorable state of China's environment. Senior Vice-Premier Wan Li, Yu Guangyuan, and others returned speaking rhapsodically about the high levels of environmental quality even in small industrialized countries such as Japan and Switzerland (Yu Guangyuan 1980). Their impressions were reinforced by critical comments that began to be expressed by foreign visitors, including estimates of excess deaths and work days lost to pollution (Swannack-Nunn 1979, Butterfield 1980, Qu Geping 1984: 225).

Economic considerations also were a factor. China began to solicit foreign aid in 1978. Donor agencies such as the World Bank and FAO (and some foreign governments as well) insisted on the incorporation of environmental assessments into project evaluations and, more importantly, included environmental improvement projects such as grasslands improvement and pollution control in their aid programs (the value of which totaled U.S. $130 million in the period 1981–85), thus making such projects more viable (World Food Program WFP/CFA, 11/12 and 13/13, 1982; JPRS CEA-85-007, Jan. 25, 1985: 82–83; RR, Aug. 15, 1985; CD, Aug. 17, 1985). The Chinese also received advanced pollution controls with the foreign plants and technology that they imported as part of their overall modernization program. The importance of environmental quality for the growing tourist industry also provided a foreign exchange rationale for pollution control and the preservation of nature in Hainan and other fragile ecologies (Enderton 1984).

Linkages also developed between environmental scientists and their counterparts abroad. These scientists helped provide the Chinese with new information and resources that would have been extremely difficult to assemble otherwise, thus strengthening their ability to advocate environmental positions at home, e.g., in defense of stricter liability laws (Mi Jian 1984; Luo Huihan 1985) and more stringent emission standards (Ling Xiaoyun 1984). In the latter case, environmentalists were able to win support for more demanding international standards in part because the government was determined to upgrade product quality and increase exports by rapidly adopting international manufacturing, measurement, and quality standards. Environmental standards were piggybacked onto the standardization drive. The "Procedures for the Management of Environmental Protection Standards" issued on October 11, 1983 (reprinted in *Urban and Rural Construction and Environmental Protection Legal Compendia* 1: 307–11), explicitly declared:

> We must actively adopt international standards and advanced standards used in foreign countries concerning environmental protection, while our fundamental environmental protection standards and our commonly used

methods and standards should be gradually strengthened to basically meet
international standards.

Perhaps the most prominent example is the World Wildlife Fund's agreement with China to support research on and preservation of the habitat of
the great panda, the reclusive animal whose lovable visage makes it a symbol
of China around the world. From the Fund's inception in 1961 it had
expressed strong interest in the panda, having adopted the animal as its
symbol. But it was not until 1979, after China's reopening to the outside
world, that the Fund was invited to send a delegation to China and help
organize a major research program, in return for which China agreed to
abide by the International Convention on Trade in Endangered Species of
Fauna and Flora despite its impact on traditional medicine (Becker 1984).
Although the effort to preserve the panda's dwindling habitat had begun
in China in the mid-1970s (*Sichuan Dongwu*, April 1985: 32–34; CD, Nov.
21, 1985), it proceeded further and faster thanks to expressions of international concern and some financial assistance.* For example, the State
Council became directly involved, ordering the delivery of emergency food
supplies in 1983–84 when the panda's precious bamboo flowered, depriving the animals of their preferred food source (ZRGGYG 413, Sept. 20,
1983: 820–22). Some ecologists may question the anthropomorphic concern for the panda, but the panda's symbolic magnetism has in turn increased support for habitat and endangered species preservation in
general, including the establishment of hundreds of nature preserves (BR,
Oct. 15, 1984: 34; *Linye Keji Tongxun*, December 1983). Indeed, Chinese
scientists eagerly seek international assistance in this regard (BR, Apr. 15,
1985: 33).

Nevertheless, international actors cannot replace the vibrant domestic
interest groups that arouse environmental concern in democracies. The
former's attention span and resources are inherently limited and are further restricted by China's determination to channel and confine foreign
influence. International influence is likely to be greatest when it meshes

with established domestic political interests on such issues as foreign trade
or when China is heavily dependent on foreign suppliers and customers,
as in the case of nuclear materials. China's decision to join the International
Atomic Energy Agency in 1983 and its public, even statutory, declamations
against nuclear proliferation seem to have been inspired in no small part
by the country's need for foreign technology to develop nuclear-power-
generating capability quickly and in large volume. Influence is also likely
to be higher under conditions of greater certainty and when China's direct

*The World Wildlife Fund's substantial influence elsewhere is indicated by its relationship
with the Department of Justice and other federal agencies in the United States to step up
enforcement of the Lacey Act and other laws intended to protect endangered species (NYT,
June 27, 1984). A similar case involves the International Crane Foundation.

costs are low or subsidized from abroad (Jacobson and Kay 1983). International influence is weakest when there is no resonance from a strong domestic political interest, as in the case of human rights, where Amnesty International's criticisms have been dismissed. Nevertheless, the international dimension became much stronger on the whole after Mao's death, although more formal consultation on issues that China still regards as domestic matters, such as foreign trade legislation, is desirable.

With regard to international influence, some studies have demonstrated how factional politics affects the pattern of attention. Coverage of Eastern Europe in China's leading economics journals favorably highlighted those aspects that reinforced China's reforms while the reform faction was in power and then emphasized economic controls after the conservative readjusters regained dominance in late 1980. Coverage similarly emphasized the relatively benign elements of policy in China's two closest friends, Yugoslavia and Rumania, while slighting more fundamental reforms in countries more faithful to the Soviet Union in foreign policy, Hungary in particular. Thus, Halpern (1985) concluded that factional politics was the dominant factor, while the media, scientists, and international links did not exert an independent effect on Chinese policy.

The situation is quite different in environmental policy. A survey of leading journals indicates that there was little or no variation over time in the pattern of references to foreign countries (tables 21 and 22). More importantly, coverage was overwhelmingly oriented toward the West, and the United States in particular, rather than toward the communist countries. It is unclear whether that is due to the more technical nature of this subject or to general agreement that Eastern European experience is of little value. Regardless of the explanation, this pattern of attention—which is mirrored in overseas study and travel experiences and especially in the dominance of English-language study—will have substantial long-term significance if it continues, with officials and scientists alike being trained to look for answers to complex questions in the West and via non-Marxist methods (RR, Nov. 16, 1983), despite the objections of ideological stalwarts (e.g., Li Kaiwang 1984; see also the controversial retraction in RR, Dec. 7, 1984, on the contemporary value of Marxism).

Moreover, environmental policy is by no means an exception in this regard. The reorientation of interest toward the West among scientists and intellectuals as well as the younger generation has become very pronounced. It has grown to such proportions that political ideologues must warn their countrymen of the need to redouble research on the theory of scientific socialism to refute the growing belief that capitalism is superior to socialism and that class analysis and Marxism are irrelevant in the modern world (GR, Feb. 10, 1986). Although this reactionary impulse gained strength in 1986, it would ultimately appear to be a futile quest, forcing the regime to resort to measures that it would prefer to avoid, such as harsh crackdowns on personal freedom or xenophobic responses to foreign influence, with

Table 21

Foreign References in <u>Huanjing Kexue</u>
(Environmental Science)

Year	Issue	USA	Japan	Other Western	USSR and E. Europe
1981	1	58	2	26	7
	2	96	11	11	7
	3	53	5	7	11
	4	64	2	24	4
	5	24	0	10	1
	6	29	10	16	6
1982	1	54	12	7	7
	2	72	3	17	1
	3	63	9	7	3
	4	58	16	16	4
	5	65	3	10	7
	6	89	13	12	7
1983	1	96	17	8	1
	2	68	4	2	9
	3	49	8	8	6
	4	44	10	9	6
	5	36	2	1	7
	6	61	4	4	13
1984	1	55	0	4	1
	2	60	2	16	9
	3	68	5	29	9
	4	38	1	4	2
	5	78	23	12	0
	6	49	3	9	1

NOTE: Classification is complicated by the
international:zation of science. I have
relied largely on journal names, so there is
bound to be some overlap between columns 3,
4, and 5. This dominance of Western and
Japanese sources is also found in China's
other leading environmental science journal,
<u>Zhongguo Huanjing Kexue</u>.

Table 22

Articles on Overseas Forestry in
<u>Zhongguo Linye</u> (Chinese Forestry)

Year	USA	Japan	Other Western	USSR and E. Europe
1981	2	2	6	0
1982	3	6	3	1 (Rumania)
1983	4	4	6	0
1984	1	2	4	0

NOTE: This pattern is also observable
in articles on technical subjects.

serious consequences for modernization if it means to seriously defend the ideological basis of its rule in other than nominal terms.

Crisis

No effort to map the policy process can ignore the random aspect in which problems, solutions, actors, and opportunities circulate in complex, unrelated patterns. The reformers' considerable success in the post-Mao era can be understood in this light. Deng Xiaoping exhibited exceptional guile and patience, carefully isolating one group of opponents at a time and awaiting their removal before tackling others to reduce the chances of a defensive coalition's forming against himself (Clarke 1985). Part of the pragmatists' skill lay in making compromises when necessary without losing sight of their ultimate goals. Such compromises in part involved waiting for windows of opportunity to open before moving forward.

One such window is the occurrence of a crisis, a sudden and unanticipated ✓ event that creates a sense of urgency among decision makers, examples of which include foreign conflicts and natural disasters.* Crises can raise the status of an agenda item by increasing the urgency of a response. Although agenda status declines after the crisis atmosphere ends, it still tends to remain higher than its precrisis level (Downs 1972). In general, however, the response itself reflects the underlying predispositions of the actors involved and does not generate an entirely novel decision (Kingdon 1984: 99–105).

Two examples concerning natural hazards and one involving foreign policy illustrate the function of crises as windows of opportunity.** The Tangshan earthquake occurred during the power struggle to succeed the dying Mao. The Gang of Four regarded the earthquake as a distraction from its campaign to assert the absolute importance of ideology in political life. Therefore, the mass media that were dominated by the Gang treated the earthquake as yet another occasion to trumpet the need for ideological fastness and to acclaim the heroism of the masses, despite the immensity of the disaster. By contrast, Hua Guofeng, who had risen to power through the bureaucracy by quietly demonstrating his competence in the service of Maoist ideals, took immediate charge of the relief effort in his capacity as

---

*Kemp (1984) found that accidents (defined as "widely publicized, unanticipated events resulting in significant loss of life, health, and/or property with the perceived probability of reoccurrence or continuance affecting a relatively large number of persons") exert a significant impact on levels of budgetary support for American regulatory agencies.

**A more idiosyncratic but no less serious crisis was the criminal assault on some members of Deng Xiaoping's official party in August 1983 near the seaside resort of Beidaihe. The Hong Kong journal *Chengming* reported that this incident accelerated a major crackdown on crime that began shortly afterward and was marked by thousands of executions (FBIS, Oct. 5, 1983: W2–8; Commentator 1983).

premier and won praise, while the Gang, which lacked direct administrative responsibility, watched from the sidelines. After Hua's accession to power, earthquake policy shifted away from a campaign-style forecast and evacuation policy toward earthquake engineering and regulation of human settlement patterns, a more bureaucratic approach, and more scientific forecasting. Had the left emerged victorious in the power struggle, the response might well have been different.

A second example involves the floods of 1981, which ravaged much of the country. The floods enabled the Ministry of Forestry and the forestry profession to advance their argument that deforestation caused flooding, despite widespread scientific doubts about its validity. The higher leadership accepted this argument but did so in a way that conformed to the broader program of the pragmatists. In particular, revegetation was acclaimed not only on its own merit but also because it was less costly and involved less construction than did engineering measures, an argument that appealed to a regime newly determined to control public spending and inflation. Even more to the point, Hu Yaobang and later Zhao Ziyang promoted private and contract responsibility woodlots to develop forestry even though this policy directly contradicted forestry's own preference for public ownership and larger-scale management.

However tempting they may be, crises do not always provide windows of opportunity large enough to change policy without risk for the proponent. With regard to foreign policy, the escalation of American involvement in Vietnam led the Ministry of Defense to favor at least a partial reconciliation with the Soviet Union to reaffirm China's security umbrella and keep the United States away from Vietnam's southern frontier. Such a rapprochement ran directly contrary to Mao Zedong's polemical posture toward Moscow. In the ensuing controversy the defense minister, Luo Ruiqing, was purged. Although Chinese military assistance to Vietnam increased, the Sino-Soviet dispute and the Cultural Revolution hampered aid, to the continuing discomfiture of Hanoi (Harding and Gurtov 1971).

Conclusions

Agenda setting is primarily a function of factional politics. Factions engage in continuing contests for power, knowing all the while that the loser may face political oblivion. By contrast, the victorious faction is largely able to determine the future agenda. In this respect, the process is heavily top-down in nature. Indeed, were the dominant faction content to simply rule society without heed for modernization in the style of emperors in a traditional regime, there would ordinarily be little need to consider the influence of anyone outside the palace itself.

The greater a faction's policy ambitions, however, the larger the pool of actors involved in agenda setting. Whether its goals involve foreign policy, modernization, or the preservation of political purity, each faction must strive for successful policy performance if it is to cement its power and fend off criticism by its rivals. Inevitably, this necessity leads dominant factions to embark on personnel shakeups and reorganizations to remove their opponents and ensure that loyalists occupy prominent positions in the bureaucracy. Thus, a cleansing of party membership rolls and the activation of control organs sooner or later follow every change in the factional balance.

But even if it could be assumed that new appointees retain their original allegiances after gaining office, loyalty without competence is a prescription for policy disaster. While many factors affect policy success, performance is ultimately dependent on the broader structure of relationships and incentives that govern policy implementation. Designing implementation so that people's energies and talents are harnessed to the dominant faction's goals is a key to success. If people instead respond in a lethargic or evasive fashion in a context of resource scarcity, the resulting policy shortcomings will lead to increased pressure by other factions.

What was most remarkable during the post-Mao era was the reformers' tolerance and even encouragement of self-interested implementation instruments that allowed individuals and organizations unaccustomed autonomy. The cost was a decline in the scope of direct controls by the elite, but that was deemed acceptable because it generated more enthusiastic and efficient responses in behalf of modernization writ large. Any concern that it would lead to environmental degradation was lessened by the regime's simultaneous commitment to raising living standards and codifying legal rights and obligations that allowed for more balanced development than the People's Republic had seen. Some issues, such as the development of tourist sites in ecologically sensitive areas, are particularly hard to resolve, but on the whole the prospect was for environmental quality to improve simultaneously with economic growth. Whether this pattern will endure hinges upon continued economic success, the avoidance of an overload of political demands and natural catastrophes, keeping the reforms from becoming simply vehicles for the furtherance of bureaucratic interests, and a smooth succession of power when Deng Xiaoping fades from the scene.

There can be no assurance of continuity in this regard, particularly in light of Hu Yaobang's dismissal and the apparent decline in Deng Xiaoping's power during the winter of 1986–87. As we have seen, however, the inevitable frictions between the private and public sectors have so far led to consolidations and adjustments rather than to reversals of the reforms (FBIS, Apr. 16, 1985: K10–11). Indeed, the momentum behind some of the policy changes that we have observed has been sufficient to propel them forward, albeit at a slower rate, even during periods of readjustment. That does not signify uniform rates of change in all policy sectors—those linked to human rights and freedom of expression being particularly resistant to meaningful reform—but it does indicate a strong underlying base of support for the reforms that will continue to surface unless forcibly suppressed at enormous cost to future development.

BIBLIOGRAPHY

Agricultural Economics Research Institute, Chinese Academy of Social Sciences (1982). *Linye Jingji Wenti* (Problems of Forestry Economics). Beijing: Zhongguo Shehui Kexue Chubanshe.

Ahn, Byung-joon (1976). *Chinese Politics and the Cultural Revolution: Dynamics of Policy Processes.* Seattle: University of Washington Press.

Aird, John S. (1982). "Recent Demographic Data From China: Problems and Prospects," in CUFM 1: 171–223.

Alchian, Armen A., and Harold Demsetz (1973). "The Property Rights Paradigm," *Journal of Economic History,* 16–65.

Amacher, Ryan C., et al. (1976). "The Economic Approach to Social Policy Questions: Some Methodological Perspectives," in Amacher et al., eds., *The Economic Approach to Public Policy.* Ithaca: Cornell University Press, 18–37.

An Pingsheng (1983). "On the Development of the Agricultural Production Responsibility System," JG (March): 5–7.

Anderson, Frederick R., et al. (1977). *Environmental Improvement through Economic Incentives.* Baltimore: Johns Hopkins University Press.

Anderson, Terry L. (1983). *Water Crisis: Ending the Policy Drought.* Baltimore: Johns Hopkins University Press.

Arrow, Kenneth J. (1963). *Social Choice and Individual Values.* 2d ed. New Haven: Yale University Press.

Ashbrook, Arthur G., Jr. (1982). "China: Economic Modernization and Long-Term Performance," in CUFM 1: 99–118.

Axelrod, Robert (1981). "The Emergence of Cooperation among Egoists," APSR 75, 2 (June): 306–18.

Baark, Erik (1981). "China's Technological Economics," AS 21, 9 (September): 977–99.

Bangongting (1982). "Joint Circular 235 on 25 City Water Conservation Conference," ZRGGYG 392, 14: 795–99.

Barnard, Chester I. (1938, 1964). *The Functions of the Executive.* Cambridge: Harvard University Press.

Barnett, A. Doak, ed. (1969). *Chinese Communist Politics in Action.* Seattle: University of Washington Press.

Bartholomew, Bruce, et al. (1983a) "*Metasequoia glyptostroboides*—Its Present Status in Central China," *Journal of the Arnold Arboretum* 64, 1 (January): 105–28.

———— (1983b). "The 1980 Sino-American Expedition to Western Hubei Province," *Journal of the Arnold Arboretum* 64, 1 (January): 1–103.

Bates, Robert H. (1981). *Markets and States in Tropical Africa: The Political Basis of Agricultural Policies.* Berkeley: University of California Press.

———— (1984). "Some Conventional Orthodoxies in the Study of Agrarian Change," *World Politics* 36, 2 (January): 234–54.

Baum, Richard (1975). *Prelude to Revolution: Mao, the Party, and the Peasant Question, 1962–1966.* New York: Columbia University Press.

————, and Frederick C. Teiwes (1968) *Ssu-Ching: The Socialist Education Movement of 1962–1966.* Berkeley: University of California Center for Chinese Studies, Research Monograph No. 2.

Baumol, William, and Wallace Oates (1979) *Economics, Environmental Policy, and the Quality of Life.* Englewood Cliffs: Prentice-Hall.

Becker, Gary S. (1981). *A Treatise on the Family.* Cambridge: Harvard University Press.

Becker, Jasper (1984). "Pandas, Politics, and the People's Republic," Associated Press (May 16).

Beijing Politics and Law Research Institute, ed. (1957). *Zhonghua Renmin Gongheguo Tudi Fa Cankao Ziliao Huibian* (Selected Reference Materials on the PRC's Land Law). Beijing: Falü Chubanshe.

Beijing Water Company (1984). "Thirty-Five Years Supplying Water to Beijing," *Chengshi Gong Shui,* 3: 9–11.

Bennett, Gordon (1976). *Yundong: Mass Campaigns in Chinese Communist Leadership.* Berkeley: University of California Center for Chinese Studies.

Berk, Richard A., et al. (1981) *Water Shortage: Lessons in Conservation from the Great California Drought 1976–1977.* Cambridge: Abt Books.

Berlin, Isaiah (1958). *Two Concepts of Liberty.* London: Oxford University Press.

Bernstein, Richard (1982). *From the Center of the Earth: The Search for the Truth About China.* Boston: Little, Brown.

Bernstein, Thomas P. (1967). "Leadership and Mass Mobilization in the Soviet and Chinese Collectivization Campaigns of 1929–1930 and 1955–1956: A Comparison," CQ 31 (July): 1–47.

——— (1977). *Up to the Mountains and Down to the Countryside.* New Haven: Yale University Press.

Biswas, Asit K., et al., eds. (1983). *Long-Distance Water Transfer: A Chinese Case Study and International Experiences.* Dublin: Tycooly International.

Bordevich, Fergus M. (1983). "Bad News in China," *Columbia Journalism Review* (July–August): 9–10.

Bowen, Elinor R. (1982). "The Pressman-Wildavsky Paradox: Four Addenda or Why Models Based on Probability Theory Can Predict Implementation Success and Suggest Useful Tactical Advice for Implementers," *Journal of Public Policy* 2, 1 (February): 1–22.

Bower, Blair T., et. al. (1977). "Incentives for Managing the Environment," *Environmental Science and Technology* 11, 3 (March): 250–54.

Boxer, Baruch (1980). "Environmental Science," in Leo A. Orleans, ed., *Science and Contemporary China.* Stanford: Stanford University Press, 463–74.

Braybrooke, David, and Charles Lindblom (1963). *A Strategy for Decision.* Glencoe: Free Press.

Brubaker, Sterling, and Emery N. Castle (1982). "Alternative Policies and Strategies to Achieve Soil Conservation," in Harold G. Halcrow et al., eds. *Soil Conservation Policies, Institutions, and Incentives.* Ankeny, Iowa: Soil Conservation Society of America, 302–14.

Bunce, Valerie (1981). *Do New Leaders Make a Difference? Executive Succession and Public Policy under Capitalism and Socialism.* Princeton: Princeton University Press.

Burns, John F. (1985). "China's Legislative Forums Are Becoming Increasingly Feisty," NYT (April 15).

Burton, Ian, et al. (1978). *The Environment as Hazard.* New York: Oxford University Press.

Butterfield, Fox (1980). "China's Leaders Waking Up to Dangers of Pollution," NYT (April 6): 1.

——— (1982). *China: Alive in the Bitter Sea.* New York: Bantam.

Cahn, Robert (1978). *Footprints on the Planet: A Search For an Environmental Ethic.* New York: Universe Books.

Cai Hanquan (1984). "Why Has Polluted Soil Become a Problem in the Suburbs of Guangzhou?" H (September): 20–21.

Caldwell, Lynton Keith (1984). *International Environmental Policy: Emergence and Dimensions.* Durham: Duke University Press.

Cao Fenglin (1982). "Grabbing the Bull by the Nose in Environmental Management Work," H (January): 2–3.

Carens, Joseph H. (1981). *Equality, Moral Incentives, and the Market: An Essay in Utopian Politico-Economic Theory.* Chicago: University of Chicago Press.

Cell, Charles P. (1977). *Revolution at Work: Mobilization Campaigns in China.* New York: Academic Press.

Central People's Government (1951). "Instructions regarding the Suitable Resolution of Forestry Rights and Clarification of Management and Protection Responsibilities," Apr. 21, in Beijing Politics and Law Research Institute (1957).

Chan, Anita K., et al. (1984). *Chen Village: The Recent History of a Peasant Community in Mao's China.* Berkeley: University of California Press.

Chang Chunyin and Kong Min (1984). "The Price of Land and the Cost Paid for Land in Socialist Economy," JY (February): 37–42.

Chang, Hsin (1984). "The 1982–1983 Overinvestment Crisis in China," AS 24, 12 (December): 1275–1301.

Chang, Parris H. (1970). "Research Notes on the Changing Loci of Decision in the CCP," CQ 44 (October–December): 169–94.

——— (1978). *Power and Policy in China.* 2d ed. University Park: Pennsylvania State University Press.

Chen Dongsheng (1980). "Research on Environmental Protection and Environmental Economics," in Yu Guangyuan et al. (1980): 110–25.

Chen Huaizhi (1982). "A Preliminary Discussion of Water Pricing with Regard to Water Conservancy Projects," *Jiage Lilun he Shijian* (May): 21–23.

Chen Lihu (1984). "Creating a Body of Local Environmental Civil Law Has Great Significance," H (May): 28–29ff.

Chen Peiyuan and Li Zhou (1984). "A Discussion of the Theory of Forest Valuation," LK 20, 3 (August): 299–306.

Chen Ren (1984). "How to Properly Address and Resolve Contradictions between Factories and the Masses," H (May): 21.

Chen Rong (1934). *Lidai Senlin Shilue ji Minguo Linzheng Shiliao* (Annotations on the Forest History of Past Centuries and Historical Materials on Forest Policy of the Republic). Nanking: Forestry Department, Nanking University.

Chen Taishan et al. (1982). "The Structure and Calculation of Stumpage Prices for Artificial Plantations," LJW, 124–43.

Chen Tung-Lei (1963). "Lei Feng," in Franz Schurmann and Orville Schell, eds. (1967). *Communist China.* New York: Vintage Books, 450–56.

Chen Tuyan (1983). "Large-Scale Establishment of Fuelwood Forests Is a Major Avenue to Solving the Rural Energy Problem," NJJ (November): 20–22.

Chen Wuyuan and Rong Yuyan (1983). "Our Rural Management System Must Be Reformed," JY (April): 63–65.

Chen Yongmi (1984). "Social Economic Returns from Forestry in Hunan," ZL (December): 14.

Chen Youxiang and Xu Gangxi (1986). "An Exploration of Strategic Issues Affecting the Environment and Environmental Science and Technology," *Huanjing Baohu Jishu Zhengce Yanjiu Tongxun* 2: 1–8.

Chen Yun (1961). "Investigation of Qingpu County," trans. in Lardy and Lieberthal (1982): 171–94.

Chen Ziqun (1985). "Effluent Fees Are an Important Economic Instrument to Promote Industrial Pollution Control," *Huanjing Guanli* (January): 18–21.

Cheng, Chu-yuan (1982). *China's Economic Development: Growth and Structural Change.* Boulder: Westview.

Cheng Yaping (1983). "The Development of Collective Industry Must Uphold the Unity of Economic and Environmental Interests," HB (May): 28–29.

Chi Weiyun (1982). "Some Economic Problems Associated with the Development of Tree Planting and Afforestation," LJW, 10–22.

China Agricultural Development Research Group (1983). "Enlightenment from the Contracting on Small River Valleys on the Household Basis," NJW (August): 20–25.

China Timber Company (1984). "Be Active in Structural Reform and Enliven Timber Circulation," *Wuzi Guanli* (November): 4–7.

Chinese Forestry Society (1985). *Zaolin Guihua Sheji* (Afforestation Planning and Design). Beijing: Zhongguo Linye Chubanshe.

Chinn, Dennis L. (1978). "Income Distribution in a Chinese Commune," *Journal of Comparative Economics* 2, 3 (September): 246–65.

——— (1979). "Team Cohesion and Collective Labor Supply in Chinese Agriculture," *Journal of Comparative Economics* 3, 4 (December): 375–94.

Chu, Godwin C. (1979). "Communication and Cultural Change in China: A Conceptual Framework," in Godwin C. Chu and Francis L.K. Hsu, eds. *Moving A Mountain: Cultural Change in China.* Honolulu: University of Hawaii Press, 2–24.

Clarke, Christopher M. (1985). "Changing the Context for Policy Implementation: Organizational and Personnel Reform in Post-Mao China," in Lampton (1987), 25–47.

Coase, Ronald H. (1960). "The Problem of Social Cost," *Journal of Law and Economics* 3, 1: 1–44.

Cobb, Roger W., et al. (1976). "Agenda Building as a Comparative Political Process," APSR 70, 1 (March): 126–38.

Cohen, Michael, et al. (1972). "A Garbage Can Model of Organizational Choice," *Administrative Science Quarterly* 17, 1 (March): 1–25.

Collier, David, ed. (1979). *The New Authoritarianism in Latin America.* Princeton: Princeton University Press.

Commentator (1983). "An Acute Struggle with the Enemy in the Political Sphere," HQ 18: 2–8.

——— (1984). "Our Policy Is One of Making the People Prosperous," RR, Mar. 29.

Compendia of Forestry Laws and Decrees (*Linye Fagui Huibian*) (1980–84). Vols. 13–17. Beijing.

Compendia of Forestry Laws and Regulations (*Linye Faling Huibian*) (1950–63). Vols. 1–12. Beijing.

Compendia of Laws and Decrees of the People's Republic of China (*Zhonghua Renmin Gongheguo Faling Huibian*) (1955–63). Vols. 1–13. Beijing: Falü Chubanshe.

Compton, Boyd (1952). *Mao's China: Party Reform Documents, 1942–1944.* Seattle: University of Washington Press.

Contemporary China's Forestry (*Dangdai Zhongguo de Linye*) (1985). Beijing: Zhongguo Shehui Kexue Chubanshe.

Council on Environmental Quality (1981). *Environmental Quality 1983.* Washington: U.S. Government Printing Office.

Crandall, Robert W. (1983). *Controlling Industrial Pollution: The Economics and Politics of Clean Air.* Washington: Brookings Institution.

——— and Paul R. Portney (1984). "Environmental Policy," in Portney, ed., *Natural Resources and the Environment.* Washington: Urban Institute Press, 47–81.

Crenson, Matthew A. (1971). *The Un-Politics of Air Pollution: A Study of Non-Decision Making in the Cities.* Baltimore: Johns Hopkins University Press.

Crook, Frederick W. (1975). "The Commune System in the People's Republic of China, 1963–1974," in U.S. Congress Joint Economic Committee. *China: A*

Reassessment of the Economy. Washington: U.S. Government Printing Office, 411–35.

Culhane, Paul T. (1980). *Public Lands Politics: Interest Group Influence on the Forest Service and the BLM*. Baltimore: Johns Hopkins University Press.

Curry, Jane Leftwich (1984). *The Black Book of Polish Censorship*. New York: Vintage.

Dacy, Douglas C., and Howard Kunreuther (1969). *The Economics of Natural Disasters: Implications for Federal Policy*. New York: Free Press.

Dales, J.H. (1968). *Pollution, Property and Prices*. Toronto: University of Toronto Press.

Dana, Samuel Trask, and Sally K. Fairfax (1980). *Forest and Range Policy: Its Development in the United States*. New York: McGraw-Hill.

Daneke, Gregory A. (1982). "The Future of Environmental Protection: Reflections on the Difference between Planning and Regulation," *Public Administration Review* 42, 3 (May–June): 227–33.

de Bary, William Theodore, et. al. (1960). *Sources of Chinese Tradition*. New York: Columbia University Press.

De Janvry, Alain (1981). *The Agrarian Question and Reformism in Latin America*. Baltimore: Johns Hopkins University Press.

Deng Jianxu (1983). "Some Problems regarding the Establishment of a Mediation Organization for Environmental Protection," HB (April): 11–12.

Deng Xiaoping (1978). "Emancipate the Mind, Seek Truth from Facts, and Unite as One in Looking to the Future," Dec. 13, in *Selected Works of Deng Xiaoping, 1975–1982*. Beijing: Foreign Languages Press, 151–65.

——— (1980). "On the Reform of the System of Party and State Leadership," Aug. 18, in BR 26, 40 (Oct. 3, 1983): 14–22.

Deng Zihui (1957). "Rely on the Massess to Complete the Great Mission of Greenifying the Motherland," ZL 1958 (February): 3–5.

Dernberger, Robert F. (1982). "The Chinese Search for the Path of Self-Sustained Growth in the 1980s: An Assessment," in CUFM 1: 19–76.

Ding Ming (1984). "An Inquiry into the Question of Water Transportation Rates in China," *Jiage Lilun yu Shijian* 4: 32–35.

Dirlik, Arif (1982). "Spiritual Solutions to Material Problems: The 'Socialist Ethics and Courtesy Month' in China," *South Atlantic Quarterly* 81, 4 (Autumn): 359–75.

Dittmer, Lowell (1974). *Liu Shao-ch'i and the Chinese Cultural Revolution: The Politics of Mass Criticism*. Berkeley: University of California Press.

——— (1977) " 'Line Struggle' in Theory and Practice: The Origins of the Cultural Revolution Reconsidered," CQ 72 (December): 675–712.

——— (1978). "Bases of Power in Chinese Politics," *World Politics* 31, 1 (October): 26–61.

——— (1980). "The Radical Critique of Political Interest, 1966–1978," *Modern China* 6, 4 (October): 363–96.

Domes, Jurgen (1977). *China after the Cultural Revolution: Politics between Two Party Congresses*. Annette Berg and David Goodman, trans. Berkeley: University of California Press.

——— (1985). *The Government and Politics of the PRC: A Time of Transition*. Boulder: Westview.

Donnithorne, Audrey (1972). *The Budget and the Plan in China: Central-Local Economic Relations*. Canberra: Australian National University, Contemporary China Paper No. 3.

——— (1981). *Centre-Provincial Economic Relations in China*. Canberra: Australian National University, Contemporary China Paper No. 16.

Downing, Paul B., and Kenneth Hanf, eds. (1983). *International Comparisons in Implementing Environmental Laws*. Boston: Kluwer-Nijhoff.

Downs, Anthony (1972). "Up and Down with Ecology—The Issue Attention Cycle," *Public Interest* 28 (Summer): 38–50.

Dreyer, June Teufel (1977). *China's Forty Millions*. Cambridge: Harvard University Press.

Du Runsheng (1984a). "Explaining China's Rural Economic Policy," BR 27, 18 (Apr. 30): 16–21.

——— (1984b). "China's Countryside under Reform," BR 27, 33 (Aug. 13): 16–21.

Duan Shaobo (1984). "Rational Utilization of Naural Resources in Shanghai," ZZ 1: 42–48.

Eckholm, Erik (1979). *Planting for the Future: Forestry for Human Needs*. Washington: Worldwatch Institute, No. 26.

Eckstein, Alexander (1968). "Economic Fluctuations in Communist China's Economic Development," in Ping-ti Ho and Tang Tsou, eds. *China's Heritage and the Communist Political System*. Chicago: University of Chicago Press, 1, 2: 691–752.

——— (1977). *The Chinese Development Model*. Cambridge: Cambridge University Press.

Editorial Committee for the Atlas of Cancer Mortality (1979). *Atlas of Cancer Mortality in the People's Republic of China*. Beijing: China Map Press.

Emerson, John Philip (1982). "The Labor Force of China, 1957–1980," in CUFM 1: 224–67.

Enderton, Catherine Schurr (1984). *Hainan Dao: Contemporary Environmental Management and Development on China's Treasure Island*. Ph.D. diss., University of California at Los Angeles.

Engels, Frederick (1940). "The Part Played by Labour in the Transition from Ape to Man," in *Dialectic of Nature*. Clemens Dutt, trans. and ed. New York: International Publishers, 279–96.

Epstein, Edward J. (1984). "Pollution Law Laid Down," *China Trade Report* (March): 4–5.

Esman, Milton J., and Norman T. Uphoff (1984). *Local Organizations: Intermediaries in Rural Development*. Ithaca: Cornell University Press.

Etzioni, Amitai (1967). "Mixed Scanning: A Third Approach to Decision-Making," *Public Administration Review* 27, 4 (July–August): 385–402.

FAO (1982). *Forestry in China*. Rome: FAO Forestry Paper No. 35.

Ferguson, Buell M., et al. (1982) *Land Use and Conservation Treatment, Flood Control, River Basin Planning, Interbasin Transfer of Water, and Microhydroelectric Generation*. Washington: U.S. Department of Agriculture Office of International Cooperation and Development.

Fisher, Anthony C. (1981). *Resource and Environmental Economics*. Cambridge: Cambridge University Press.

Fletcher, Merlon Don (1974). *Workers and Commissars: Trade Union Policy in the People's Republic of China*. Bellingham: Western Washington State College, Program in East Asian Studies, Occasional Paper No. 6.

Forestry Development Section, Agricultural Economics Institute, Academy of Social Sciences (1983). "An Initial Plan of Strategy for China's Forestry Development," NJW 5: 34–38.

Frederick, Kenneth D. (1982). "Water Supplies," in Paul R. Portney, ed. *Current Issues in Natural Resource Policy*. Washington: Resources for the Future, 216–52.

Freeman, A. Myrick, III (1979). *The Benefits of Air and Water Pollution Control: A Review and Synthesis of Recent Estimates*. Prepared for the Council on Environmental Quality.

Frohlich, Norman, et al. (1971). *Political Leadership and Collective Goods*. Princeton: Princeton University Press.

Gao Fengxiang (1973). "Halt Stream Pollution, Recover Wastes and Transform Them into Treasures," in Quanguo Huanjing Baohu Huiyi Mishuchu, ed., *Huanjing Baohu Jingyan Xuanbian* (Selected Experiences in Environmental Protection). Beijing: Renmin Chubanshe.

Gao Yusheng (1981). "How to Better Incorporate Environmental Protection in the National Economic Plan," HB (May): 1–3.

Gardner, B. Delworth (1983). "Water Pricing and Rent Seeking in California Agriculture," in Terry L. Anderson, ed., *Water Rights: Scarce Resource Allocation, Bureaucracy, and the Environment*. Cambridge: Ballinger, 83–113.

Gisser, Micha, and Ronald N. Johnson (1983). "Institutional Restrictions on the Transfer of Water Rights and the Survival of an Agency," in Terry L. Anderson, ed., *Water Rights: Scarce Resource Allocation, Bureaucracy, and the Environment*. Cambridge: Ballinger, 137–65.

Goffman, Erving (1961). *Asylums: Essays in the Social Situation of Mental Patients and Other Inmates*. Garden City: Anchor.

Gold, Thomas B. (1984). " 'Just in Time!' China Battles Spiritual Pollution on the Eve of 1984," AS 24, 9 (September): 947–74.

Goldman, Marshall I. (1972). *The Spoils of Progress*. Cambridge: MIT Press.

Goldman, Merle W. (1971). *Literary Dissent in Communist China*. New York: Atheneum.

——— (1979). "The Media Campaign as a Weapon in Political Struggle: The Dictatorship of the Proletariat and Water Margin Campaigns," in Godwin C. Chu and Francis L.K. Hsu, eds. *Moving A Mountain: Cultural Change in China*. Honolulu: University of Hawaii Press, 179–206.

Gong Fanwen and He Naihui (1982). "A Discussion on Forest Value and the Theoretic Price of Timber in China," LK 18, 2 (May): 177–84.

Government Administration Council (1951). "Instructions regarding the Appropriate Disposition of Forest Rights and Clarification of Management and Protection Responsibilities," Apr. 21, in *Zhonghua Renmin Gongheguo Minfa Cankao Ziliao* (Reference Materials on the Civil Law of the PRC). Beijing, 1956–57.

——— (1953). "Instructions concerning the Stimulation of the Masses for Afforestation, Tending, and Protection Work," July 30, in *Zhongyang Renmin Zhengfu Faling Huibian* (Legal Compendia of the Central People's Government). Beijing, 1953, 235–39.

Greer, Charles (1979). *Water Management in the Yellow River Basin of China*. Austin: University of Texas Press.

Gregory, Kenneth (1978). "China's Rivers," *Geographical Journal* 144, 2 (July): 194–99.

Grindle, Merilee S., ed. (1980). *Politics and Policy Implementation in the Third World*. Princeton: Princeton University Press.

Guo Huan (1974a). "Focus on Environmental Protection Work," HQ (September): 11–15.

——— (1974b) "Accent on Environmental Protection," PR 17, 45 (November 8): 9–11.

Guo Li'ai (1985). *Jianzhu Sheji Weisheng Shencha* (An Examination of Public Health Considerations in Architecture and Design). Harbin: Heilongjiang Kexue Jishu Chubanshe.

Gustafson, Thane (1981). *Reform in Soviet Politics: Lessons of Recent Policies on Land and Water*. Cambridge: Cambridge University Press.

Halpern, Nina P. (1985). "Learning from Abroad: Chinese Views of the East European Economic Experience, January 1977–June 1981," *Modern China* 11, 1 (January): 77–109.

Hammond, Thomas H. (forthcoming). "The Political Implications of Organizational Structures or 'Which Buck Stops Where?' "

—— and Gary J. Miller (forthcoming). "A Social Choice Perspective on Expertise and Authority in Bureaucracy."

Han Gangli (1985). "Some Proposals on How to Enliven Timber Circulation," *Wuzi Guanli* (January): 17–18.

Han Yongwen (1985). "Unearth the Potential for Timber Conservation and Substitution, Ensure Coordinated Economic Development," *Wuzi Guanli* (August): 17–18.

Hansen, John Mark (1985). "The Political Economy of Group Membership," APSR 79, 1 (March): 79–96.

Hardin, Garrett (1968). "The Tragedy of the Commons," *Science* 162 (Dec. 13): 1243–48.

—— (1981). "Ending the Squander-archy," in Herman E. Daly and Alvaro F. Umana, eds. *Energy, Economics and the Environment*. AAAS Selected Symposia 64. Boulder: Westview.

Hardin, Russell (1982). *Collective Action*. Baltimore: Johns Hopkins University Press.

Harding, Harry (1981). *Organizing China: The Problem of Bureaucracy 1949–1976*. Stanford: Stanford University Press.

—— and Melvin Gurtov (1971). *The Purge of Lo Jui-ch'ing: The Politics of Chinese Strategic Planning*. Santa Monica: Rand.

Harper, Paul (1969). "The Party and the Unions in Communist China," CQ 37 (January–March): 84–119.

He Huanyan and Chu Xuejin (1984). "China's Agricultural Statistics," in State Statistics Bureau Research Institute of Statistical Science, ed. *Zhongguo Shehuizhuyi Tongji Gongzuo de Jianli yu Fazhan* (The Origins and Development of China's Socialist Statistical Work). Beijing: Zhongguo Tongji Chubanshe, 101–9.

He Naihui (1982). "On the Danger of the Yangtze River Becoming the Second Yellow River." LJW, 176–90.

He Tingxian (1983). "Initial Discussion on the 'Two Households' in Forestry and Their Management Characteristics in Guizhou Province," NJW (September), 40–42.

He Weicheng (1982). "A Preliminary Analysis of Beijing's Water Resources," ZZ 3: 12–20.

He Yanxian (1984). "A New Trend in the Development of Specialized Households in Forestry," NJW (November): 40–42.

Heffron, Florence (1983). *The Administrative Regulatory Process*. New York: Longman.

Henan Fuguo Xian Party Committee (1973). "Do Tree Planting on the Four Sides in a Big Way, Build a Surplus in Timber," in Ministry of Agriculture and Forestry, Forestry Bureau (1974). *Lühua Zuguo* (Greenify the Motherland). Beijing: Nongye Chubanshe, 7: 22–26.

Hinton, William H. (1983). "A Trip to Fengyang County: Investigating China's New Family Contract System," *Monthly Review* (November): 1–28.

"Historical Review: Establishment and Development of the Chinese Society of Environmental Economics," ZHK 4, 1 (February 1984): 4–9.

Hofheinz, Roy, Jr. (1977). *The Broken Wave: The Chinese Peasant Movement 1922–1928*. Cambridge: Harvard University Press.

Hooper, Beverly (1985). *Youth in China*. Ringwood, Australia: Penguin.

Hou Jianqiu (1984). "Some Fundamental Questions regarding Environmental Protection Work," H (January): 2–5.

Hou Xueyu (1982). "On the Orientation of Making Use of Mountains and Hills in the South," NJW (November): 25–30.

—— (1983). "Some Suggestions on Forest Type," ZL (June): 35–36.

Hou Zhizheng et al. (1982). "A Preliminary Discussion of Conditions regarding Fiberboard and Particleboard Production," LJW, 144–53.

Howe, Christopher, and Kenneth R. Walker (1977). "The Economist," in Dick Wilson, ed. *Mao Tse-tung in the Scales of History.* Cambridge: Cambridge University Press, 174–222.

Hu Jiwei (1979). "Report on a Series of Struggles in the Top Echelons of the CCP," FBIS, Aug. 15, 1980, U1–17.

Hu Jushun (1983). "An Effective Way to Solve the Timber Shortage Problem on the Plains," NJW (July), 53–55.

Hu Tongwen (1983). "Correctly Understanding Xishuangbanna," DZ (May): 2–3.

Hu Yaobang (1982). "Create a New Situation in All Fields of Socialist Modernization," BR 25, 37 (Sept. 13): 11–40.

——— (1983). "On Problems in Political and Ideological Work," HQ 1 (January): 2–10.

Hu Zhengchang (1983). "Arguments about the Management Policy and Methods for Secondary Forests," *Dongbei Linxueyuan Xuebao* 11, 4 (December): 12–22.

Hua Guofeng (1975) "Mobilize the Whole Party, Make Greater Efforts to Develop Agriculture and Strive to Build Tachai-Type Counties throughout the Country," Oct. 15, in PR 18, 44 (Oct. 31): 7–10ff.

——— (1978). "Unite and Strive to Build a Modern, Powerful Socialist Country!" PR 21, 10 (March 10): 7–40.

Hua Qingyuan (1971). "Comprehensive Utilization Requires Us to Promote the Good and Discard the Harmful," HQ (October): 54–59.

Huang Daoxia (1983). "What Are the Differences between a Cooperative and a Collective Econonmy?" HQ 7 (Apr. 1): 46–47.

Huang Faruo (1985). "Shifting Relocation Policy from Resettlement to Economic Development," ZS (January): 6–8.

Huanggang Prefecture, Hubei, Bureau of Water Conservancy and Electric Power et al. (1974). *Management of the Meichuan Reservoir Irrigation Project.* Beijing: Shuili Dianli Chubanshe. In Nickum (1981), 77–159.

Hyde, William F. (1980). *Timber Supply, Land Allocation, and Economic Efficiency.* Baltimore: Johns Hopkins University Press.

——— (1981). "Compounding Clear-cuts: The Social Failures of Public Timber Management in the Rockies," in John Baden and Richard L. Stroup, eds. *Bureaucracy vs. Environment: The Environmental Costs of Bureaucratic Governance.* Ann Arbor: University of Michigan Press, 186–202.

Hyman, Eric L. (1983). "Pulpwood Tree Farming in the Philippines from the Viewpoint of the Smallholder: An Ex Post Evaluation of the PICOP Project," *Agricultural Administration* 14: 1–27.

Ingram, Helen, et al. (1983). "Replacing Confusion with Equity: Alternatives for Water Policy in the Colorado River Basin." Presented at the Colorado River Working Symposium, Santa Fe, N. Mex.

Ishikawa, Shigeru (1983). "Chinese Economic Growth since 1949–A Reassessment," CQ 94 (June): 242–81.

——— (1984). "China's Economic System Reform: Underlying Factors and Prospects," in Neville Maxwell and Bruce McFarlane, eds. *China's Changed Road to Development.* Oxford: Pergamon, 9–20.

Jacobsen, Harold K., and David A. Kay (1983). "Conclusions and Policy," in idem., eds. *Environmental Protection: The International Dimension.* Totowa: Allanheld, Osmun, 310–32.

Jencks, Harlan W. (1982). *From Markets to Missiles: Politics and Professionalism in the Chinese Army, 1945–1981.* Boulder: Westview.

Jia Bangjie (1983) "Some Proposals for the Reform of Irrigation Management Work," ZS (June): 46–48.

Jiang Bikun and Guo Rui, eds. (1980). *Huanjing Baohu Fa Jianghua* (A Discussion on Environmental Protection Law). Zhangjiakou: Falü Chubanshe.

Jiang Yingguang (1983). "On Several Theoretical Questions of Eco-economics," JY (October): 56–60.

Jin Qi (1984a) "Greening China by Contract System," BR 27, 14 (Apr. 2): 4.

——— (1984b) "China Expands Flexible Policies," BR 27, 19 (May 7): 4.

Jin Ruilin and Cheng Zhengkang (1983). "An Analysis of Crimes Relating to Environmental Damage," ZHK (April): 71–76.

Jing Ping (1983). "We Must Stabilize the Area Sown in Grain," HQ 5: 32–33.

——— (1984) "Do Well the Merger of Unity and Separation, Perfect the Unified Production Contract Responsibility System," HQ 4: 25–26.

Joffe, Ellis (1965). *Party and Army: Professionalism and Political Control in the Chinese Officer Corps, 1949–1964.* Cambridge: Harvard University, East Asian Research Center.

Joint Editorial (1978). "Transform China in Spirit of Foolish Old Man Who Removed Mountains," BR 21, 10 (Mar. 10): 44–47.

Jones, Charles O. (1975). *Clean Air: The Policies and Politics of Pollution Control.* Pittsburgh: University of Pittsburgh Press.

——— (1984). *An Introduction to the Study of Public Policy.* 3d ed. Monterey: Brooks/Cole.

Kapp, K. William (1974). *Environmental Policies and Development Planning in Contemporary China and Other Essays.* The Hague: Mouton.

Kau, Ying-mau (1969). "The Urban Bureaucratic Elite in Communist China: A Case Study of Wuhan, 1949–1965," in A. Doak Barnett, ed. *Chinese Communist Politics in Action.* Seattle: University of Washington Press.

——— (1973). *The People's Liberation Army and China's Nation Building.* White Plains: IASP.

Kautsky, John H. (1969). "Revolutionary and Managerial Elites in Modernizing Regimes," *Comparative Politics* 1, 4 (July): 441–67.

Keidel, Albert (1983). "Incentive Farming," CBR 10, 6 (November–December): 12–14.

Kellison, Robert C., et al. (1982). "Forest Tree Improvement in the People's Republic of China," *Journal of Forestry* 80, 10 (October).

Kelman, Steven (1981). *What Price Incentives? Economists and the Environment.* Cambridge: Auburn House.

——— (1983). "Economic Incentives and Environmental Policy: Politics, Ideology, and Philosophy," in Thomas C. Schelling, ed. *Incentives for Environmental Protection.* Cambridge: MIT Press, 291–331.

Kemp, Kathleen A. (1984). "Accidents, Scandals, and Political Support for Regulatory Agencies," *Journal of Politics* 46, 2 (May): 401–27.

Kingdon, John W. (1984). *Agendas, Alternatives, and Public Policies.* Boston: Little, Brown.

Kinzelbach, Wolfgang K.H. (1981). "Environmental Problems in the People's Republic of China." Presented at the Third International Conference on Energy Use Management, West Berlin, Oct. 26–30.

——— (1983). "China: Energy and Environment," *Environmental Management* 7, 4: 303–10.

Kneese, Allen V., and Charles L. Schultze (1975). *Pollution, Prices, and Public Policy.* Washington: Brookings Institution.

Kong Fanwen and He Naihui (1982). *Mucai Jiage* (Wood Prices). Beijing: ZL Chubanshe.

Kraus, Richard Curt (1981). *Class Conflict in Chinese Socialism.* New York: Columbia University Press.

Krier, James E., and Edmund Ursin (1977). *Pollution and Policy: A Case Essay on*

California and Federal Experience with Motor Vehicle Air Pollution 1940–1975. Berkeley: University of California Press.

Krutilla, John V., et al. (1983). "Public versus Private Ownership: The Federal Lands Case," *Journal of Policy Analysis and Management* 2, 4 (Summer): 548–58.

LaBounty, J.F. (1982). "Assessment of the Environmental Effects of Constructing the Three Gorges Project on the Yangtze River," in S.W. Yuan, ed. *Energy, Resources and Environment: Papers Presented at the First U.S.-China Conference on Energy, Resources and Environment 7–12 Nov. 1982.* New York: Pergamon, 583–90.

Lampton, David M. (1977). *The Politics of Medicine in China: The Policy Process, 1949–1977.* Boulder: Westview Press.

——— (1983). "Water Politics," CBR (July–August): 10–17.

———, ed. (1987). *Policy Implementation in Post-Mao China.* Berkeley: University of California Press.

Lan Xiuliang (1984) "Some Reflections on the Changes in Moral Atmosphere Brought On by the Rural Reforms," GR (Nov. 19).

Lardy, Nicholas R. (1983). *Agricultural Prices in China's Modern Economic Development.* Cambridge: Cambridge University Press.

——— and Kenneth G. Lieberthal, eds. (1982) *Chen Yun's Strategy for China's Development.* Armonk: M.E. Sharpe.

Lau Yeefui et al. (1977). *Glossary of Chinese Political Phrases.* Hong Kong: Union Research Institute.

Lave, Lester B., and Gilbert S. Omenn (1981). *Cleaning the Air: Reforming the Clean Air Act.* Washington: Brookings Institution.

Lee, Terence R. (1969). *Residential Water Demand and Economic Development.* Toronto: University of Toronto Press.

Lei Kai (1985) "On China's Effluent Fee System," *Faxue Yanjiu* 5: 23–26.

Lewis, David K. (1969). *Convention: A Philosophical Study.* Cambridge: Harvard University Press.

Li Baihang (1984). "Doubts about the Policy Decision on Establishing Fuel Forest Bases," *Jingji Wenti Tansuo* (August): 30–33, trans. in JPRS CEA-85-004, Jan. 16, 1985: 3–9.

Li Boning (1983). "Water Conservancy Must Provide the Insurance for Doubling Output," *Nongye Jishu Jingji* (April): 1–5.

Li Chaobo (1979). "Strive to Raise the Level of China's Environmental Management," in Yu Guangyuan et al. (1980), 41–51.

——— (1980). "Environmental Protection Should Be Included in the State Plan," HB (April): 1–2.

Li, Choh-Ming (1962). *The Statistical System of Communist China.* Berkeley: University of California Press.

Li Fang (1961). "State Forest Plantations," PR (July 28): 11–12.

Li Jinchang (1983). "Focus on Analyzing the Actual Magnitude of Environmental Problems," HB (July): 2–4.

——— (1984a) "Everyone Should Be Concerned about Environmental Strategy," HB (January): 5–7.

——— (1984b). "Some Thoughts on a Comprehensive Indicator System for the 'Three Lives'" HB (May): 2–4ff.

Li Jinyao (1982). "Why Did I Take Responsibility for Over 70 Hectares of Wasteland?" RR (Feb. 6).

Li Kaiwang (1984). "A Discussion on the Object and Task of Socialist Environmental Economics," HK 5, 2 (April): 67–70.

Li Kaixin (1983). "Concentrate Material Strength to Guarantee the Construction of Keypoint Projects," HQ 429 (Sept. 1): 16–19.

Li Keliang (1982). "On China's Forestry Modernization Construction," LJW, 51–65.

Li Rongchun (1984). "Forestry Production Co-ops Are a Good Way to Develop Collective Forestry," NJW (October): 33–34.

Li Weiwu (1984). "The Strategy to Develop Agricultural Production in Hubei Province," NJW (March): 21–29.

Li Yangming (1982). "Raise Our Knowledge and Propel Environmental Protection Work Forward," HB (August): 2–5.

—— (1984). "How to Attain the Strategic Aims of Environmental Protection in China," HB (February): 2–3.

Li Yuanzhu (1983). "Problems Facing Mountainous Areas in Grain Production," NJW (June): 32–33.

Li Zhangong (1984). "Environmental Standard Setting and Pollution Control Should Focus on Economic Rationality," in Chinese Environmental Economics, Management, and Law Society, ed. *Lun Huanjing Jingji* (On Environmental Management). Nanjing: Kexue Jishu Chubanshe, 201–8.

Li Zhankui et al. (1982). "Quickly Turn Around the Passive Situation of Overly Intensive Felling in China's Key Forest Areas," NJW (January): 9–12.

—— (1984). "Bringing People's Initiative into Full Play to Speed Up the Economic Construction of the Taihang Mountains Region," NJW (April): 3–9.

Li Zhengke (1982). "Develop the Best Features of the Mountains and Restore Ecological Balance," LJW, 169–75.

Li Zhixue (1985). "We Cannot Underestimate Flood Control Problems along the Middle and Lower Liao River," ZS (March): 12–13.

Li Zhongxuan (1957). "Modes of Dominant Use Felling," ZL (August): 30–31.

Liang Heng and Judith Shapiro (1983). *Son of the Revolution*. New York: Knopf.

Liang Xi (1955). "Address on the Topic of Forestry Development." Presented at the First Session of the First National People's Congress; in *Wu Nian Lai de Caizheng Jingji Gongzuo* (Financial and Economic Work in the Last Five Years). Beijing: Caizheng Jingji Chubanshe.

—— (1956). "The Basic Conditions of Forestry Work in 1956 and the Tasks Ahead for 1957," ZL (December): 1–8.

Liao Shiyi et al. (1983). "Discussion on the Economic Essence of Forest Price and the Model for Calculating Prices of Man-Made Forests," LK 19, 2 (May): 181–90.

Liaoning Forestry Society et al. (1982). *Dongbei de Linye* (Forestry in the Northeast). Beijing: ZL Chubanshe.

Lieberthal, Kenneth G. (1971). "Mao versus Liu? Policy towards Industry and Commerce: 1946–1949," CQ 47 (July–September): 494–520.

—— (1976). *A Research Guide to Central Party and Government Meetings in China, 1949–1975*. White Plains: International Arts and Sciences Press.

—— (1978). *Central Documents and Politburo Politics in China*. Ann Arbor: University of Michigan, Center for Chinese Studies, Michigan Papers No. 33.

—— (1980). *Revolution and Tradition in Tientsin, 1949–1952*. Stanford: Stanford University Press.

Lifton, Robert Jay (1961). *Thought Reform and the Psychology of Totalism*. New York: Norton.

Lijphart, Arend (1971). "Comparative Politics and the Comparative Method," APSR 65, 3 (September): 682–93.

Lin Changgeng (1982). "An Exploration of the Issue of Speed of Forest Development in China," LJW, 23–35.

Lin, D.Y., and M.F. Yule (1916). *Chapters on China and Forestry*. Shanghai: Commercial Press.

Lin Ling and Zhang Lixian (1983). "The Peasants Welcome Private Hills," ZL (November): 17–18.

Lin Senmu and Zhou Shulian (1981). "To Reduce the Scale of Capital Construction Is to Gain the Initiative in Economic Work," HQ 3: 9–13.

Lin Wenshan (1983). "Speaking about a Commune Member Who No Longer Is Willing to Do Contract Guarantee Forestry," HQ 2: 49.

Lin Zheng (1983). "Differences between Responsibility Hills and Private Hills," ZL (October): 24.

Lindblom, Charles E. (1977). *Politics and Markets: The World's Political-Economic Systems*. New York: Basic Books.

Ling Xiaoyun (1984). "Formulating Correct Environmental Policies in Light of China's Economic Conditions," in Chinese Environmental Management, Economics, and Law Society et al., eds. (1983). *Lun Huanjing Jingji* (On Environmental Economics). Nanjing: Jiangsu Kexue Jishu Chubanshe, 37–47.

Linye Gongzuo Zhongyao Wenjian Huibian (Compendia of Important Documents in Forestry Work). Vols. 5–8. Beijing: Zhongguo Linye Chubanshe.

Liu, Changming, and Laurence J.C. Ma (1983). "Interbasin Water Transfer in China," *Geographical Review* 73, 3 (July): 253–70.

Liu Chengdong (1957). "Genuinely Strengthening Afforestation Work in the South Is an Important Way to Relieve China's Timber Shortage," *Senlin Gongye Tongxun* (September): 1–5.

Liu Jinkai and Shi Xizhai (1984). "An Important Avenue to Resolving the Capital Problem in Afforestation," ZL (November): 17.

Liu Mingxu (1984). "Carrying Out the Responsibility System Produces Visible Results in Pest Control," *Heilongjiang Linye* (March): 4–5.

Liu Pufeng (1983). "Tianjin Must Step Up Greenification," ZL (July): 7–8.

Liu Shaoqi (1958). "The Present Situation and the Party's General Line for Socialist Construction," May 5, in Robert R. Bowie and John K. Fairbank, eds. (1962). *Communist China 1955–1959: Policy Documents with Analysis*. Cambridge: Harvard University Press, East Asian Series No. 10.

Liu Tianji (1980). "Strengthen Environmental Management, Use Management to Expedite Control," in Yu Guangyuan et al. (1980), 174–86.

Liu Wen (1980). "A Sketch of Environmental Economics," in Yu Guangyuan et al. (1980), 63–95.

Liu Xunhao (1983). "Some Views on Agricultural Development in the Arid Loess Plateau," NJJ (September): 5–7.

Liu Yun (1984). "Suggestions on Solving the Problem of Inaccurate Afforestation Claims," ZL (August): 34–35.

Liu Yunfa and Wang Wanxin (1983). "The Route to Water Economizing Irrigation in Arid Areas," NJJ (September): 11–12.

Liu Zeng, ed. (1983). *Guoying Linchang Guanli* (State Forest Farm Management). Beijing: ZL Chubanshe.

Liu Zhanjiu (1983). "Ways to Solve Drought Problem in Gullied Loess Hills," NJJ (December): 32–34.

Liu Zhijie (1983). "Problems regarding the Establishment of Responsibility Systems for Timber Forests in Collective Forestry Regions," ZL (June): 8–9.

——— (1985). "Summing Up Historic Experiences in Collective-Owned Forest Regions in South China to Bring About a Great Advance in China's Forestry," 4: 5–8.

Liu Zhuangfei, ed. (1982). *Guoying Linye Jihua Guanli* (Planned Management in State Forestry). Beijing: ZL Chubanshe.

Lockett, Martin, and Craig R. Littler (1984). "Trends in Chinese Enterprise Management, 1978–1982," in Neville Maxwell and Bruce MacFarlane, eds. *China's Changed Road to Development*. Oxford: Pergamon, 61–82.

Long Dehuai (1984). "What Harm Can Air Pollution Cause You?" H (November): 6–7.

Lu Baifu and Yuan Zhenyu (1983). "Several Problems regarding the Procurement of Agricultural and Sideline Commodities," JY (May): 65–69.

Lu Changmiao and Fu Lixun (1984). "Research on How Chinese Household Energy Should Develop," ZHK 4, 5: 34–37.

Lu Qi (1984). "Energy Conservation and Its Prospects," BR 27, 46 (November 12): 20–23.

Lu Qinzhi et al. (1983). "Some Important Problems in Promoting Water Transportation in China," JY (January): 55–60.

Lu Rizhou and Du Zhuangye (1984). "Some Problems Associated with the Perfection of the Household Unified Production Guarantee Responsibility System," HQ 4: 27–33.

Lu Weiguo and Wang Mingshui (1985). "Our Views on Issues Involving the Lifting of the State Timber Procurement Monopoly in Collective Forest Districts," LJ 4: 33–37.

Lu Yun (1984). "Li Ruihuan—Tianjin's Mayor Is a Builder," BR 27, 40 (Oct. 1): 21–25.

Lucas, An Elissa (1980). "Changing Medical Models in China: Organizational Options or Obstacles?" CQ 83 (September): 461–89.

Lundqvist, Lennart J. (1980). *The Hare and the Tortoise: Clean Air Policies in the United States and Sweden.* Ann Arbor: University of Michigan Press.

Luo Hanxian (1983). "Use Natural Resources Thoroughly," BR 26, 17 (Apr. 25): 22–24.

Luo Huihan (1985). "On the Issue of 'No-Fault Liability' in the Environmental Law System," *Faxue Zazhi* 4: 6–8.

Ma Hong (1984). "Strive to Succeed in Our Environmental Protection Work," HB (February): 4–7 and (March): 2–5.

Ma, Laurence J.C. (1981). "Water Supply in Beijing." Presented at the Midwest Regional Seminar on China, Urbana, Dec. 5.

Maass, Arthur, and Raymond L. Anderson (1978) . . . *And the Desert Shall Rejoice: Conflict, Growth, and Justice in Arid Environments.* Cambridge: MIT Press.

MacFarquhar, Roderick, ed. (1960). *The Hundred Flowers.* New York: Praeger.

——— (1974 and 1983). *The Origins of the Cultural Revolution.* Vols. 1 and 2. New York: Columbia University Press.

MacGregor, J.J. (1972). "A Critique of Criteria Sometimes Used In Judging Forest Policies," in *Proceedings of the Seventh World Forestry Congress,* Buenos Aires, Oct. 4–18.

McCloskey, H.J. (1983). *Ecological Ethics and Politics.* Totowa: Rowman and Littlefield.

McGregor, Eugene B., Jr. (1981). "Administration's Many Instruments," *Administration & Society* 13, 3 (November): 347–75.

McIntyre, Robert J., and James B. Thornton (1978a). "On the Environmental Efficiency of Economic Systems." *Soviet Studies* 30, 2 (April): 173–92.

——— (1978b). "Urban Design and Energy Utilization: A Comparative Analysis of Soviet Practice." *Journal of Comparative Economics* 2, 4 (December): 334–53.

McMillen, Donald H. (1979). *Chinese Communist Power and Policy in Xinjiang, 1949–1977.* Boulder: Westview.

Mao Yushi (1982). "Three Fundamental Problems in Environmental Economics," JY (July): 60–63.

Mao Zedong (1945). "The Foolish Old Man Who Removed the Mountains," in *Selected Works of Mao Zedong.* Beijing: Foreign Languages Press, 1967, 3: 271–74.

——— (1949). "Report to the Second Plenary Session of the Seventh Central Committee of the Communist Party of China," Mar. 5, in *Selected Works of Mao Zedong*. Beijing: Foreign Languages Press, 1967, 4: 361–75.

——— (1955). "On the Cooperative Transformation of Agriculture," July 31, in *Selected Works of Mao Zedong*. Beijing: Foreign Languages Press, 1977, 5: 184–207.

——— (1956). "On the Ten Great Relationships," in Stuart Schram, ed. (1974). *Chairman Mao Talks to the People: Talks and Letters, 1956–1971*. New York: Pantheon, 61–83.

——— (1959). "Speech at the Lushan Conference," July 23, in *Mao Zedong Sixiang Wansui* (Long Live Mao Zedong Thought), 1969, 294–305.

——— (1964). "Talks with Mao Yuan-hsin," July 5, in Stuart Schram, ed. (1974) *Chairman Mao Talks to the People: Talks and Letters, 1956–1971*. New York: Pantheon, 142–50.

——— (1967). "Twenty Manifestations of Bureaucracy," trans. in JPRS 49826 (Feb. 12, 1970): 40–43.

Margolis, Howard (1983). *Selfishness, Altruism and Rationality: A Theory of Social Choice*. Cambridge: Cambridge University Press.

Maxwell, Neville (1979). "The Tachai Way, Part I: Learning from Tachai" and "The Tachai Way, Part II: The Fourth Mobilization," in Neville Maxwell, ed. *China's Road to Development*. 2d ed. New York: Pergamon, 41–70 and 71–95.

Mazmanian, Daniel A., and Paul A. Sabatier (1983). *Implementation and Public Policy*. Glenview: Scott, Foresman.

Mi Jian (1984) "On Civil Liability for Environmental Pollution," *Faxue Yanjiu* 3: 60–62.

Miller, Gary, and Terry M. Moe (1983). "Bureaucrats, Legislators, and the Size of Government," APSR 77, 2 (June): 297–322.

Ministry of Communications (1983). "Plans for Structural Reforms of Shipping along the Changjiang River," Mar. 10, in State Economic Commission Economic Structural Reform Bureau, ed. *Zhongguo Jingji Guanli Zhengce Faling Xuanbian* (Compendia of Policies and Laws regarding Chinese Economic Management). Beijing: Jingji Kexue Chubanshe, 1: 285–89.

Ministry of Finance (1985). "A Discussion of Whether Afforestation Is a Type of Capital Construction," LJ 4: 41–44.

Ministry of Forestry (1952). "Instructions regarding Spring Afforestation Work in 1952," Feb. 16, in *Linye Faling Huibian* (Compendia of Forestry Laws). Beijing, 1952, 2: 9–11.

Ministry of Forestry Afforestation Management Section (1983). *Linye Shengchan Chengbao Zeren Zhi* (Production Responsibility Systems in Forestry). Beijing: ZL Chubanshe.

Ministry of Forestry Policy Research Section (1981). "Carry Out the Governance of Forestry according to Law," HQ 5: 27–31.

Ministry of Forestry Technical Economics Research Section (1983). *Zhongguo Linye Gaikuang* (Chinese Forestry Conditions). Beijing: ZL Chubanshe.

Ministry of Urban and Rural Construction (1983). *Quan Guo Gongye Xitong Fangzhi Wuran Jingyan Jiaoliu Hui* (National Industrial System Pollution Control Experiences Exchange Conference). Beijing: Zhongguo Huanjing Kexue Chubanshe.

Ministry of Water Conservancy (1957). "Report of Some Opinions regarding the Assessment and Utilization of Water Fees in Irrigation Districts," Dec. 27, in *Compendia of Laws and Regulations of the People's Republic of China*, 7: 377–79.

——— (1980). "Report on Basic Experiences in Water Conservancy Work During the Past Thirty Years and Opinions on the Future," Oct. 6, in ZRGGYG 17: 528–37.

"Minutes of the National Academic Seminar on the Development of Forestry" (1984), NJW (February): 11–14.

Mishima, I. (1951). "Opinions concerning the Natural Regeneration of *Pinus koraiensis*," in *Zhongguo Linye Lunwen Ji 1950–1951* (Articles on Chinese Forestry 1950–1951). Beijing: ZL Bianji Weiyuanhui, 1952, 338–57.

Montjoy, Robert S., and Laurence J. O'Toole, Jr. (1979). "Toward a Theory of Implementation: An Organizational Perspective," *Public Administration Review* 39, 5 (September–October): 465–76.

Myers, Norman (1975). "China's Approach to Environmental Conservation," *Environmental Affairs* 5, 3: 33–63.

Nagel, Thomas (1970). *The Possibility of Altruism*. Oxford: Clarendon Press.

Nantong Municipal Environmental Protection Bureau (1982). "How Did We Develop Environmental Statistics Work?" HB (November): 6–7.

Nash, Roderick (1982) *Wilderness and the American Mind*. 3d ed. New Haven: Yale University Press.

Nathan, Andrew J. (1973). "A Factionalism Model for Chinese Politics," CQ 53 (March): 34–66.

—— (1976). "Policy Oscillations in the People's Republic of China: A Critique," CQ 68 (December): 720–33.

National Environmental Protection Conference Secretariat, ed. (1973). *Huanjing Baohu Jingyan Xuanbian* (Selected Experiences in Environmental Protection). Beijing: Renmin Chubanshe.

National Environmental Protection Conference Small Group Office (1973). *Gongye "Sanfei" Paifang Shixing Biaojun* (Provisional Standards for Industrial "Three Wastes" Emissions). Beijing: Zhongguo Jianzhu Gongye Chubanshe.

Naughton, Barry (1983). "The Price System," CBR 10, 5 (November–December): 14–18.

Nicholson, Norman K. (1981). "Applications of Public Choice Theory to Rural Development—A Statement of the Problem," in Russell and Nicholson (1981), 17–41.

Nickum, James E. (1974). *A Collective Approach to Water Resource Development: The Chinese Commune System, 1962–1972*. Ph.D. diss., University of California at Berkeley.

——, ed. (1977). *Hydraulic Engineering and Water Resources in the People's Republic of China: Report of the United States Water Resources Delegation* (August–September 1974). Stanford: Stanford University, U.S.-China Relations Program.

—— (1978). "Labor Accumulation in Rural China and Its Role since the Cultural Revolution," *Cambridge Journal of Economics* 2: 273–86.

——, ed. (1981). *Water Management Organization in the People's Republic of China*. Armonk: M.E. Sharpe.

Noll, Roger (1982). "Leasing the Air: An Alternative Approach to Regulation?" *Engineering & Science* 46, 1 (September): 12–17.

Northwest Military and Political Commission (1951). "Several Regulations Ordering the Coordination of Land Reform and the Resolution of Disputes over Forestry Rights," Nov. 19, in Beijing Politics and Law Research Institute (1957).

Nove, Alec (1983). *The Economics of Feasible Socialism*. London: Allen & Unwin.

Oksenberg, Michel (1969). "Policy Formulation in Communist China: The Case of the 1957–1958 Mass Irrigation Campaign." Ph.D. diss., Columbia University.

—— (1970). "Getting Ahead and Along in Communist China: The Ladder of Success on the Eve of the Cultural Revolution," in John Wilson Lewis, ed. *Party Leadership and Revolutionary Power in China*. Cambridge: Cambridge University Press, 304–47.

—— (1977). "The Political Leader," in Dick Wilson, ed. *Mao Tse-tung in the Scales of History*. Cambridge: Cambridge University Press, 70–116.

—— (1982). "Economic Policy-Making in China: Summer 1981," CQ 90 (June): 165–94.

O'Leary, Greg, and Andrew Watson (1982). "The Production Responsibility System and the Future of Collective Farming," *Australian Journal of Chinese Affairs* 8 (July): 1–34.

Olson, Mancur (1965 and 1971). *The Logic of Collective Action*. Cambridge: Harvard University Press.

Ophuls, William (1977). *Ecology and the Politics of Scarcity*. San Francisco: W.H. Freeman.

Ouchi, William G. (1980). "Markets, Bureaucracies, and Class," *Administrative Science Quarterly* 25, 1 (January): 29–41.

Pannell, Clifton W. (1982). "Less Land for Chinese Farmers," *Geographical Magazine* 54 (November): 324–29.

—— and Laurence J.C. Ma (1983). *China: The Geography of Development and Modernization*. London: Arnold.

Parish, William L., and Martin King Whyte (1978). *Village and Family in Contemporary China*. Chicago: University of Chicago Press.

Parry, B. Thomas, et al. (1983). "Changing Conceptions of Sustained-Yield Policy on the National Forests," *Journal of Forestry* 81, 3 (March): 150–54.

Parsons, Howard L., ed. (1977). *Marx and Engels on Ecology*. Westport: Greenwood.

Peng Dehuai (1959). "Talks at the Meetings of the Northwest Group of the Lushan Meeting," July 3–10, in *The Case of Peng Dehuai 1959–1968*. Hong Kong: Union Research Institute, 1968, 1–5.

People's Procuracy (1983). *Renmin Jiancha Xuanbian* (Selections from People's Procuracy). Beijing: Falü Chubanshe.

Perkins, Dwight H. (1966). *Market Control and Planning in Communist China*. Cambridge: Harvard University Press.

—— (1976). "A Conference on Agriculture," CQ 67 (September): 596–610.

Perry, Ronald W., et al. (1981). *Evacuation Planning in Emergency Management*. Lexington: Lexington Books.

Peterson, Albert S. (1982). "China: Transportation Developments, 1971–1980," in CUFM 1: 138–70.

Petrick, Richard L. (1981). "Policy Cycles and Policy Learning in the People's Republic of China," *Comparative Political Studies* 14, 1 (April): 101–22.

Phelps, Charles E., et al. (1978). *Efficient Water Use in California: Executive Summary*. Santa Monica: Rand.

Pillsbury, Barbara L.K. (1978). "Factionalism Observed: Behind the 'Face' of Harmony in a Chinese Community," CQ 74 (June): 241–72.

Polachek, James M. (1983). "The Moral Economy of the Kiangsi Soviet (1928–1934)," *Journal of Asian Studies* 42, 4 (August): 805–29.

Polinsky, A. Mitchell (1979). "Controlling Externalities and Protecting Entitlements: Property Right, Liability Rule, and Tax-Subsidy Approaches," *Journal of Legal Studies* 8, 1 (January): 1–48.

Polsby, Nelson W. (1984). *Political Innovation in America: The Politics of Policy Initiation*. New Haven: Yale University Press.

Popkin, Samuel L. (1981). "Public Choice and Rural Development—Free Riders, Lemons, and Institutional Design," in Russell and Nicholson (1981), 43–80.

Pressman, Jeffrey L., and Aaron Wildavsky (1979). *Implementation*. 2d ed. Berkeley: University of California Press.

"Provisional Regulations for the Management of State Forests in the Northeast" (1950), in Compendia of Forestry Laws and Regulations (1950–63), 2: 29–33.

Pye, Lucian (1981). *The Dynamics of Chinese Politics*. Cambridge: Oelgeschlager, Gunn
& Hain.

Qian Zhengying (1985). "Speech to the Conference on Exchanging Experiences on
the Multipurpose Utilization of Water Resources and Solving the Navigation
Problems Caused by Water Projects and Dams," Jan. 25, in ZS (April): 2–6.

Qiang Xiaochu (1983). "Uphold the Principle of Seeking Truth from Facts," HQ
430 (Sept. 16): 9–11.

Qu Geping (1982). "Strengthen the Supervisory Capability of Environmental Management," HB (August): 6–8ff.

—— (1983). "Basic Aspects and Key Lessons regarding China's Environmental
Problems," HB (August): 2–5.

—— (1984). *Environmental Problems and Strategy in China* (in Chinese). Beijing:
Zhongguo Huanjing Kexue Chubanshe.

Qu Shuye (1984). "Critical Aspects of Carrying Out the Single Ledger in Timber,"
ZL (February): 32.

Qu Yaoguang (1983). "Water Resources and the Construction of a Commodity
Grain Base in the Hexi Corridor," DZ (October): 4–5.

Reese, Craig (1983). *Deregulation and Environmental Quality: The Use of Tax Policy to
Control Pollution in North America and Western Europe*. Westport: Quorum.

Reidinger, Richard B. (1980). "Water Management by Administrative Procedures
in an Indian Irrigation System," in E. Walter Coward, ed. *Irrigation and Agricultural Development in Asia: Perspectives from the Social Sciences*. Ithaca: Cornell
University Press, 263–88.

Ren Guofu (1985). "Using Economic Instruments to Inspire Enterprises to Control
Pollution," *Huanjing Guanli* (January): 21–23.

Reynolds, Bruce L. (1982). "Reform in Chinese Industrial Management: An Empirical Report," in CUFM 1: 119–37.

Richman, Barry M. (1969). *Industrial Society in Communist China*. New York: Vintage
Books.

Rogers, Peter (1983). "The Future of Water," *Atlantic* 240, 7 (July): 80–92.

Rose-Ackerman, Susan (1977). "Market Models for Water Pollution Control: Their
Strengths and Weaknesses," *Public Policy* 25, 4 (Fall): 383–406.

Rosen, Stanley (1985). "Prosperity, Privatization, and the Communist Youth
League," *Problems of Communism* 34, 2 (March–April): 1–22.

Ross, Lester (1980a)."Forestry Policy in China," Ph.D. diss., University of Michigan.

—— (1980b)."Forestry in the People's Republic of China: Estimating the Gains
and Losses," *China Geographer* 11: 123–37.

—— (1983a)."Changes in Water Policy in the People's Republic of China," *Water
Resources Bulletin* 19, 1 (February): 69–72.

—— (1983b). "Flood Control Policy in China: The Policy Consequences of Natural
Disasters," *Journal of Public Policy* 3, 2 (May): 209–32.

—— (1984) "Earthquake Policy in China," AS 24, 7 (July): 773–87.

—— (1987). "Obligatory Tree Planting: The Role of Campaigns in Policy Implementation in Post-Mao China," in Lampton (1987), 225–52.

—— and Mitchell A. Silk (1985). "Post-Mao China and Environmental Protection:
The Effects of Legal and Politico-Economic Reform," *UCLA Pacific Basin Law
Journal* 4, 1–2 (Spring–Fall): 63–89.

—— (1987). *Environmental Law and Policy in the People's Republic of China*. Westport:
Quorum Books, Maryland Studies in Chinese Law and Politics No. 8.

Rudolph, Jorg-Meinhard (1984). "China's Media: Fitting News to Reality," *Problems
of Communism* 33, 4 (July–August): 58–67.

Russell, Clifford S. (1979). "What Can We Get from Effluent Charges?" *Policy Analysis*
5, 2 (Spring): 155–80.

―――― (1982). "Externality, Conflict, and Decision," in Kent A. Price, ed. *Regional Conflict and National Policy*. Baltimore: Johns Hopkins University Press.

―――― and Norman K. Nicholson, eds. (1981). *Public Choice and Rural Development*. Washington: Resources for the Future.

Schell, Orville (1984). "A Reporter at Large," *New Yorker* 59, 49 (Jan. 23): 43ff.

Schelling, Thomas C., ed. (1983). *Incentives for Environmental Protection*. Cambridge: MIT Press.

Schram, Stuart R. (1973). "Introduction: The Cultural Revolution in Historical Perspective," in Schram, ed. *Authority, Participation and Cultural Change in China*. Cambridge: Cambridge University Press, 1–108.

―――― (1984). " 'Economics in Command?' Ideology and Policy since the Third Plenum, 1978–1984," CQ 99 (September): 417–61.

Schran, Peter (1976). *Guerrilla Economy: The Development of the Shensi-Kansu-Ninghsia Border Region, 1937–1945*. Albany: State University of New York Press.

Schumacher, E.F. (1973). *Small Is Beautiful: Economics as if People Mattered*. New York: Harper & Row.

Schurmann, Franz (1968). *Ideology and Organization in Communist China*. 2d ed. Berkeley: University of California Press.

Selden, Mark (1971). *The Yenan Way in Revolutionary China*. Cambridge: Harvard University Press.

Sen, Amartya (1973). *On Economic Inequality*. Oxford: Clarendon Press.

Shambaugh, David L. (1984). *The Making of a Premier: Zhao Ziyang's Provincial Career*. Boulder: Westview.

Shen Guansheng (1982). *Jianchuan Fazhi, Yifa Zhilin* (Strengthen the Legal System and Rely on Law to Govern Forestry). Beijing: ZL Chubanshe.

Shen, H.W. (1979). "Some Notes on the Yellow River," *EOS: Transactions of the American Geophysical Union* 60, 31 (July 31): 545–47.

Shen Ji (1984). "A Preliminary View on the Effectiveness of Controlling the Larch Caterpillar by *Trichogramma dendrolimi* (Matsumura)," *Dongbei Linxue Yuan Xuebao* 12, 3 (September): 21–27.

Shen Xin (1984). "Preliminary Discussion of the Administration of the Special Management Law," ZHK 4, 2 (April): 29–32.

Sheng Chijing (1950). "A Discussion of Several Problems in Forestry," ZL (January): 15.

Shi Hongwen (1985). "The Benefits of Effluent Fees," *Huanjing Guanli* (January): 24–25.

Shi Yinsen (1982). "A Preliminary Discussion of the Relationship between Implementing Stumpage Prices and Increasing the Utilization of Forest Resources," LJW, 114–23.

Shirk, Susan L. (1982). *Competitive Comrades: Career Incentives and Student Initiatives in China*. Berkeley: University of California Press.

Shubik, Martin (1982). *Game Theory in the Social Sciences: Applications and Solutions*. Cambridge: MIT Press.

Shue, Vivienne (1980). *Peasant China in Transition: The Dynamics of Development toward Socialism, 1949–1956*. Berkeley: University of California Press.

Sigurdson, Jon (1977a). *Rural Industrialization in China*. Cambridge: Harvard University Press.

―――― (1977b). "Water Policies in India and China," *Ambio* 6, 1: 70–76.

Silk, Mitchell A. (1985). "China's Marine Environmental Protection Law: The Dragon Creeping in Murky Waters," *Review of Socialist Law* 11: 249–73.

Skinner. G. William, and Edwin A. Winckler (1969). "Compliance Succession in Rural Communist China: A Cyclical Theory," in Amitai Etzioni, ed. *Complex Organizations: A Sociological Reader*. 2d ed. New York: Holt, Rinehart and Winston, 410–38.

Skogerboe, Gaylord V. (1983). "Agricultural Water Management and the Environment," in Biswas et al. (1983), 35–64.

Smil, Vaclav (1978). "China's Energetics: A System Analysis," in U.S. Congress Joint Economic Committee. *Chinese Economy Post-Mao*. Washington: U.S. Government Printing Office, 323–69.

——— (1984). *The Bad Earth: Environmental Degradation in China*. Armonk: M.E. Sharpe.

Solinger, Dorothy J. (1982). "The Fifth National People's Congress and the Process of Policy Making: Reform, Readjustment, and the Opposition," AS 22, 12 (December): 1238–75.

——— (1983). "The 1980 Inflation and the Politics of Price Control in the PRC." Presented at the Workshop on Policy Implementation in China, Columbus, Ohio, June 20–24, in Lampton (1987), 81–118.

Song Zongshui (1982). "The Problem of Estimating a Forest's Ecological Function," NJW (June): 29–33.

——— (1983a). "An Effective Way to Enlarge Forest Cover," NJW (January): 10–12.

——— (1983b). "The Economic Effects Are Good for the Development of Forestry on Mountainous and Hilly Land in South China," NJW (May): 44–45.

Song Zuowen (1985). "A Discussion of Economic Reform in Sichuan's Forest Industry Enterprises," LJ 6: 13–18.

Special Commentator (1984). "On Lessons and Experiences from China's Environmental Protection Work," HB (January): 2–4.

Sproule-Jones, Mark (1982). "Public Choice Theory and Natural Resources: A Methodological Explication and Critique," APSR 76, 4 (December): 790–804.

State Commodities General Bureau (1981). "On the Main Points in the Communique of the National Commodities Bureau Chiefs Conference," June 15, in ZRGGYG 361 (Sept. 5): 423–24.

State Council (1981). "Decision on Strengthening Environmental Protection Work in the Economic Readjustment Period," Feb. 24, in ZRGGYG 351 (Apr. 25): 103–7.

——— (1984a)."Circular on Promoting Urban Water Conservation in a Big Way," June 19, in ZRGGYG 436 (July 20): 515–17.

——— (1984b) "Decisions regarding the Strengthening of Statistical Work," ZRGGYG 422 (Mar. 20): 3–6.

——— (1984c). "Decisions on Environmental Protection Work," May 8, in ZRGGYG 431 (Apr. 30): 319–22.

——— (1985). "Procedures regarding the Calculation, Assessment, and Management of Water Charges on Water Conservancy Projects," JR, July 31, 1985.

State Economic Commission et al. (1981). "Circular on Strengthening the Management of Water Conservation," Sept. 14, in ZRGGYG 370 (Nov. 30): 744–48.

State Planning Commission et al. (1983). "Explaining Some Problems in the Regulations concerning the Acquisition of Land for State Construction," June 9, in ZRGGYG 410, 15: 715–18.

State Statistical Bureau (1983). "Communique on Fulfillment of China's 1982 National Economic Plan," Apr. 29, in BR 26, 19 (May 19).

——— (1985a) *Zhongguo Gongye de Fazhan 1949–1984* (The Development of Chinese Industry 1949–1984). Beijing: Zhongguo Tongji Chubanshe.

——— (1985b) *Zhongguo Nongye de Guanghui Chengjiu 1949–1984* (The Glorious Achievements of Chinese Agriculture 1949–1984). Beijing: Zhongguo Tongji Chubanshe.

——— (1985c) *Zhongguo Shehui Tongji Ziliao* (Statistical Materials on Chinese Society). Beijing: Zhongguo Tongji Chubanshe.

Su Yuzhang (1984). "Some Opinions on How to Raise the Efficiency of Capital Investment in Forest Industry," *Senlin Jianshe* 1984, 1: 2–5.

Sui Wenchang and He Zhuanjia (1983). "The Present System of People's Communes in the Countryside Needs Reform," JY (February): 76–78.

Sun Jingbo (1983). "Reevaluating Forestry Resources," *Nengyuan* 2: 11–13.

Sun Xiangming (1984). "Was This a Counterrevolutionary Incident?" H (October): 24–25.

Suttmeier, Richard P. (1974). *Research and Revolution: Science Policy and Societal Change in China.* Lexington: Lexington Books.

———— (1982). "Research, Innovation, and the Chinese Political Economy," in CUFM 1: 489–513.

Swannack-Nunn, Susan L. (1979). *Environmental Protection in the People's Republic of China.* Washington: National Council for U.S.-China Trade.

Taga, Leonore Shever (1976). "Externalities in a Command Society," in Fred Singleton, ed. *Environmental Misuse in the Soviet Union.* New York: Praeger, 75–100.

Tai Qisheng (1984) "Atmospheric Pollutants and Beijing's Populace: Their Ultimate Consequences and Ways to Reduce Them," HB (June): 16–19.

Tang Ke (1972). "China's Stand on the Question of Human Environment," PR 15, 24 (June 16): 5–8ff.

Tang Polin (1957). "Resolve Problems Affecting Implementation of the Dominant Use Felling Regulations," ZL (May): 41.

Tao Zhenni (1982). "Beijing on the Brink of the 21st Century," BR 25, 33 (Aug. 16): 26–28.

Taylor, Serge (1977). "The Politics of Charges," in Frederick R. Anderson et al. *Environmental Improvement through Economic Incentives.* Baltimore: Johns Hopkins University Press, 145–91.

Thompson, James D. (1967). *Organizations in Action: Social Science Bases of Administrative Theory.* New York: McGraw-Hill.

Thompson, James T. (1981). "Public Choice Analysis of Institutional Constraints on Firewood Production Strategies in the West African Sahel," in Russell and Nicholson (1981), 119–52.

Tian Chunsheng (1984). "Preliminary Analysis of Ground Water Characteristics and Trends in Quality in China," ZHK 4, 2 (April): 34–40.

Tian Jiyun (1984a). "Further Develop Commodity Production and Circulation," HQ 6: 6–12.

———— (1984b). "Price System Due for Reform," trans. in BR 28, 4 (Jan. 28): 16–19ff.

Tietenberg, Thomas (1984). *Emissions Trading: An Exercise in Reforming Pollution Policy.* Baltimore: Johns Hopkins University Press.

Titmuss, Richard (1971). *The Gift Relationship: From Human Blood to Social Policy.* New York: Pantheon.

Tong Pingya (1984). "Agricultural Development in China's Arid Lands," DZ (March): 2–3.

Townsend, James R. (1968). *Political Participation in Communist China.* Berkeley: University of California Press.

Travers, S. Lee (1982). "Bias in Chinese Economic Statistics: The Case of the Typical Example Investigation," CQ 91 (September): 478–85.

Tsou, Tang (1976). "Prologemenon to the Study of Informal Groups in CCP Politics," CQ 65 (March): 98–114.

———— et al. (1982) "The Responsibility System in Agriculture: Its Implementation in Xiyang and Dazhai," *Modern China* 8, 1 (January): 41–103.

Tucker, William (1977). "Environmental and the Leisure Class," *Harper's* (December): 49–56ff. See also letters to the editor in February 1978 issue.

U.S. Water Resources Council (1978). *The Nation's Water Resources, 1975–2000. The Second National Water Abstract.* Vol. 1. Washington: U.S. Government Printing Office.

Veilleux, Louis (1978). *The Paper Industry in China from 1949 to the Cultural Revolution.* Toronto: University of Toronto–York University Joint Centre on Modern East Asia.

Vermeer, E.B. (1977). *Water Conservancy and Irrigation in China: Social, Economic and Agrotechnical Aspects.* The Hague: Leiden University Press.

—— (1982). "Rural Economic Change and the Role of the State in China, 1962–1978," AS 22, 9 (September): 823–42.

Vogel, Ezra F. (1969 and 1971). *Canton under Communism: Programs and Politics in a Provincial Capital, 1949–1968.* New York: Harper Torchbooks.

Wai-Kown, D.C. Chan, et al. (1984). "Insuring the China Trade," CBR 11, 1 (January–February): 20–21.

Walder, Andrew G. (1983). "Organized Dependence and Cultures of Authority in Chinese Industry," JAS 43, 1 (November): 51–76.

—— (1984). "The Remaking of the Chinese Working Class, 1949–1981," *Modern China* 10, 1 (January): 3–48.

Walker, Kenneth R. (1965). *Planning in Chinese Agriculture: Socialization 1956–1962.* London: Frank Cass.

—— (1984). "Chinese Agriculture during the Period of the Readjustment," CQ 100 (December): 783–812.

Wallace, Michael B. (1983). "Managing Resources That Are Common Property: From Kathmandu to Capitol Hill," *Journal of Policy Analysis and Management* 2, 2 (Winter): 220–37.

Wan Li (1983). "Raise Our Knowledge, Strengthen Leadership, and Resolutely Do Obligatory Tree Planting Well," ZL (February): 3–5.

Wang Baozhen (1984). "Comprehensive Control of Urban Water Pollution," ZHK 4, 2: 5–11.

Wang Changsheng (1983). "Quadrupling the Gross Value of Output and the Problem of Water Resources," HQ 11: 36–39.

Wang Dianwen (1983). "Forestry Development and Timber Economizing Must Be Simultaneously Emphasized," ZL (April): 11–12.

—— (1985). "Some Problems in Reforming the Economic System in State Forest Districts," LJ 4: 1–5.

Wang Hongzha (1984). "The Problem of Urban Water Supply during the Past Thirty-Five Years," *Chengshi Gong Shui* 3: 3–6.

Wang Jianzheng (1983). "Some Questions regarding the Establishment and Perfection of the Forestry Responsibility System," ZL (March): 9–11.

Wang Mingzhong (1983). "Lessons of Exploitation and Utilization of Natural Resources from the Disastrous Floods of Sichuan Province," ZZ 2: 7–11.

Wang Qingyi and Gu Jian (1983). "How Will China Solve Energy Problem?" BR 26: 35 (August 29): 13–18.

Wang Weimin (1980). "Effluent Fees Advance Environmental Protection Work," HB (May): 26–27.

Wang Wende and Qiao Zhangbao (1983). "A New Channel for Preventing Soil Erosion in an Effective Way," NJW (May): 6–9.

Wang Yanxiang (n.d.). "Resource Pricing for Sustainable Development," mimeographed.

Wang Yijun (1984). "Taking Timber and Grain Production as Well as Their Profits as a Whole into Consideration Is a Good Method for Improving the Forestry Responsibility System," NJW (October): 37–39.

Wang Youchen (1984). "An Investigation of Problems Affecting Forestry Construction in the Mountainous Regions of South China," *Jingji Dili* 3: 191–94, trans. in JPRS CAG 85-001, Jan. 3, 1985, 68–76.

Wang Zhangfu (1983). "The Cultivation of Forest Resources Should Chiefly Rely on Expansion from Within through Reproduction," JY (March): 77–78.

—— and Wang Enling (1983). "Forest Protection and Forestry Development Are Great Strategic Measures," ZL (January): 7–8.

—— and Zhang Jianguo (1981). "Preliminary Discussion on Forest Value in China," LK 17, 2 (May): 194–201.

Wei Zhenwu (1950). "Rational Felling and Utilization of Forests," ZL (February): 31–33.

Wei Zhongyi and Ren Hongzun (1983). "Groundwater Exploitation in the Jinglu Region and Its Effects on the Environment," DZ (August): 2–4.

Weil, Martin (1982). "The Baoshan Steel Mill: A Symbol of Change in China's Industrial Development Strategy," in CUFM 1: 367–93.

—— (1983). "Coal Slurry in China," CBR (July–August): 21–24.

Weisskopf, Michael (1983). "To Save Junk Is to Serve Socialism," *Washington Post* (Oct. 22).

Wen Quan (1984). "Helping to Boost the Economy of the Mountain Areas by Showing Greater Concern for Forestry Workers," NJW (October): 41–43.

Westoby, Jack C. (1979). " 'Making Green the Motherland': Forestry in China," in Neville Maxwell, ed. (1979). *China's Road to Development*. 2d ed. New York: Pergamon, 231–45.

Whyte, Martin King (1973). "Bureaucracy and Modernization in China," *American Sociological Review* 38, 2 (April): 149–163.

—— (1974). *Small Groups and Political Rituals in China*. Berkeley: University of California Press.

—— and William L. Parish (1984). *Urban Life in Contemporary China*. Chicago: University of Chicago Press.

Wilford, John Noble (1983). "China Quake Forecasts Found Based on Guesses," NYT, June 1.

Williamson, Oliver E. (1975). *Markets and Hierarchies, Analysis and Antitrust Implications: A Study in the Economics of Internal Organization*. New York: Free Press.

Wilson, James Q., ed. (1980). *The Politics of Regulation*. New York: Basic Books.

Woodward, Dennis (1982). "A New Direction for China's State Farms," *Pacific Affairs* 55, 2 (Summer): 231–51.

World Bank (1981). *Accelerated Development in Sub-Saharan Africa: An Agenda for Action*. Washington.

Wren, Christopher S. (1983). "Chinese Mobilize for New Flooding," NYT, July 12.

Wu Furen (1983). "On Developing Research on Enviro-Economic Impacts and Establishing an Assessment Reporting System," in Chinese Environmental Management, Economics, and Law Society, ed. *Lun Huanjing Jingji* (On Environmental Economics). Nanjing: Jiangsu Kexue Jishu Chubanshe, 78–84.

Wu Jinghe (1983). "An Analysis of the Forestry Economic Structure in Zhejiang Province," NJW 4: 16–22.

Wu Wen and Chen Enjian (1982). "Our Views to the Resolution of China's Rural Energy Requirements." Presented at the Joint U.S.-China Science Policy Conference, Washington, D.C., Jan. 9–12, 1983.

Wu Yicai (1983). "Reduced Water Cultivation Is an Important Route to Developing Wet Paddy Farming in the North," NJJ (July): 19–21.

Wu Zhonglun (1982). "Talking Further about Forests and Floods," in *Senlin yu Shuizai*. Beijing: ZL Chubanshe.

Wylie, Raymond F. (1980). *The Emergence of Maoism: Mao Tse-tung, Ch'en Po-ta, and the Search for Chinese Theory, 1935–1945*. Stanford: Stanford University Press.

Xu Wuchuan and Chen Daping (1982). "Discussion of the Theory of Timber Price and Its Calculated Model," LK 18, 1 (February): 71–79.

Xu Xing (1983). "Conservative Systems Reforms," *Cheng Ming* (November), trans. in JPRS CPS-84-011, Feb. 1, 1984: 110–17.

Yan Anyun (1984). "The Nature and Prospects of the Family-Run Forestry Farm," NJW (December): 36–38.

Yang Furong (1985). "The Tertiary Sector Should Be Vigorously Developed in Forestry Regions," LJ 4: 12–14.

—— et al., eds. (1982). *Linye Shengchan Jingji Zeren Zhi* (An Economic Responsibility System for Forestry Production). Beijing: ZL Chubanshe.

Yang Qicheng (1982). "Talking about the Problem of Water Resource Utilization in Our Country," DZ (December): 2–3.

Yang Rongshen (1983). "Genuinely Enhance the Foundation Role of Agriculture in China," JY (September): 15–19.

Yang Tao (1982). "A New Way to Manage Forestry Production," *Fujian Lun Tan* (March): 83–86, reprinted in *People's University Agricultural Economics Reprints* 14: 111–14.

—— (1984a). "The Development of the Ecological Economy in the Mountainous Areas as Shown on the Forestry Farm Run by Li Jinyao," NJW (April): 14–16.

—— (1984b). "Development of Commodity Production Is Essential for Invigorating Forestry Production in China," *Nongye Jingji Jishu* (October): 36–40, trans. in JPRS CAG-85-009, Mar. 6, 1985: 36–45.

Yang Xinzheng (1980). "A Preliminary Discussion of the Issue of Effluent Charges," in Yu Guangyuan et al. (1980), 197–205.

Yang Yu and Wang Shikui (1983a). "The Forestry Responsibility System Advances China's Forestry Development," ZL (May): 2–3.

—— (1983b). "An Investigation of Forestry Production Responsibility Systems in Plains Districts," ZL (June), 2–4.

Yang Zhanru (1982). "The Basic Conditions concerning the Imbalance between Logging and Cultivating and the Destruction of Forests in Heilongjiang, and How to Turn the Situation Around," in LJW, 154–63.

Yang Zhong (1982). "Mobilize and Work Hard to Create a New Situation in Forestry Construction," ZL (November): 3–6.

—— (1983a). "Science and Technology Is the Key to Creating A New Visage," ZL (February): 11–14.

—— (1983b). "Firmly Establish and Perfect Forestry Production Responsibility Systems," ZL (August): 2–3ff.

—— (1986). "Research on Forestry Policy Must Correspond to the Requirements of the Reforms," LJ 3, 4: 1–8.

Yao Wenyuan (1975). "On the Social Basis of the Lin Piao Anti-Party Clique," PR 18, 10 (Mar. 7): 5–10.

Ye Yuhui (1984). "The Rational Utilization of Natural Resources Ought to Be an Important Element in Economic Return," JY (April): 77–79.

Yin Jinghua (1983). "Discussing Logging and Regeneration in the Yichun Forestry District," *Heilongjiang Linye* (December): 12–13.

Yong Wentao (1982). "Two Trends Confronting Forestry," NJW 9: 14–18.

Yu, Frederick T.C. (1967). "Campaigns, Communication, and Development in Communist China," in Daniel Lerner and Wilbur Schramm, eds. *Communication and Change in Developing Countries*. Honolulu: East-West Center, 195–215.

Yu Guangyuan (1980). "Environmental Problems, Work, and Science," in Yu Guangyuan et al. (1980), 1–40.

—— (1984). "A Visit to an Ecological Farm," JY (March): 2–8.

————et al. (1980). *Lun Huanjing Guanli* (On Environmental Mangement). Taiyuan: Shanxi Renmin Chubanshe.

Yu Hong (1970). "Stress Multiple Utilization," HQ (April): 22–26.

Yu Yongzhi and Sun An (1984). "Study on Controlling Effect of *Trichogramma dendrolimi* Mats. on Larch Caterpillar," *Dongbei Linxue Yuan Xuebao* 12, 3 (September): 28–36.

Yuan Tonggong (1982). "Riches from the 80 Percent Mountainous Portion of the Land," NJW (February): 38–40.

Zang Zhifeng (1983). "Pay Attention to the Study of the Theory of Insurance under Socialism," JY (September): 35–37ff.

Zeng Jianhui (1983). "To the Northwest Plateau," *Liaowang* (September): 2–7.

Zeng Yibing (1983). "Environment and Flood—Learn from Experience of Flood in August 1981 in Southern Shaanxi," ZHK 3, 6: 41–42.

Zhang Bo et al. (1983). "Why Did the Mountainous Areas Fail to Achieve a Greater Economic Growth?" NJW (December): 12–16.

Zhang Chunqiao (1975). "On Exercising All-Round Dictatorship over the Bourgeoisie," PR 18, 14 (April 4): 5–11.

Zhang Jianguo (1979). "Strengthen Research in Forestry Economics, Speedily Develop Forestry Production," JY (January): 42–46.

————(1982). "A Preliminary Discussion of Chinese Style Forestry Modernization," LJW, 36–50.

Zhang Jingfu (1982). "Do the 'Three Fixes' Well to Develop Forestry," ZL (April): 4–5.

Zhang Kexia (1957). "Positively Transform the Forest Resource Shortage in China," ZL (May): 6–8.

Zhang Nan (1982). "Divert Huanghe River Water to Tianjin," BR 25, 34 (Aug. 23): 19–25.

Zhang Qinwen (1983). "Consider Mechanized Dryland Agriculture to Realize Vast Economic Benefits," NJJ (August): 1–3.

Zhang Tong (1983) "Opinions regarding the Reform of the Timber Cost Structure and Realignment of Timber Prices," ZL (April): 37–38.

Zhang Wenqi et al., eds. (1982). *Linye Qiye Zhuyao Jingji Jishu Zhibiao.* (Major Economic and Technical Norms for Forestry Enterprises). Beijing: ZL Chubanshe.

Zhang Zhida (1985). "A Major Economic Law for Developing Forestry in China," LJ 1: 16–20.

Zhao Jie and Peng Yishang (1983). "Multipurpose Afforestation in Farming Areas with Few Trees," NJW (February): 18–20.

Zhao Mingguang (1984). "Springtime in Forestry Is Welcomed in Xiyang County," ZL (August): 4–5.

————(1985). "The Plaint of Specialized Households Engaged in Forestry," ZL (January): 7.

Zhao Ziyang (1985). "Relax Agricultural Commodity Prices, Advance the Reorganization of Village Commercial Structure," HQ 3: 10–13, trans. in JPRS CRF-85-008, Apr. 3, 1985: 14–20.

Zhao Zongliu (1981). "Economic Readjustment and Environmental Protection," JY (May): 67–73.

Zheng, D.R., and R. Salib (1982). "AQCS for Coalfield Plants in the People's Republic of China," in S.W. Yuan, ed. *Energy, Resources and Environment: Papers Presented at the First U.S.-China Conference on Energy, Resources and Environment 7–12 November 1982, Beijing, China.* New York: Pergamon, 121–31.

Zheng Xiaojing (1973). "Promote the Comprehensive Utilization of Waste Products in a Big Way, Transform the Harmful into the Beneficial," in National Environmental Protection Conference Secretariat (1973), 24–29.

Zhong Xingfan (1982). "Some Perspectives regarding Problems in Forestry Economics," in LJW, 1–9.

Zhongguo Jianzhu Gongye Chubanshe, ed. (1975). *Huanjing Baohu Wenxian* (Essays on Environmental Protection). Beijing.

Zhongguo Linye Editorial Committee (1953). *Xin Zhongguo de Linye Jianshe*. Beijing: Shenghuo Shudian.

Zhongguo Linye Gongyuehui, ed. (1973). *Dianning Cailiao Xuanbian* (Selected Materials on Models). Beijing: Nongye Chubanshe.

Zhou Fuxiang (1980). "A Discussion of Some Issues in Environmental Economics," in Yu Guangyuan et al. (1980), 126–39.

Zhou Fuyang (1982). "Economic Policy and the Solution of Problems in Environmental Protection," HQ 13: 27–30.

Zhou Jinhua (1981). "Appraising the Dazhai Brigade," BR 24, 16 (Apr. 20): 24–28.

Zhou Xu and Chen Qizhong (1984). "An Examination of Sichuan's Level of Forest Cover in 1962," *Sichuan Linye Keji* 4, 1: 65–66.

Zhou Zishi (1983). "Some Opinions on Reform of Investment," ZS (June): 45–46.

Zhu Bangchang (1983). "Rational Utilization of Hilly Areas Is of Great Significance to the Transformation of China's Land," NJW (May): 39–43.

Zhu Hanxue and Zhang Zhao (1983). "The Economic Benefits from Putting Resources to Use a Second Time," in Chinese Environmental Management, Economics and Law Society, ed. *Lun Huanjing Jingji* (On Environmental Economics). Nanjing: Jiangsu Kexue Jishu Chubanshe, 240–47.

Zhu Laidong (1981). "Water in Tianjin Municipality," DZ (November): 5–6ff.

Zhu Qinfang (1984). "Major Economic and Social Achievements (II)," BR 27, 41 (Oct. 8): 28–31.

Zhu Zanping (1984). "On the Motivating Force in Developing Forestry in the Collective Forestry Areas of South China," NJW (November): 36–39, trans. in Ross and Silk (1987).

Ziegler, Charles E. (1980). "Soviet Environmental Policy and Soviet Central Planning: A Reply to McIntyre and Thornton," *Soviet Studies* 32, 1 (January): 124–34.

——— (1982). "Economic Alternatives and Administrative Solutions in Soviet Environmental Protection," *Policy Studies Journal* 11, 1 (September): 175–87.

Zivnuska, John A. (1974). "Forestry Investments for Multiple Uses among Multiple Ownership Types," in Marion Clawson, ed. *Forest Policy for the Future: Conflict, Compromise, Consensus*. Washington: Resources for the Future, 221–79.

Zweig, David L. (1983). "The Politics of Rural Prosperity: Social Conflicts and the 'Seedlings' of Capitalism in Rural China." Presented at the Midwest Regional Seminar on China, Chicago, Dec. 3.

——— (1987). "Context and Content in Policy Implementation: Household Contracts in China, 1977–1983," in Lampton (1987), 255–83.

INDEX